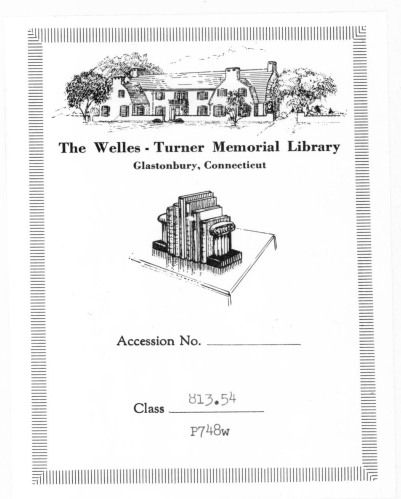

The Welles - Turner Memorial Library
Glastonbury, Connecticut

Accession No. _____

Class ___813.54___

P748w

The Way the
Future Was

The Way the Future Was:

A Memoir

Frederik Pohl

A Del Rey Book

BALLANTINE BOOKS • NEW YORK

A Del Rey Book
Published by Ballantine Books

Copyright © 1978 by Frederik Pohl

Photo credits:
Jay Kay Klein: p. 5, bottom; p. 6, bottom; p. 9; p. 10; p. 11,
top; p. 12; p. 13; p. 14, top; p. 16.
All other photographs are from the author's personal collection.

Manufactured in the United States of America

First Edition: August 1978

Library of Congress Cataloging in Publication Data

Pohl, Frederik.
    The way the future was.

    1. Pohl, Frederik. 2. Authors, American—20th
century—Biography. 3. Science fiction, American—
History and criticism. I. Title.
PS3566.036Z47   813'.5'4 [B]   78-19050
ISBN 0-345-27714-7

For Carol,
who shared in so much of it,
and made it so much nicer.

Contents

1

As It Was in the Beginning

When I first encountered science fiction, Herbert Hoover was the President of the United States, a plump, perplexed man who never quite figured out what had gone wrong. I was ten years old. I didn't know what had gone wrong, either.

A boy of ten is not without intelligence. It seems to me that then I was about as educable and perceptive as I was ever going to be in my life. What I did lack was knowledge. Was something bad happening in the world? I had no way of knowing. It was the only world I had ever experienced. I knew we moved a lot. I suspected that it was because we couldn't pay the rent, but that wasn't any new thing in my ten-year-old life. My father had always been a plunger. There were times when we lived in suites in luxury hotels, and times when we didn't live anywhere at all, at least as a family. My father would be in one place, my mother in another, and me with some relative until they could get it together again. The name of the game that year was the Great Depression, but I didn't know I was playing it. And at some point in that year of 1930 I came across a magazine named *Science Wonder*

Stories Quarterly, with a picture of a scaly green monster on the cover. I opened it up. The irremediable virus entered my veins.

Of course it isn't really true that there is no cure for the science-fiction addiction, because every year there are thousands of spontaneous remissions. I have wondered from time to time why it is that any number of kids can discover science fiction and some will abandon it in a year, others will keep a casual interest indefinitely but never progress beyond that, while a few, like me, will make it a way of life. I suppose both seed and soil are needed. Damon Knight says that, as children, all we science-fiction writers were toads. We didn't get along with our peers. We had no close friends and were thus thrown on our own internal resources. Reading, particularly science fiction, filled the gaps. A more charitable explanation might be that most science-fiction readers were precocious kids who got little reward from the chatter of their subteen schoolmates and looked for more stimulating companionship in print. Either way, Damon was hooked, and so was I, and so were some ten or twenty thousand people all over the world who comprise the great collective family called "science fiction."

I do, however, deny that I was a toad.

Actually, I was quite a good-looking ten- or twelve-year-old. I have the pictures to prove it. My reflexes were okay, and I could handle myself at sports. Never much of a ballplayer, but a good swimmer and a good marksman from the age of ten on. I did not, it is true, spend a great deal of time with my peers. I missed four years out of the beginning of my school career, partly from moving, partly from maternal stubbornness. Every time I went to school I got sick. Not just sniffles or Monday-morning fevers, but thumping good cases of all the UCD. The law said I had to go to school at a certain age, and so obediently my parents

sent me off; I got whooping cough and was in bed
for a month. They sent me back; I got sick again, with
something else; sent me again, and I came home with
scarlet fever. In the 1920s, that was no fun. It meant
a Board of Health quarantine sign on the door, all my
possessions baked in an oven for two hours, and
nothing for me, for weeks on end, but to lie in bed
and wish I had something to do. Well, I did have
something to do. I read. I don't remember a time
when I couldn't read, and the Bobbsey Twins and
Peewee Harris kept me content when I couldn't go
out and skate.

After my mother came to the conclusion that the
New York City public-school system was proposing to
kill her only child with its diseases, she kept me out
of school entirely. It helped that we moved so often.
Even so, from time to time the truant officer would
come around to complain. She would inform him that
she herself was a fully accredited teacher, a graduate
of Lehigh State Teachers College and well able to
tutor her son at home. Perhaps she was. I don't remember any lessons, only books in endless supply. But
that is not a bad way of getting an education.

When I was around eight the world finally caught
up with us, and I started school. They had a little
trouble placing me. By age, I should have been a grade
or two lower down. In terms of some of the specifics
children learn, I was hardly performing at kindergarten level; when the principal asked me to write my
name, I smiled sweetly and said, "I'll print it for
you." (There are no penmanship lessons in *Huckle-
berry Finn*.) But in reading and general knowledge of
the world I was well up there with the big kids, and
so they compromised on 4-A. It wasn't so bad. The
only thing I can find to object to in my grammar-
school career was that I don't remember learning anything in it.

My father, he was a traveling man. When he was around twenty-two he was a machinery salesman, and one of his accounts was Flegenheimer's iron and steel works, near Allentown, Pennsylvania. There my mother, a redheaded Irish girl two or three years older than he, worked as a secretary. They got married in 1917. The next year my father was drafted. He spent a few weeks in basic training, prepping to go to France to kill off the Kaiser and finish World War I, but the Armistice came before they got around to him. He got out without ever having gone overseas. On the twenty-sixth of November in 1919 I was born. The next week my father left for the Panama Canal, where he had a job waiting. My mother and I followed, and I spent my first Christmas at sea.

They tell me that the Canal Zone was not a bad place to be—assuming, of course, that you were American, employed, and white. We had servants, including one immense black lady whose only job was taking care of me. But we didn't stay there. My father spent his life convinced there was something better than what he had, if he could only find it. We chased it to places like Texas, New Mexico, and California over the next couple of years. By the time I was old enough to be aware of where I was, we were back in Brooklyn. And there, in one neighborhood or another, we stayed all through my childhood.

Depression or none, Brooklyn was a warm and kindly place to me. There was much to do, and little to fear. I can remember a few rough times—schoolboy fistfights, once or twice a tentative advance from some sad, predatory gay, a time or two when older kids carried a practical joke a touch too far. But nothing that made me afraid. What I remember best are pleasures. Penny candy and Saturday movie-matinees. Sunday drives to my grandparents' home in Broad Channel, gimcrack little house that old Ernst Pohl had built with his own hands on tidal water, with killies to be seen from the plank walks that reached out to the stilted summer houses behind it. Cattail marshes you could lose yourself in, four or five blocks from my house. Summer camp at Fire Place Lodge, where I learned to ride a horse, paddle a canoe, and hit what I aimed at with a .22. Once or twice a year we would take the Lehigh Railroad to visit my mother's family in Allentown. All I remember of them are character tags: the leap-year aunt who had had fewer birthdays than I because she was born on the twenty-ninth of February, the uncle who drank (I remember my tiny mother taking a bottle away from her six-foot-four brother and pouring it down the sink), the cousin who played the violin.

A ten-year-old is a piece of unexposed film. I soaked up all the inputs that fell on me without sharing them. I perceived quite early that I was a reader, and most of the people I came in contact with were not. It made a barrier. What they wanted to talk about were things they had eaten, touched, or done. What I wanted to talk about was what I had read.

When it developed that what I was thinking and reading was more and more science fiction, the barrier grew. I don't want to give the impression that I read only science fiction. Perhaps I would have if I could, but there wasn't enough of it to meet my needs. Since I had the good luck to learn to read long before I saw the inside of a school and so did not associate it with drudgery, I read quickly and easily; and if I didn't understand all the words, I could usually get the drift, confident that sooner or later the words would fit themselves into a context. One reason for this catholicity of taste was that I had very little control over what reading matter was available to me. At ten, I had not achieved the sophistication of buying books for myself or belonging to a library; I took what turned up in the house or what I could borrow from friends. That first issue of *Science Wonder* was heaven, but I didn't realize that the fact that it was a magazine implied that there would be other issues for me to find. When another science-fiction magazine came my way, a few months later, it was like Christmas. That was an old copy of the *Amazing Stories Annual,* provenance unknown. Given two examples, I was at last able to deduce the probability of more, and the general concept of "science-fiction magazines" became part of my life.

That *Amazing Stories Annual* contained the complete text of Edgar Rice Burroughs's *The Master Mind of Mars,* all red-skinned princesses and mad scientists and huge, four-armed, talking white apes. I doted on it. The cover enslaved me before I turned a page: bright buckeye painting of Ras Thavas, the crazy old organ transplanter of Barsoom, leaning over the sweet, dead form of a beautiful Martian maiden into which he proposed to transplant some rich old hag's brain. I couldn't wait to read it; having read it, at once read it again; having all but memorized it, attained the wisdom to go looking for more. I found more. I found back-number magazine stores where I could pick up 1927 *Amazings* and 1930 *Astoundings* for the nickel or dime apiece that even my ten-year-old budget could afford. I found second-hand bookstores, scads of them, which turned out to have science-fiction *books*: all the rest of the Burroughs oeuvre, originally published in the Grosset & Dunlap editions for a dollar and now available to me, hardly damaged, for as little as a dime. It was something of a blow to find that Burroughs had written books about other things than the planet Barsoom. I tried Tarzan as an experiment and didn't much like it—talking great apes were not wonderful enough for me—but there were half a dozen other Mars books, plus books about Venus, Pellucidar, and the Moon.

All of these interesting places appeared to have sensibly organized native civilizations, with beautiful princesses to win and important deeds of valor to do; more, they had useful and exciting inventions, like radium rifles and airships propelled by the secret rays of the sun. I got my first public-library card around then. Although I was ghettoized into the children's section without appeal, I found tons of Jules Verne and a smattering of H. G. Wells. Verne was bread and butter, enough to survive on, at least; Wells was pure delight. And now that my antennae were sensitized, I discovered children's books that showed the same stigmata: Carl H. Claudy, Roy Rockwood, even, although contemptibly old-fashioned and watered-down, Tom Swift.

My uncle Bill Mason turned out to be King Midas for me. He was my war-wounded uncle, gassed in the Argonne in World War I and eking out some sort of a livelihood on his disability pension, an occasional job of watch repairing, and what he could grow on a rented acre of ground in Harlem, Pennsylvania. He took me off my parents' hands now and then in the summer, not so much to give me a vacation as to get me away from the polio scare that enlivened most pre-Salk city summers. I enjoyed going to the farm. We could swim behind the dam in the little brook, hunt ginseng in the woods, engage in butting contests with the neighbor's bull calves. I was even allowed to fire the family shotgun now and then.

I wasn't much use as a farmhand, but neither were my two cousins. The three of us put much more effort into the avoiding of work than into the doing of it. When trapped, we could feed the chickens and gather the eggs. We could cut a little brush and pick potato bugs off the vines. What we did as much as we could was hide.

After some research, I found the perfect hiding place

in the farmhouse attic. My grandfather lived on the same farm, and he grew his own tobacco. The attic was where he cured it, so that it smelled of ripening tobacco and a sour-salty tang of heat. But that wasn't the marvelous thing about it. The truly marvelous thing was that in a corner of the attic was a treasure-trove of old pulp magazines, hundreds of them.

Only a few were science-fiction magazines. Quite a lot were Westerns or queer things like submarine stories and sports magazines, but many were golden. Someone had been a big fan of Frank Munsey's old *Argosy*, then a weekly pulp magazine selling for a dime, each issue packed with half a dozen shorts and installments of four different serials. And what serials! Borden Chase novels about sandhogs digging the Holland tunnel. Eight-parters about adventure in ancient Greece or Rome. I knew nothing of history, but I knew a good story when I read one, and these stories awakened my interest in the classic ages in a way that nothing in school ever did. (I have no doubt that in the long run I owe the fact that I am the *Encyclopedia Britannica*'s source for the Roman emperor Tiberius to those old pulp novels.) Derring-do among Soviet collective farms and in American steel mills. Medical adventures with Dr. Kildare. Exploration of every corner of the Earth. The literary style was peremptory, and someone was getting hit over the head on every page, but they were *grand*. And among them was the occasional pure vein of science fiction. I read A. Merritt's *The Moon Pool* up in that attic, with the temperature a hundred and four under the eaves, and Ray Cummings and Otis Adelbert Kline, and I only stopped when someone dragged me away. Or when the sun went down. The house had neither electricity nor running water, and after dark there were only limited options. You could sit in the kitchen by the kerosene lantern and listen to Whisperin' Jack Smith on the battery radio. Or you could go to bed.

So in the two years from age ten to twelve I managed to read every scrap of science fiction I knew to exist: every back issue of *Amazing* and *Wonder* and *Astounding*, most of *Weird Tales*, all the books I could find in second-hand stores, friends' homes, and the children's section of the library; everything. My head was popping with spaceships and winged girls and cloaks of invisibility, and I had no one to share it with.

The house we lived in when I was ten was at 2758 East 26th Street in Brooklyn.

A few months ago I did a nostalgic thing. I was driving to Kennedy Airport in my rented Avis car, about to catch a plane to Budapest and, astonishingly, with an hour or two to spare. On impulse I got off the Belt Parkway at Sheepshead Bay, hunted around, and found that very house, the first time I had seen it since I left it forty-five years earlier.

When we lived there, the house had been of the style called "semidetached," which meant that it shared a common building wall with the next-door house on one side. It wasn't semidetached any more. The house next door had been neatly amputated, sacrificed to the building of the Belt, but 2758 was still there, a corner house now, and not really looking very old.

The whole neighborhood was much changed. When New Yorkers say that, what they generally mean is that the blacks and Hispanics have moved in. That isn't so, but it is all built up now. In 1930 it wasn't like that. Most of one side of the big block was an actual farm devoted to growing Italian tomatoes. One of the best things I found to do on late summer nights was to steal and eat them by the pound, fresh off the vine, warm, powdery with some no doubt damaging chemical residue on their skins, but delicious beyond any tomato I have tasted since.

I thought of knocking on that door and asking to look around. But I have no recollection of what the house was like inside. I know which room had to be my room—the back one on the second floor—because I can remember spying out that window into the bedroom of the house across the driveway. But I don't know what the room looked like.

Beyond the house I remember spying into was a vacant lot where we once dug an underground clubhouse. Beyond that was another semidetached house inhabited by a family named Abbot. They had been family friends for years, before either of us lived on that block, and remained so through countless moves of both families until we lost touch in World War II. Griffith and Daisy Abbot were British-born and kept ties to the homeland. Every week or two they received packets of Papers from Home in the mail, mostly children's weeklies like *Puck*, primitive color-comics about Robin Hood and about somebody named Val who adventured around the English countryside in a "caravan." When the five Abbot kids were through with them, I inherited them, and puzzled in my ten-year-old way over this strange language that seemed to be English but sometimes wasn't. We all played street games like Green Light and King of the Hill. We played other games, too. In one of them we decided to hang somebody—I suppose the game was Rustler and Posse, carried out to its logical Saturday-matinee conclusion—and I was given the starring role. My mother caught sight of what was going on out of the kitchen window and came storming out just as the noose was stretching my neck. On the far side of Sheepshead Bay, reached by a wooden pedestrian bridge, was Oriental Point and a small, primitive, very probably polluted bathing beach. It was about half an hour's walk, and we all walked it over and over again all through the summers. I saw my first dead man there. He was a very ripe one, two weeks drowned and hauled up on the beach pending someone's coming to take him away; I almost stepped on his chest, being busy woolgathering at the time. He smelled. Out along our own side of the bay, in the general direction of Queens and Long Island, there was not much between our house and the new Floyd Bennett Field except tidelands and bulrushes. They were marvelous to roam around in. You could get lost in a minute, and see nothing made by man for an hour. Now they are all high-rise apartments, built on God-knows-what foundations.

It was a nice place to be. But the money ran out, and we could no longer pay the rent on the house. In the winter of 1931 we moved into a tiny apartment downtown.

The words "the money ran out" cannot be understood in the context of the 1970s as they were in that quite different ambience of 1931.

Nearly half a century later, money never quite runs out. I don't mean there are no poor people any more. Of course there are, and enough squalor and misery to stock a planet. But when trouble strikes in the 1970s, there is one additional option. You can surrender to it. You collect unemployment insurance, or you go on welfare; if you're evicted, some bureau picks you up and finds you a place to live; if you're sick, there are agencies to pay your doctor bills. In 1931 you could not surrender because there was no one to give up to. You could find a soup kitchen to get something to eat. But no one would keep your family together, and no one would pay your rent.

The other side of the coin in the Great Depression

was that the landlords were in as much trouble as
you were. There were plenty of apartments to rent,
and it was a buyer's market. To persuade you to take
his apartment in the first place, the landlord would
give you the first two months free; you paid the third
month and moved after the fourth.

Or so my family seemed to do, in one year in which
we lived in four different apartments. Our first apartment after 26th Street was in a high-rise just off Grand
Army Plaza, with its livery stables and luxury flats.
We made our way down Flatbush Avenue a few blocks
at a time, winding up in a cold-water flat * on Dean
Street, at the bottom of Park Slope. (Then things
began to improve, and a year or so later we were back
up at the top of the Slope again.)

Even in those years, the pit of the Great Depression,
that part of Flatbush Avenue was a bustling, lively
street, seamed with trolley tracks, lined with shops of
all kinds. The merchants might have had trouble paying their rent, but they put on a busy front. There
were three motion-picture theaters in that eight-block
stretch, and they told the story of the Depression
more clearly than the stores did. At the top of the
hill, the Bunny Theater was open, but not as a theater;
it had been turned into an indoor miniature golf
course. At the foot of the hill, the Atlantic was
shuttered, hoping for better times. The only one that
was functioning was the Carlton, in between, and it
wasn't prospering greatly. On Tuesdays they would
let you in for nothing if you would drop a can of food
into a bin to feed the hungry of the neighborhood.

None of the people I knew personally had anything
to do with bread lines or baskets for the poor. They
weren't "poor." They didn't think of themselves as
poor, only broke. In the war for survival they were

---

* "Cold-water" flats had hot water; what they didn't have
was central heating.

outnumbered and surrounded, but they had not surrendered (if only because there was no agency to surrender to) and they had not, yet, been wiped out. Of the totally defeated, I only encountered one, and him only at long range.

The shuttered Atlantic Theater was a nice place for a twelve-year-old to spend an hour or two on an idle Saturday, climbing the fire escape, four stories of strap-iron stairs and landings. From the top landing you could look down like a god on the people strolling Flatbush Avenue. I went there often. But on one Saturday, as I started up the stairs, I perceived that something was different. The top landing seemed to be full of cardboard cartons. I ghosted up the steps, silent as any kid stalking the strange, and saw that the top landing had been walled with flattened cardboard. Inside the room he had built, sitting on the floor, doing nothing because having nothing to do, was a white-haired old man.

When I say "the money ran out," what I mean is him. Even at twelve I could figure out his story. He was alone, and broke, and had nowhere to go. He managed to get one sparse meal on the bread lines every day, and he had the clothes he stood up in, and that was all. He had no other place to live. There were such things as municipal lodging houses, true. But there were an awful lot of penniless, hopeless, homeless men, and so the "munies" were full.

I tiptoed unseen back down the stairs to ponder this. For the first time in my life I was moved to charity. I took some eggs out of the icebox, hard-boiled them, put them in a paper bag, sneaked back up the steps, and left them for him. A day later I stole back and found a note he had left for me, penciled almost illegibly on a scrap of the paper bag: God-bless-you-unknown-stranger, and Thanks.

And a day or two after that his cardboard nest had

been taken apart and carried away, and he was gone.

The thing about my friend of the fire escape was that there were so many of him. You saw him all over, thousands and thousands of him, in every city of the land. Younger versions of him shoveled snow, in their black dress shoes and double-breasted business suits—the only clothes they had to wear, and the only thing they could find to do. They prayed for snow. An inch of snow was a dollar's worth of shoveling. You saw him in his improvised huts, cardboard or sheet tin, in the parks and the vacant lots, whole communities of him. And he could be you. My own grandfather would have been one of him if there had not been my mother or my uncle to take him in.

The communities of homeless men were called "Hoovervilles," an honor our President did not like and had not sought. How much of the blame for the Great Depression belonged to Hoover, really? I tried to answer that question once, in a book that I worked on for several years, decades after the fact.* Hoover did not plant the seeds, they were sown over the boom years of the 20s, in easy credit buying and mad stock swindles. But he did nothing to respond to the crisis. Herbert Hoover was a decent, capable man, who boasted of his kindly, fatherly record of providing food for the needy in the battle-damaged Europe of World War I. He could not see the point of giving help to people who were merely out of work, and so history, and Franklin Delano Roosevelt, assigned him the blame for the whole thing.

A few years ago I was on Long John Nebel's all-night radio talk show, and the conversation turned to the Depression. With great joy I plunged into an

---

* After fifty thousand words of copy and three-quarters of a million words of notes, I decided I didn't like the book and bought back the contract, so it is, and may well remain, unpublished.

analysis of who had been at fault. I described Hoover's flat refusal to provide food or jobs for the needy, and his callous cruelty (or cowardice?) when he permitted MacArthur and Eisenhower to drive the bonus marchers away from their encampment on Anacostia Flats. I drew a picture of him as a frightened and closed-minded man who had neither the wisdom to see that fundamental change was needed nor the courage to admit mistakes, and as I was soaring through my peroration Long John passed a note to me across the studio table: "Did you know he's listening to you?" It was so. The dying ex-President didn't sleep well in his Waldorf suite, and it was his custom to tune in Long John on the radio by his bed through the long nights. That was a shock. I had been thinking of him as a symbol for so long that it had never occurred to me that he was still a living, hurting old man.

I had another shock, but a pleasant one, when I was writing my book on the Depression: I found a newspaper story about my friend of the fire escape, and a third of a century after the fact learned the end of his story. The beginning was just about what I had deduced. He had had a job, but the job closed; had money in the bank, but the bank went broke; had a room but couldn't pay the rent; and so the landlord turned him out and kept his clothes and workmen's tools (he was a carpenter) against the unpaid bill. The police found him on the theater fire escape and chased him away, but a newspaper reporter happened to cover the story. The publicity resulted in his getting admitted to a municipal shelter; so, in a sense, his story had at least a happy ending.

But I've always wondered who was turned out of the municipal lodging house to make room for my friend.

And all this had its effect on science fiction, not only on my own work but on that of many writers; not only in affecting moods and themes but in practical, tangible ways. Magazines were a Depression business. If you couldn't afford fifty cents to take the family to the movies, you could probably scrape up a dime or twenty cents to buy a magazine, and then pass the magazine back and forth to multiply the investment. And talk was cheap. One reason for the growth of science-fiction fan clubs in the 30s was that you could get an evening's worth of entertainment out of two nickels spent on the subway.

There is a populist, anti-establishment tone to a lot of the science fiction of the 30s, and in fact to all science fiction everywhere. One of the reasons has to do with its flowering in an age in which anyone could plainly see that the Establishment had screwed up the world. Rich people got a very bad press in almost all newspapers, magazines, books, plays, and films, and nowhere worse than in science fiction. Rich people were "Steel"—power behind villainous Blackie Du-Quesne and evil adversaries of good, pure Richard Ballinger Seaton—in *The Skylark of Space*. They were the pitifully empty Eloi of *The Time Machine*, the smug and corrupt legless master race of *The Revolt of the Pedestrians*, the maniac gulgul-collectors of *The Blue Barbarians*.

Of course, that tradition is older than the Depression,* but the climate of the times encouraged it, and even encouraged that kind of thinking about the unthinkable which is one of the hallmarks of some kinds of science fiction: talk of social change. The 30s seethed with proponents of social change: Anarchists and Technocrats, Single-Taxers and four or five brands of Marxists, Father Coughlin and Upton Sinclair, Ham

* In fact, most of the stories I have just named were written before 1929.

and Eggs and Thirty Dollars Every Thursday. Science fiction both reflected and sparked events in the outside world. When you invent a new civilized planet, you have to invent a new society to inhabit it; when you invent a new society, you make a political statement about the one you live in. Every writer is in some sense a preacher. (Why else would anyone write a book?) With or without intent, with or without awareness of what they were doing, the science-fiction writers were preaching.

James Blish once had a theory that science-fiction writing was the specific consequence of some historical event, as Parkinson's Syndrome was considered to be the late aftereffect of the world influenza epidemic of 1920. He could not identify the event, but he based his theory on the observation that, of all major science-fiction writers alive a decade or two ago, more than half had been born within a year or two of 1920.

Jim's theory doesn't now seem as plausible as it did when he proposed it, because there are too many new writers showing their faces: Samuel R. Delany, Larry Niven, even a few who were actually being born just about when Jim was developing his theory, such as George R. R. Martin. But there's some truth to it, at least in the sense that science fiction does clearly show the impact of the social confusion and experimentation of the 30s. For all of us who were born between, say 1915 and 1920—Isaac Asimov, Ray Bradbury, Arthur C. Clarke, and a lot of others—the world of the 30s, which was the world of the Great Depression, was where we grew up, and where we formed our conceptions of the universe.

2

Let There Be Fandom

In the Beginning there was Hugo Gernsback, and he begat *Amazing Stories*.

In the fullness of time, about three years' worth, a Depression smote the land, and *Amazing* was riven from him in a stock shuffle; whereupon he begat *Air Wonder Stories* and *Science Wonder Stories*, looked upon them and found them incomplete, and joined them one unto the other to be one flesh, named *Wonder Stories*. And Hugo looked upon the sales figures of *Wonder Stories* and pondered mightily that they were so low. Whereupon a Voice spake unto him, saying, "Hugo, nail those readers down," so that he begat the Science Fiction League, and thus was Fandom born.

If there had not been a Science Fiction League, it would have been necessary to invent one. The time was ripe. In the early 30s, to be a science-fiction reader was a sad and lonely thing. There weren't many of us, and we hadn't found each other to talk to. A few activists had tried to get something going, digging addresses out of the letter columns of the science-fiction magazines and starting tiny correspondence clubs, but the largest of them had maybe a dozen members, and for the rest of us we had the permanent consciousness of being alone in a hostile world. The hordes of the unblessed weren't merely disinterested in science fiction, they ridiculed it.

From Gernsback's point of view, what he had to sell was a commodity that a few people wanted very much indeed but most people wouldn't accept if it were given away free. He couldn't do a lot about recruiting new readers, but he was aware that there were a great many in-and-outers, people who would buy an issue of *Wonder Stories* now and then, and thus were obviously prime prospects, but had not formed the every-month addiction that he sought. Well, sir. The arithmetic of that situation was pretty easy to figure. If the seventy percent of his readers who averaged three issues a year could be persuaded to buy every issue, he would *triple* his sales. These were the visions of sugarplums that danced in Hugo Gernsback's mind. He had a special need to think of something, because by the early 30s even the magazine industry was grinding down under the Depression. Even the science-fiction magazines. Three of them existed, but they were reducing their size, cutting their prices, dropping back from monthly to every-other-month publication; in 1933 *Astounding* went out of business entirely, and then for a brief little while there were only two. (A few months later Street & Smith bought the magazine from the wreckage of the Clayton group of pulps and started it up again.) What Hugo hoped for from the Science Fiction League was a plain buck-hustle, a way of keeping readers loyal.

What we fans hoped for from it was Paradise. As soon as the notice appeared I rushed to join, but my membership number was 490, even so. I didn't mind. I was thrilled to think that there were 489 others like me, when I had in my whole life seen only one or two. The announcement promised that chapters would be chartered in all major cities; club news would be published in every issue of the magazine, members would be encouraged to become each other's pen pals—what fun! Hugo promised that some of the members would be foreign—imagine discussing *Spacehounds of IPC* or *The Man Who Awoke* with someone who lived in England or Australia! Imagine joining a chapter, sitting in a room filled with people who knew what you meant when you used terms like "time machines" or "ray guns," and didn't laugh! Imagine just knowing people who did not think science fiction was junk.

But, you know, in all honesty, a lot of it was.

Although I have devoted my life to science fiction, I don't *like* all of it. What I do like I often like very much, but that is only a minor fraction of what is written and published. Ted Sturgeon defined the situation exactly, in what has come to be called Sturgeon's Law: "Ninety percent of science fiction is crud, but then ninety percent of everything is crud."

John Campbell used to say that he was the world's greatest expert on bad science fiction because he had read more of it than anyone else alive. He based his claim on having read *Astounding*'s slush pile of unsolicited manuscripts, eighty or ninety of them every week, for thirty-four straight years, and surely no one else could challenge that record while he lived. But now John has gone to that great editorial resting place in the sky, and I think I may have inherited his mantle. I don't really know how much I have read, but the best estimate I can make is that, allowing for everything—books, magazines, unpublished manuscripts, everything—I must have read something in excess of 5×10^8 words of science fiction in my life. That's half a billion words, or almost twice as many as are contained in all the books published in the United States in any one year.

Even so, even after all of that, every now and then something grabs me around the groin, compels my full attention, and does not let me go. Not until I have finished the story, at least, and if it is really good, *not even then.* (What is best about the best science fiction is not merely the pleasure it gives while you are reading it, but the long serial thoughts it stirs in the mind of the reader for days and months afterward.) Because I have read so much, that doesn't happen very often any more, but it still does happen. There are still new thoughts to be comprehended and new insights to be explored.

But in the early 1930s—for me as one fledgling, but for almost all science-fiction readers simply because the field itself was so new—almost *all* the ideas were new! Revelation followed revelation. Fresh perception piled on revolutionary insight.

It is quite possible, I realize, that some of the ideation in *Air Wonder* or *Astounding Stories of Super-Science* was not quite as fresh and innovative as it seemed at the time. There was (and still is) much borrowing, which the more naive among the readers (myself certainly included) were simply not equipped to recognize.

No matter. Whether or not the satirists borrowed from Voltaire and the adventure writers cribbed from Verne and the humanists copied their perceptions of feeling from *True Story*—no matter how hallowed or tawdry the sources, no matter how often the story had been told, to us it was still the first time. This is what is now diagnosable as the *Star Trek* syndrome. As science fiction goes, *Star Trek* isn't much. There's not a fresh idea in all the three years of it put together, nothing that has not been done before, and usually much better, in the pages of some science-fiction magazine or book. But the people who saw *Star Trek* numbered *forty million.* The overwhelming majority of them had never been exposed to anything like it before. They had never really thought about the possibility of life on other planets, or time travel, or what it would be like to cruise through space, or how other societies might resemble (or differ from) our own, until they caught it on the boob tube, and to them it was Revelation. To them. To us, decades earlier. Above all, to me.

When you have that sort of experience, your very glands shriek out to share it—cellar Christians whispering the Gospel by the flickering light of oil lamps—and so the Science Fiction League fell on ripe ground. We were, boy, ready!

Sadly, the Science Fiction League did not in the long run do much for *Wonder Stories.* The readers joined up, but they did not recruit new ones; and the ones who joined were unanimously the ones who had been reading every issue, anyway. The magazine limped along for a few more years, stalling its creditors and underpaying its writers when it paid them at all, and before the end of the decade was sold to the knacking shop of the Thrilling Group.

But whatever the SFL did for Gernsback, it did an awful lot for us practitioners of the solitary vice of science fiction. It got us out of the closet and into Fandom, leading directly to such group orgies as the worldcons of today, with casts of thousands openly engaged in the celebration of sf.

I had, as it happened, met one or two fellow fans before that.

One was a boy in my eighth-grade class in Public School 9 in Brooklyn. That was a close-knit class to begin with, because we were all united in a bond of common terror. Our teacher, Maude Mary Mahlman, was nine feet tall, ferocious of mien, and possessed of compound eyes, like a fly, so that even when she seemed to be looking at the blackboard or a student across the room, at least one facet was always and unwinkingly fixed on *me*. She told us that herself, and I believed every word she said. For a time. Then my courage came back. By the end of the term I had learned to look industrious when daydreaming, and I actually wrote a short science-fiction story, my very first, under her eyes on a drowsy May morning in English class. (The story had something to do with Atlantis. That's all I remember, except that it was awful.)

In the same class, Owen Jordan sat nearby, and lived nearby to my home. We would walk home together and sometimes stop off at his house or mine to play chess, and he was the one who tuned me in to the existence of the magazine I had not previously known existed, *Astounding*. The first issue he loaned me had a cover illustrating the story "Manape the Mighty," and so naive (or despairing) was I that I read only that story and returned it to him before he pointed out that all the other stories in the issue were science fiction. But we lost touch shortly after that. We graduated from grammar school, and I went off to Brooklyn Tech.

There was no high school specializing in science fiction, which is what really interested me. There was not yet even a High School of Science, and perhaps that's a pity, because I think I might have liked being a physicist or an astronomer. What there was, was Brooklyn Technical High School. It was said to give many courses in science, which I recognized as being some part of science fiction, and besides, it was an honor school, requiring a special examination for entrance, which appealed to my twelve-year-old snob soul.

Brooklyn Tech was a revolutionary concept in high

schools, dedicated to the quick manufacture of tech-
nologists. In 1932 its own building was still under
construction, and it was housed temporarily in a
sprawl of out-of-date schools and one abandoned factory, at the Brooklyn end of the Manhattan Bridge,
where the laboratories and workshops could be accom-
modated.

In my second term, my home room was in Annex 1,
identified as Brooklyn PS 1 at the time it was built,
probably around the time of the Civil War. (Or the
Punic.) It was by all odds the dingiest structure I
have ever spent much time in. The toilets were
plugged and foul. Leaking pipes overhead left white
nacre on the walls. The heating system was a mockery,
and the time was February of 1933, cold as hell.
Fortunately, only a few of my classes were in Annex 1.
In midmorning I shifted to Annex 5, a much newer,
nicer school next to a playground, six or seven face-
frozen blocks away. Then in the afternoon I had
classes in the Main Building, the whilom factory, just
on the other side of the constant truck rumble of
Flatbush Avenue. After the first few days I noticed
that I was dodging the trucks in the company of the
same tall, skinny guy with glasses—he looked quite
a lot like me, or actually quite a lot handsomer than
me—and he turned out to be a science-fiction fan. His
name was Joseph Harold Dockweiler, but he wasn't
terribly pleased with it, and a few years later he
changed it to Dirk Wylie.

Dirk was the sort of best friend every young person
should have. Our interests were similar, but not identi-
cal. We were much of the same age, and almost iden-
tically of the same stage of growth, so that we
discovered the same things about the world at the
same time: girls, smoking, drinking, reading, science
fiction. If you mapped a schematic diagram of Dirk
onto one of me, nearly all the points at the centers

of our personalities would match exactly. Off to one side was my growing interest in politics and society, which Dirk found unexciting; off to another, his in weapons and cars, which I shared at most tepidly.

Dirk lived in Queens Village, an hour from Tech by subway and bus. Like me, he was an only child. Like me, he had no close ties with the kids next door. Like me, he had a tolerant home environment, willing to let him grow on his own. Like me, he had a Collection.

The possession of a Collection is one of the diagnostic signs of Fandom. Another is Trying to Write, and Dirk shared that symptom with me, too. We found out these things about each other within the first week after our meeting, after which there was no question that, at least until further notice, we two loners were going to be Best Friends. So we were. We stayed Best Friends. When we were old enough, we even married two girls who themselves were Best Friends, and were Best Men at each other's weddings.

Although we were schoolmates, school was the least part of both our lives. There was much more education in the outside world. Partly it was because of Brooklyn Tech itself, splendid school but not for us. It was necessary to declare a specialty at the end of the first year, so that at the age of thirteen I committed myself to a lifelong career as a chemical engineer, which was nonsense. (I uncommitted myself a few years later by dropping out of high school without graduating.) Not all of it was unpleasant. There was a lot of how-to-do-it in the curriculum, and we found ourselves operating machine tools and casting molten iron into greensand cope-and-drag molds, and that was fun. Lab work in chemistry and physics was enjoyable, and the math courses were challenging, but the rest was a washout. Both Dirk and I were readers, and so it was our custom to read our textbooks all the way through in the first week of any term, and so the rest of the term was unendurable tedium. But the excitement of the world outside never waned.

I count it one of the great good fortunes of my life that I grew up with all the resources of one of the world's greatest cities within my reach. Young kids of the 70s, I do devoutly pity you, stuck in your pasteurized suburban developments except when Mom chauffeurs you into town. I had the city streets, always exciting in themselves, and I had the subways.

Of all the modes of mechanized urban transport man has devised, the subway is the most nearly perfect. I love them all, from the creaky tiny cars of Budapest to the shiny streamliners of Toronto, under ground and above. Moscow's is beautiful. London's is marvelously efficient. Paris's runs engagingly from the super-technological to the quaint. But first loves are best, and New York's subways are what I grew up on. In the days of my youth the five-cent fare was sacred, and so for a nickel you could be carried from the Bronx to Coney Island, from sylvan Flushing to Wall Street. If you were a young boy and willing to take minor risks (jail, electrocution, things like that), you didn't even need the nickel. I was six years old when I learned that you could ride free from the Avenue H station of the BMT just by climbing over the exit doors. If I chose to visit friends in Sheepshead Bay, I could ride there free, and ride back at the same economical rate just by climbing an embankment, stepping carefully over the third rail, and entering the platform of the station there. When we moved to Kings Highway there was another embankment, equally easily breached. The Seventh Avenue subway station, near Grand Army Plaza, could be penetrated by winding oneself through the exit stiles. They kept adults out, but there was enough give in them to let a hundred-pound kid slip through. Of the major lines, the BMT's defenses were the leakiest; the IRT was built on a less carefree plan, but you could take the BMT to Queens, where the two lines ran together, and thus enter the forbidden pathways of the IRT at only the small cost of an extra hour or so of travel time.

If you chose to go somewhere past the ends of the subway lines, there was a further natural resource of free transportation in the form of trucks and trolley cars. They weren't as much fun. You were exposed to the weather, and there was always the chance of falling off. Or of being caught; while once you were into the subway system, you were as serene as any paying fare. But the whole city was open to exploration, and I explored it systematically from the age of six on.

I didn't always steal rides. There were times when I walked because it was my whim to walk that time, as any lordly millionaire might wave his limousine away for a nice day's stroll. Walking is the best way to know a city, which is why I feel quite at home in, say, London, and even now am a stranger in Los Angeles. And for most of my high-school career, my companion in exploration was usually Dirk Wylie.

Sometimes we explored geography, sometimes other things. Not a part of his Collection, but hidden behind the *Amazings* and the Edgar Rice Burroughs novels he had publications of another sort. They had titles like *Spicy Western Stories* and *Paris Nights*, soft-core porn that I had never seen and that inflamed my pubescent glands a lot. In return I conducted him to his first burlesque show, doing the same for his.

It wasn't *my* first burlesque show. Not by, even then, a number of years. When I was a little kid, five or so, my parents had taken me with them to the Oxford Burlesque, near where Atlantic and Flatbush avenues met in Brooklyn. I liked the baggy-pants comedians, didn't understand what the stripping was all about, but was thrilled to be included in something Grown-up. I kept in touch with the Oxford, one way or another, all through my childhood. When my parents stopped taking me, as soon as I was old enough to pass the ticket taker's scrutiny, I went by myself; and in the famine period between I would still skate down to the nearby Loft's soda fountain, and often enough I'd see the chorus girls, makeup an inch and a quarter deep around their eyes, sipping sodas through a straw and gazing at themselves in the mirrored walls.

In our sophomore year at Brooklyn Tech, the New Building at last was completed and we moved in. How modern and grand it seemed! Five or six stories tall, with an athletic field on the roof, shiny, clean laboratories instead of the jagged zinc of the old factory, an auditorium with air conditioning and the fullest projection facilities; the thing even had a radio station of its own. Pretty Fort Greene Park was just across the street, and the concentrated heart of Brooklyn's downtown only a five-minute walk away. The magnetism was too powerful to resist; Dirk and I walked there every afternoon, to go to a burlesque theater, or a movie, or just to explore.

Let me tell you about Brooklyn. For the first part of Brooklyn's life it was not a conquered province of New York City, it was a competitor. Even after the consolidation it still competed. Brooklyn had its own baseball team (the Dodgers), its own library system (better than New York's in every respect, except for, maybe, the Fifth Avenue reference facility), its own parks (after Frederick Law Olmsted designed Central Park in Manhattan, he took what he had learned to Brooklyn and laid out the even more spectacular Prospect Park), its own museums, its own zoo. Downtown Brooklyn had its own department stores—

Namm's, Loeser's, A & S—and I still think they were nicer than, and almost as big as, Macy's or Gimbels. Downtown Brooklyn had four or five first-run movie houses, including the Brooklyn Paramount, as lavish a marble-staired temple as any in the world, at least until the Radio City Music Hall came along. On Fulton Street it even had legitimate theaters, with the same sort of bills as theaters in Boston or Chicago. Road companies of Broadway shows played there after the New York runs had closed, and sometimes Broadway shows opened there for tryouts before risking the metropolis across the river.* And all these marvels, stores and shows, bookshops and burlesques, parks and playgrounds, were within our grasp. If Brooklyn palled, New York was just across the bridge; often enough we walked across the East River and up Broadway as far as Union Square to check out the second-hand book and magazine stores on Fourth Avenue. School could not compete. Outside it we were learning the world.

Which was changing.

The Depression had settled in, but Franklin Delano Roosevelt was inaugurated a week or two after Dirk and I met, and there was talk of a New Deal. Society seemed to be evolving into something new before our eyes. So was science. We heard about things like relativity and the expanding universe—not just in the sf magazines, but even on the radio. The world seemed to be into science fiction almost as much as Dirk and

---

* I saw a preview of *George White's Scandals of 1934* there weeks before it hit Broadway. I was no big White fan, but that one had been advertised as having a sort of science-fiction theme, something about how the Earth looked to Martians. The science-fiction part was contemptibly unimaginative, of course, but I rather liked the songs, and may be the only living person in America who still knows the words to "The Fellow Who Loves You." It was lucky I saw it in Brooklyn, because when the show hit Broadway it folded at once.

I were, at least in a nuts-and-bolts way. Airplanes were almost common in the sky, whereas a few years earlier it had been reason enough for housewives to leave the dishes in the sink and run outside to gawk at a plane. There were dirigibles, and the new Empire State Building, almost a quarter mile of masonry stretching up to scrape the sky, was topped with a mooring mast for blimps (or for King Kong to cling to). There was a kid in our classes at Brooklyn Tech who actually *flew* —yes, had a real pilot's license, spun the prop, took off, landed, was full of stories about how you could walk into an unseen spinning propeller and be chopped into ground round before you knew it, about hairy landings in the fog and storms aloft. I had fantasies about getting a plane of my own, preferably one of the swallow-tailed or heart-shaped or magnetically driven jobs out of *Wonder Stories*, challenging my friend to a race and beating his ass off. I knew that that was fantasy. But what but fantasy was it that he was doing, every Saturday at Floyd Bennett Field?

In a way that had never happened before in the history of the human race, the world was looking into the future. Most especially Dirk and I. Most particularly through science fiction. When the Science Fiction League came along, we both sent our applications off at once, and almost by return mail I got a postcard from a man who identified himself as one George Gordon Clark. He was, he announced, Member 1 of the Science Fiction League. Not only that, he had been authorized to form Chapter 1; and I was invited to attend Meeting 1.

It was at night, and most of an hour away by subway, but I would not have missed it for rubies.

When G. G. Clark started the Brooklyn Science Fiction League, I do not think he knew what he was getting into.

Clark was a grown-up adult human being, in his late twenties or thereabouts. He had a job, and he had a Collection that made even Dirk's look sick.* Clark not only had every copy of every science-fiction magazine ever published, but they had that fresh-from-the-mint look of having been bought new from the corner candy store, rather than being picked up second-hand. He even had a few variorum editions, such as a copy of *Amazing Stories* on which one plate of the three-color cover had failed to print, so that it was all ghostly blues and greens. He also had more sf books than I had ever seen in one place before, and he even had science-fiction fan magazines, of which I had never previously even heard.

I think Clark must have been less than delighted with us scruffy adolescents who turned up in response to his postcard. Not one of us was within ten years of his age. At least one—Arthur Selikowitz, a tall, skinny polymath who entered Rensselaer Polytechnic Institute not long after at the age of thirteen—could not then have been quite eleven. At our first meeting the first thing we did was to elect Clark chairman. There was no alternative. Not only did he rank us all (Member 1), but it was his hall. We met some of the time in his cellar library (allowed to touch The

---

* Mine was sick to begin with. I had a fair number of books and magazines, but no place to put them, except for what space I could make by pushing the dishes and cans of soup off some kitchen shelves. That strikes me as odd. There were not many books in my house when I was a kid, except my own. My father read nothing but Westerns, which he kept on the top shelf of his bedroom closet. My mother did not seem to read much at all, which is strange: she was a pretty literate person, could recite poetry at great length, had been valedictorian of her graduating class, even once held a minor editorial job with *St. Nicholas Magazine* for a brief time. (A happy one for me; she used to bring home the review copies of children's books.) But I was fifteen before I lived in a house with a real bookcase.

Collection only one at a time, and with Clark hovering vigilantly by), sometimes in a rented classroom of a nearby public school. The term "nearby," of course, refers to its proximity to Clark. All the rest of us had to travel miles.

It is hard for me to remember what we did at these meetings, and I think the probable reason for that is that we did very little. There was a certain amount of reading the minutes and passing amendments to the bylaws, and not much else. After a while we decided to publish a mimeographed fan magazine of our own. I became its editor (largely, I think, because I owned my own typewriter), and it may have been the first place in which words of mine were actually published.

I haven't seen a copy of *The Brooklyn Reporter* in many years and doubt that there was much in it worth reading, but it was marvelously exciting to me then. My words were going out to readers all over the country! (Not very *many* readers, no. But quite geographically dispersed.) People I never saw were writing letters to comment on what I had done. It was through *The Brooklyn Reporter* that I first met Robert Lowndes —only as a pen pal at first, because he lived in faraway Connecticut and neither of us could see any way of bridging that near-hundred-mile distance. But we became good friends by correspondence, quickly found interests in common (we both were addicted to popular songs), and shared others: he initiated me into Baudelaire, Mallarmé, and J. K. Huysmans, and I introduced him to James Branch Cabell.

You see, what we science-fiction fans mostly wanted to do with each other's company was to talk—about science fiction, and about the world. Robert's Rules of Order didn't seem to provide for much of that, so we formed the habit of The Meeting After the Meeting. After enduring an hour or so of parliamentary rules, we troops would bid farewell to our leader and walk in a body to the nearest station of the El. On the way we would stop off at a soda fountain. This had three very good features: it gave us an informal atmosphere for talk, it supplied us with ice-cream sodas, and it got rid of G. G. Clark, so that we kids could be ourselves. The only bad part of it was that we had to adjourn the regular meetings pretty early, since none of us were old enough to stay out very late. But, considering what was happening at the regular meetings, that was no sacrifice.

I really don't know why the meetings had to be so dull. I wonder why it never occurred to any of us to invite some real-live science-fiction *writer* to come and bask in our worship. That would have been a thrill past orgasm for every one of us, maybe even for Clark. It wouldn't have mattered who the author was, and I'm sure some would have come. For one thing, if anyone had ever suggested it to Hugo Gernsback, he would surely have flogged any number of them into our arms to boost sales.

I know why it didn't occur to me. I was simply too naive. I wasn't aware that writers lived in places where they could be met. I don't know where I thought they did live. I may have thought they were mostly dead— that seemed to be the case with Mark Twain and Voltaire and a lot of my other favorites. If they were alive, I suppose I assumed they occupied some tree-lined, gardened, pillared suburb of something like heaven. But still, why didn't the idea occur to someone more sophisticated than I?

Well, in a way it did. After a while two Real Pro Writers did in fact come to our meetings.

They weren't *top* pros; in fact, I had never heard of either of them until they showed up. And they weren't there to help promote *Wonder Stories,* either

. . . oh, my, no. Their names were John B. Michel and Donald A. Wollheim.

To fourteen-year-old me they were immensely impressive high-powered types. Not physically. Neither were most of the rest of us fans; to some extent, Damon Knight's toad theory is descriptive enough. I started out lucky enough, but somewhere just before I got into science fiction I went swimming one day at the St. George Pool, huge indoor saltwater marvel, and went off the high board, meaning to see how close I could come to the tiled bottom. I came real close. When I got out of the water and looked in the bronze wall mirrors, I found I had knocked off a front tooth; and so, for the next couple of decades until a dentist shamed me into doing something about it, when I smiled I smiled gold.* So did Bob Lowndes. Clark was sort of belligerently defensive-looking most of the time. Cyril Kornbluth, when he came along, was short and pudgy, Jack Gillespie looked like an Irish jockey, Walter Kubilius was incredibly tall and wraithy, six-feet-eight or thereabouts, and maybe all of a hundred pounds. All of us came to understand early on that it was not on our looks that we would make our way in the world.

Both Wollheim and Michel had really bad complexions, and Donald had mannerisms that I suppose had origins within his own head, but gave the appearance of skeptical contempt for everything around him. Donald always carried a rolled-up umbrella. He rarely looked directly at the person he was talking to, but stared forty-five degrees to starboard, wry half-smile on his face, in moments of concentration a finger at his nose. Johnny was a self-taught cynic, and talked

---

* I also had pimples, not many, but prominently located, usually on the end of my nose and big enough to be visible as soon as I was. Donald used to call that one my "auxiliary nose," bless his darling heart.

that way. Donald's voice was gruff and abrupt. They were both smart as hell. Not only that. They were far more mature than the rest of us, including Clark; Johnny was a year or two older than I, and Donald a year or two older than that. (He had to be all of nineteen.) But the real clincher, the thing that elevated both of them to at least veneration, if not actual sanctity, was that they both had actually been paid for work published in a professional science-fiction magazine. Johnny had earned his letter by winning some sort of contest, in which he supplied a plot that some other writer—I think it was Clifford D. Simak—wrote a story around. Donald had done even better than that. A story entirely of his own creation, "The Man from Ariel," had been published.

And, it turned out, that was why they were with us. They were mad. Hugo Gernsback wasn't paying his writers. Johnny had finally collected his five dollars, but not without endless annoyance, and Donald had not been paid in full even then. They had come to the Brooklyn Science Fiction League to tell us their stories, and to seek vengeance.

All this inside information was revelatory to me. It was more exciting than anything that had happened to me before, at least since I discovered science fiction, maybe since I discovered sex. I don't know what airy-fairy assumptions I had made about the mechanisms by which real authors supported themselves through their work. I suppose, if I thought at all, I guessed that once your work appeared in print, the government, or somebody, handed you a blank checkbook, which you filled out as you needed, or chose to want, their money.

Now that I have had forty-some years of dealing with publishers on my own, and some of them even more reluctant than Hugo to cough up the scratch, I can see the picture in full holographic 3-D. Gernsback was not alone. Other publishers have been known to stiff their authors. It is a matter of how much money is coming in, call it X, and how much is going out: Y. When X $\geq$ Y, all is serene. But when X $<$ Y, then you have the problem of eleven holes in the dike and only ten fingers to plug them with. When you can't pay all the bills, which bills do you pay? You placate the people who can hurt you the most. You pay your own salary, or at least enough to keep you going. You pay the printers, because if you don't they won't print your next issue, and then you're out of business. You pay your paper supplier, because if you don't he won't give the printer any paper to print your next issue on. Out of what's left you pay at least enough of your taxes, rent, and utilities to keep things from being turned off. And then you start to think about the writers.

All this is, of course, immoral. Without the writers none of the other things matter in the least. But it is the way it is, and one reason for it is that writers do not write only for money. They write to be published. All writers like to be paid for what they write, but few would stop writing just because the money was sparse or hard to collect. And those few are easily and instantly replaced out of the immense pool of millions, literally millions, of would-be writers who would sell their sisters to Buenos Aires for the chance to have one story published anywhere, paid for or not.

Of course, the stories written by the pros are probably likely to sell more copies for you than the cleaned-up salvage from the slush pile. But maybe you can't afford to be choosy. If given the choice between publishing a magazine with so-so stories (but stories you can get) and a magazine made up of blank pages because the really good writers won't give you any more credit, which would you do? You would probably hold your nose and publish. If you didn't, your place, too, might well be taken by some would-be publisher ready to fill the vacuum.

Not all publishers think that way—in fact, let me put on the record right now that the business ethics in publishing seems to me a lot more praiseworthy than in most industries. But some do, even in the best of times. And in the Depression that was the Law of Nature, red in tooth and fang. Clayton's *Astounding* had paid its writers punctually and well. Clayton's *Astounding* also had gone bust in 1933. *Amazing* and *Wonder* were a whole lot less benevolent, but they were still alive.

It's interesting to try to calculate just how much money Gernsback traded the good will of his writers for. It probably was not very much—in the thousands, but probably not in the tens of thousands. But then there wasn't all that much money around in the science-fiction field at that time. In the mid-30s there were only three science-fiction magazines, often bimonthly. I estimate that the total amount paid to writers by all three of them in an average year was not much over fifteen thousand dollars. Allowing for pseudonyms, there may have been as many as fifty individuals selling stories to one or another of them in that period, and what they had to divide among themselves in return for feeding all us famished fans the fiction we lived on was something like six dollars per week per writer.

I could have made that calculation at the time, if I had wanted to. I didn't want to. I didn't care.

Listening to the wisdom that flowed from Johnny Michel and Don Wollheim was like standing on the mountain, staff in hand, while the Voice spoke from the burning bush. I could not believe I was so lucky, and I wanted to be part of it.

I came back from the meetings and reported all

this Gospel to Dirk, who cursed his parents for settling in Queens Village, so far from Bay Ridge and the Brooklyn Science Fiction League, and worked out stratagems for making the next meetings with me. We came. We sat at the feet of the masters, in one soda fountain or another, while the ice cream melted in our sodas and our malteds went flat, and we resolved to be just like them.

And when it turned out that Johnny and Donald were inviting us to join a crusade to set these iniquities aright, we took it as not debatable that we should sign up at once. What Donald proposed was that all we SFL members should secede, start our own clubs, assert our independence of The Evil One, and let the world know him for what he was. It sounded great. We thrilled to the idea of causing so much commotion and trouble for Gernsback that he would perforce reform. Or kill himself. Or be driven from the society of human beings; choice of any or all of the above; and so we entered into the great world of science-fiction feuds.

3

Science-fiction Samizdat

The fanzines are the underground press of science fiction. They come in all shapes and sizes, the contents as varied as the format. Some is very good. The best article I have ever read on hand-to-hand combat in space was written by Harry Harrison and published in the fanzine *Amra*. All that I know about mescaline comes from a fanzine article by Bill Donaho. Damon Knight made his original reputation as a science-fiction critic by a surgical dissection of the quivering flesh of A. E. van Vogt, in a fanzine article when van Vogt was at the height of his popularity.

Some of it, on the other hand, is not very good at all, because there are no standards of excellence that fanzines must meet. Not *any*. All it takes to publish a fanzine is the will to make it happen, and maybe access to somebody else's mimeograph machine, and in a pinch you can get by without the latter. (There have been carbon-copied fanzines, limited to as many sheets of paper as you can roll into a typewriter.) Consequently there is a lot that is not very interesting to read even by the standards of the fellow who wrote it ("Gosh, friends, this is lousy, isn't it?"), and even a hostile reception does not necessarily keep a fanzine from continuing ("Wow, gang, you really slammed the lastish, but wotthehell, we'll keep plugging").

Reflecting the fact that everything is always getting bigger, there are some pretty spectacular fanzines these days, professionally printed, illustrated handsomely, even one or two, like Andy Porter's *Algol*, which, my God!, actually pay their contributors. Charlie Brown's news-fanzine, *Locus*, sells a couple thousand copies an issue. (We were lucky to get rid of twenty-five, most of them free.) But the lower end of the spectrum stays pretty much the same, and that's where most of the action is. No matter how deficient in redeeming social virtues a fanzine may seem to you and me, it always has one: it is educating the person who puts it out. Ray Bradbury got his start in fanzines. So did a couple dozen of the best other science-fiction writers around.

When I got my hands on the levers of power in *The Brooklyn Reporter*, I didn't think of it as a training program. I thought of it as fun, scary fun in a way, because I perceived that I could make a fool out of myself in a more public fashion than I had ever been able to do before. But pleasure apart from that.

What we printed was a mix of what interested us, and although we did not consciously think out the probability that that would also be what interested those other people just like us who would hopefully be our readers, still that's a good way of being an editor. We printed news of what was going on in our club ("Eight members present at the last meeting, and Joseph Harry Dockweiler joined"), reviews of the professional science-fiction magazines ("The newest Van Manderpootz story is about a professor who has spectacles that can see into the future. It's a hack idea, but Weinbaum's comic treatment saves it"), gossip about the pros ("Doc Smith has just completed the mathematical calculations for his next Skylark novel, which runs to one hundred thousand words, or longer than the serial will be"), and letters. Oh, yes, letters, lots of letters, and probably they were the most interesting things in many of the magazines. Some fanzines, like the long-lasting West Coast *Voice of the Imagi-Nation,* printed nothing else.

We also published amateur stories and poems. Usually they had been rejected by all the pros, for good reason. Sometimes they were a kind of writing for which professional markets did not seem to exist. My favorite of the fanzines I edited was a tiny quarter-size mimeographed job named *Mind of Man,* and what it was mostly about was playing with words. *MoM* was tiny, infrequent, and died at an early age, but I loved it. The contents owed something to Lewis Carroll and quite a lot to James Joyce (whose "work in progress," later called *Finnegans Wake,* was running in batches in a strange little magazine called *transition*). There was also a little science fiction in *Mind of Man* now and then, but you had to look pretty close to find it; then, as now, there was no rule that the contents of an sf fanzine had to have anything to do with sf. I wrote nearly everything published in it, including a lot of, ah, poetry? Call it that—

> Necroptic life, in Thursday bliss,
> Exploits the winnowed worker's brawn,
> While taurine canines gently kiss
> With urine the aurescid lawn.

I would guess that the total circulation of *Mind of Man* ran well into two figures, and that counts the pass-arounds; but there were those who liked it. Even years later, once or twice people have quoted poems from it from memory, and I was immensely flattered. And other fanzine editors would ask me to do "something like that" for them.

That's one of the sinful temptations editors put in the way of writers: "Say, Joe, I loved *Catch-22*; why don't you write something like that for me?" It's a bad thing for writers, but fortunately I was immune to that temptation at that time. I didn't know how to write "something like that" again. I wasn't really sure how I had come to write "that" in the first place.

While we were staining our fingers with mimeograph ink, our eyes were still firmly fixed on the professional magazines. They looked like Heaven.

To their editors and writers, I am sure they looked a lot less than heavenly; the Depression was still with us, sparing nor man nor magazine. But *figurez-vous*, even at half a cent a word, a five thousand-word story would fetch twenty-five dollars. Twenty-five dollars happened to be what my mother earned every week and supported both of us on. But, of course, the money was not the point.

So I wrote my stories, and I sent them out. I didn't actually finish very many of them; I was given to beginning stories, reading what I had written, deciding it was awful, and throwing it away. In that judgment I was no doubt right, but if I had known then what I know now, I would have forced myself to finish them, anyway, for the practice and the discipline. Of the hundreds upon hundreds of sheets of paper I covered with typing in the mid-1930s, only a few dozen wound up as "finished" stories, mostly very short, and with them I assaulted the professional editors.

The conventional and best way to submit stories is to mail them in. That cost money, maybe a dime each way for each submission. I quickly realized that for half that much I could take the subway to the editors' offices and hand the stories over myself, at the negligible expense of a few hours of my own time.

Moving in the company of Real Pros like Don

Wollheim had given me some sophistication. To appear in any professional science-fiction magazine would be total ecstasy, but some magazines offered more ecstasy than others, or at least more money, and so I started at the top.

Astounding had gone down the tube as a member of the Clayton pulp chain, but Street & Smith had bought into the wreckage, and it was back in business. Its editor was a man named F. Orlin Tremaine, and it was housed in a dilapidated old slum on Seventh Avenue, a block below Barney's clothing store. I have no idea when the building was new, probably sometime in the Middle Jurassic. The lower floors were filled with printing presses, shaking the whole structure as they rolled. The building had a hydraulic elevator. To make it go up or down, the operator had to tug on a rope outside the car itself. The building had long since been declared a hazard by the fire marshal, and so smoking was prohibited everywhere in it. (That didn't actually stop anybody, it only inconvenienced them a little. When John Campbell became editor a little later on, he kept a copper ashtray on his desk, copper because of its high thermal conductivity, and whisked it into a drawer when the early-warning system announced the presence of a fire warden.) To get from the reception room to any editor's office involved going up and down staircases, squeezing past rolls of paper stored to feed the ground-floor presses, reveling in the fascinating smells of printer's ink and rotting wood.

I didn't get past the reception room the first couple of times. I was met at the desk by a diffident young male assistant to Tremaine; he took the manuscript from my grubby young hands, flipped through it, and announced that I didn't have my name and address typed in the upper right-hand corner of the first page. It was on the last page, I told him. Well enough, he said, but it's *supposed* to be on the first one. He also pointed out that standard typing paper was 8½ x 11 inches and plain white, while what I was using was several inches longer than that and had narrow blue lines down the left-hand margin. Sorry about that, I said. (I didn't tell him the reason. My mother worked in a law office at that time, and legal cap was what she filched to bring home to me.) But he allowed me to leave the story with him, and a week or two later I got a penny postcard from Street & Smith, announcing that it was "ready for pickup." The card was a printed form, from which I deduced that I was not the only writer who had more time than postage stamps.

I came to see a great many of those cards over the years. Tremaine never bought a word from me, or even came very close. But he was nice about it. After the first couple of submissions he began inviting me down to his office to chat, and toward the end of his tenure even took me out to lunch now and then.

I cannot tell you how much this inflated me, not only in my own ego but in the estimation of my fellow fans. Heaven knows what he got out of it. Since I was editing several fanzines at the time, it is possible that he mistook me for some kind of power figure among the readers, but I don't really think so. I think Tremaine was just a good guy.

He was also a good editor. John Campbell is the worshipped god in the pantheon of *Astounding*, but Tremaine did some smart things. It was not his fault that he knew nothing at all about science fiction when he took it on; Street & Smith bought it and handed it to him as a chore, and that was that. He did his best to learn, and he succeeded. He published some incredible rot. He even wrote some of the sappiest of it, or at least so gossip says: "Warner Van Lorne," one of the most frequent bylines in his magazine, was

supposed to be Tremaine himself. But he did some
very smart things. (Including hiring John Campbell to
succeed him when he was moved upstairs.) I liked
him, respected him, missed him when he left, and
wondered if this young punk Campbell would ever
measure up to Tremaine's standards.

Tremaine was no scientist, and so *Astounding* during
his tenure was likely to come up with some galumph-
ing horrors, but the virtue of that defect was that he
was able to publish some pretty fascinating stuff that
any scientifically trained person would never touch. Not
just stories. *Astounding* ran nearly the complete works
of Charles Fort, in interminable serial form, compendia
of curious and inexplicable happenings: minnows falling from a clear sky, strange lights of airships seen
before airships were invented. The towering flights of
fantasy in the Tremaine *Astounding* were an attractive
change from the nuts-and-bolts gadgetry of Gernsback's *Wonder* or the stilted stodge of T. O'Conor
Sloane's *Amazing.*

Nevertheless, as *Astounding* didn't seem to want
to buy what I had to sell, I took my wares to the others,
too. *Wonder Stories* was a grubby kind of magazine,
full of self-glorifying little digs at the competition,
such as long lists of titles of stories published in other
magazines under the heading "Stories We Reject Appear Elsewhere." (Don Wollheim said it should have
read "Stories We Don't Pay For Appear Elsewhere.")
Yet it had two things going for it. One was that the
major find of the mid-30s, a new writer named Stanley
G. Weinbaum, turned up there long before he was
seen in any other magazines. Weinbaum was great;
his first story, "A Martian Odyssey," still appears on
most lists of all-time best science fiction. Well it
should. Weinbaum invented in it a character of a
sort no one had thought to create before, an ostrich-
shaped alien creature named Tweel who didn't think,

talk, act, or look like a human, but was nevertheless
a *person*. All other writers in the field, once the egg
had been demonstrated to stand on its end, immediately began to invent personalized alien creatures
of their own, and have continued to do so ever since.

The other thing that made *Wonder* attractive was
that they had mighty nice rejection slips. From
Astounding I never even saw a slip, just the penny
postcard that told me to come and carry away another
corpse, but most magazines printed up little three-by-
five or so forms, along the general lines of

> We regret that your submitted material is not
> suitable for our needs at this time, but thank
> you for submitting it.
>   THE EDITORS

Wonder's were nothing like that. I usually wrote very
short stories, hardly having the confidence to tackle
anything much over two thousand words, and so it
seemed to me more than once that *Wonder's* rejections
were longer than the stories concerned. There was a
form letter signed by Hugo himself, benignly explaining how strict his standards were. There was a printed
check-off sheet, listing thirty or so reasons for rejection:

( ) Plot stale
( ) Errors in science
( ) Material offensive to moral standards

and lots more. And, to take the sting out of it, there
was a jolly little "translation" of a "Chinese rejection
slip." ("Your honorable contribution is so breath-
takingly excellent that we do not dare publish it, since
it would set a standard no other writer would be able
to reach.") It was almost fun to be rejected by
Wonder. Impersonal fun, though. Hugo Gernsback
was by no means as gregarious a personality as F. Orlin
Tremaine.

Their offices were on Hudson Street in lower Manhattan, and Dirk and I hiked over there from Brooklyn Tech a time or two. We milled around in the anteroom, under the original oil paintings of covers from his gadget and radio magazines, but we never got past the reception desk. After about two visits the girl made it clear to us that we never would, and so for submissions to *Wonder* I scraped up stamp money.

I never got past the reception desk at *Amazing*, either, but T. O'Conor Sloane, Ph.D., did something for me no other editor had done. He made me a pro. Sloane was quite an old man, white-bearded and infirm of gait. He was a marvel to me just on account of age—my own grandfather, who died around that time, was only in his sixties, and Sloane was at least a decade or two past that. But he was amiable and cordial enough; he would totter out to meet me, chat for a moment, and retire with that week's offering in his hand.

His talent as a science-fiction editor was not, I am sorry to say, marked. His scientific attitudes had been fixed somewhere around the rosy twilight of his career, say 1910, and anything since then he dismissed as fantasy. He put himself firmly on record as denying that any human being would ever leave the surface of the Earth in a spaceship, and to us Skylark addicts that was diagnostically treason. What he published was a queer mix of flamboyant space adventure and barely imaginative stories of exploration, all heavily weighted with his interminably balanced blurbs, editorials, and comments on letters.

I cannot resist describing one set of the space adventures for you. They began with a story called "The Jameson Satellite," written by Neil R. Jones. "The Jameson Satellite" was about a very rich university professor who had nothing much to do with his money and nobody to leave it to. He decided to use it to make himself the dandiest tomb a fellow could have, and so he built in his backyard a rocket ship, big and powerful enough to take his body into orbit, where it would circle Earth, preserved by the absolute zero of space, until the end of time. After a while, it all came about as he planned. He died. His executor had his unembalmed corpse loaded into the rocket, they lit the fuse, and *zap*, there went all that was mortal of Professor Jameson right into orbit.

But there was more. The Earth rolled along. Time passed. The human race became extinct, the sun itself grew cold—and yet Jameson was still there in the deepfreeze. And then, in the fullness of time, strangers came poking around. They were machine-men called Zoromes. They had once had fleshly bodies, more or less like you and me (except that they had tentacles and a few other peculiarities of anatomy), and when they discovered the Jameson satellite with its cargo of still-fresh meat, it was no trouble for them to do with the human corpse what they had done with their own bodies long and long ago: They built him a machine body, took out his brain, thawed it, and stuck it into the machine. And so thereafter, for endless adventures, Professor Jameson lived once again as the Zorome called 21MM392.

The Zorome stories were among the most popular series of the 1930s, and not just with me. There was another reader, a youngster named Bob Ettinger, who liked them as much as I did. A few decades later, when Ettinger was grown up and a scientist on the faculty of a Midwest university, he remembered old Professor Jameson's deepfreeze and wondered just how much science was in that science fiction. So he dug into the biochemistry and the physics, checked out what was known about the effects of liquid gas temperatures on animal tissue, even costed the current quotations for liquid helium and triply insulated containers big

enough to hold you and me . . . and evolved the pro-
posal described in his book, *The Prospects of Immortality*, for freezing everyone who dies until such
time as medical science figures out how to thaw him
out and repair him. Right now there are a couple of
dozen corpsicles in the United States (Walt Disney
is supposed to be one of them) waiting for that great
thawing-out day. It is not yet clear whether they will
make it or not; as Bob Ettinger says, they're halfway
there; they've frozen quite a few but haven't thawed
any out yet.* But if they do make it, they will owe
quite a bit to Neil R. Jones and 21MM392.

In my personal scale of priorities, the fact that
Sloane gave the world the freezing program is somewhat overshadowed by the fact that he gave me my
first paid publication ever. It wasn't a story, it was a
poem (called "Elegy to a Dead Planet: Luna," and
if you feel for any reason that you must read it—I
don't know why that would be so—you can find it in
a book called *The Early Pohl*). People ask me from
time to time when I made my first sale. For me, that's
hard to answer. I wrote the poem in 1935. Sloane accepted it in 1936. It was published in 1937. And I was
paid for it in 1938.

Funny thing. I never had another line in *Amazing*,
from that day to this. Sloane actually accepted another poem, and I had bright hopes of laying stories
on him as well, but before anything could be published,
much less paid for, *Amazing* too was sold to the
knackers, and Sloane disappeared from the science-
fiction scene. The new owners made it sell better than
it ever had, but by publishing fairly simple-minded
stories—or so I judged them; the objective facts are

* Ettinger is an admirably levelheaded scientist, with an engaging sense of humor. When I asked him once how come there
were so few frozen prospects, he shrugged and said, "Many are
cold, but few are frozen."

that I didn't care much for what they published, and
they didn't care much for what I wrote, and after a
while I stopped even trying them. By then I had found
more hospitable markets, anyway. But there's a certain
nostalgia. You never forget your first sale.

But I am ahead of myself; before I became a Pro
I had a few years of fandom to get through, and
things had happened in my personal life, too.

My parents separated when I was thirteen years old,
not amicably. My plunging father took one shortcut
too many and wound up in trouble with the law, not
just creditor trouble but grand jury trouble. I was
never told the details. One day he was gone, and my
mother told me he would not be coming back to live
with us any more; it was three or four years before
I saw him again, but, in all candor, I didn't much
mind. He had seemed a guest in the house all along.
He traveled a lot, and even when he was technically
at home he was away most of the days, and a lot of
the nights.

Looking back at it objectively, it must not have
been a tranquil time for me. Yet I don't know where
the scars are. Like all writers, I spend a lot of time
exploring the inside of my own head, and once or
twice I've had professional help in the rummaging
around. Like all human beings, I have childhood pains
or worries or yearnings unmet that still show up in a
barroom or on a couch; how strange that any of the
race survives, when we are all so vulnerable in childhood. But I did not feel very bad about my parents
at the time. The focus of my life had moved out of
the home long before then, perhaps when I learned to
live vicariously through books, certainly when I found
the world of science fiction to explore. In school and
at home I was still a child, the passive object of what
the authority figures chose to do; but in science fiction

I could be a maker and shaker on my own. Well, no. Not entirely on my own. Don Wollheim was the leader of our junta and the planner of our coups, but we were at the least his kitchen cabinet, Johnny Michel, and a little later Bob Lowndes, and I, and we four marched from Brooklyn to the sea, leaving a wide scar of burned-out clubs behind us. We changed clubs the way Detroit changes tailfins, every year had a new one and last year's was junk.

1934 was the year of the BSFL. 1935 was the year of the ENYSFL, later the ILSF. 1936 was the year of the ICSC, later the NYB-ISA. By 1937 we had got tired of initials, and of laying our cuckoos' eggs in other people's nests, and we formed The Futurians.*

The Brooklyn SFL lasted barely a year, just barely long enough for us to find each other. It did not survive the invasion of the barbarians. G. G. Clark did not much care for Donald and Johnny, and must have resented being shoved off the seat of power. ("Am I not Member One? Was I not chartered to possess Chapter One by Hugo himself?") But Hugo had chartered chapters everywhere he could, on whatever flimsy pretext any member had the gall to offer him. Dave Kyle even started a chapter in Monticello, New York, of which the entire membership was pseudonyms of his own. There was already another chapter in Brooklyn, the ENYSFL, and we birds of passage flew on.

The East New York SFL was the fiefdom of a high-

---

* BSFL: The Brooklyn Chapter of the Science Fiction League, formed by George Gordon Clark. ENYSFL: The East New York (another part of Brooklyn) chapter of the same. ILSF; The same group, gone public and renamed the Independent League for Science Fiction. ICSC: International Cosmos-Science Club. NYB-ISA: The New York Branch of the same, now retitled the International Scientific Association, but still a pure sf fan club regardless.

schooler named Harold W. Kirshenblit ("KB"), who also had a big cellar his parents allowed him to use for meetings. You took the BMT as far as it went, and then walked. KB was a livelier, sharper article than Clark, willing to make and shake with us, and in no time Donald talked him into seceding from *Wonder Stories* and creating a new worldwide competitor to the SFL. Donald was not alone—Johnny and I helped in every way we could—but it was Donald's wrath that moved us all, and his decision, I think, to point up what was going on by naming the new construct the Independent League for Science Fiction. Lowndes showed up in the flesh at the ILSF and immediately joined the team. For the next five years or so we four stuck together, called ourselves "the Quadrumvirate," and made our presence known wherever we were. At the end of a year East New York had no further charms, and so we all moved on to Astoria, Queens, where William S. Sykora had a club in *his* basement. Having a house with a basement was a lot like owning a catcher's mitt; you could always start a game of your own.

Will Sykora was a medium-sized man with enormous sloping shoulders. He had immense self-confidence* and a bump of arrogance that comported ill with our own collective and individual bumps of arrogance. Nevertheless, he had a group that seemed to be *doing* things. He had called it the International Cosmos Science Club, but on reflection "cosmos" seemed to take in a bit more territory than was justified, and so he changed it to the International Scientific Association. (It wasn't international, either, but then it also wasn't scientific.)

* "There's nothing hard about being a pro science-fiction writer. I could sell *Astounding* a story if I wanted to. It would take maybe three weeks to figure out what they want."—I heard, and marveled greatly thereat.

Both the BSFL and the ILSF had published club journals, but they didn't amount to much. The ISA's magazine was something else. It was called *The International Observer*, and, at least when we spread ourselves on a special issue, it was something to see. I became its editor, and I recall the immense pride of holding in my hand one issue, forty or more pages long, cover silk-screened in color by Johnny Michel, inside with hand-lettered titles and justified margins and even a little bit of art; I think that may have been the biggest fanzine published at that time, and I was supremely certain it was the best.

An issue of a magazine is a kind of work of art. The *IO* was not just something that had come off a distant printing press, it was a personal part of my life; I had typed every stencil with my own hands, run them off with Johnny and the others on his mimeograph machine, folded the cover and punched in the staples. To me it was a creation. I think maybe there is some criticism that could be made of that *auteur* approach (what makes me suspect it is that although I clearly remember the scent of the mimeograph ink and the heft of that issue in my hand, I can barely remember a word of what it said inside). But publishing itself is a joy apart from the contents of what it is you publish, something like building ship models in a bottle.

Indeed, it turned out that we sf fanzine people were not alone in the world; there was a whole society of amateur journalists who weren't interested in science fiction but were addicted to the smell of printer's ink. Just as in science fiction, there were feuds and splits among them. The two leading clubs were called the National Amateur Press Association and the United Amateur Press Association of America, and Johnny and Donald and I quickly joined them to see what we could learn.

They were not, in the long run, exactly what I wanted to do with my life. I went to a few meetings. I even went with Donald on the long, thrilling train ride to Boston to attend a weekend amateur-journalist convention, a great excitement to me because I had almost never traveled without some member of my family. They were pretty good people, and I admired what they could do that I could not: most of them owned their own cold-type printing presses, real letterpress instead of the mimeos and hectographs of sf fandom. But most of what was in the magazines they published was *about* the magazines they published, and it seemed a little too incestuous for my blood. When my first year's membership dues expired, I dropped out.*

With only three science-fiction magazines and hardly any science-fiction books we were on near-starvation rations of sf-in-print. But there were snacks to be had

---

* There was a kind of sequel to that. In the 1960s I wrote a fair amount for *Playboy* and was delighted to do so: not only did they pay an order of magnitude better than the science-fiction magazines, but from time to time I got to meet Hefner and the bunnies. I survived through several changes of editors and thought nothing of it when a new fellow named Robie Macauley became fiction editor. I sent him a few stories, and he bought a reasonable proportion of them.

Then one day I happened to be in Chicago on other business, and stopped by the Playboy Building to cement relationships. Turned out Robie had been an ay-jay himself; more, it turned out that we had actually met at that Boston convention, back in the teen-age dawn of time. We had a very pleasant chat, cutting up old touches and parting on the best of terms. Wow! Every young writer's dream come true! The buy-or-bounce guy at a major market turns out to be a boyhood chum! But it didn't work out that way. I never again sold a word to *Playboy* in all the years Robie was fiction editor. Well. I'm sure it was only coincidence. But all the same, every once in a while I wondered just what I might have said or done, forty years ago in Boston.

elsewhere, and once in a while a full meal. And a lot of the nourishment came from science-fiction films. The 30s were the great years of the film for everyone, not just science-fiction fans. Every hamlet had its own million-dollar Palace of the Movies, plush carpets and tinkling fountains, architecturally a bastard son of the Bolshoi out of the Baths of Caracalla. Most were left over from the manic expansion of the 20s, but nerve was seeping back into the builders. The Radio City Music Hall opened when I was around thirteen. The Music Hall didn't care much for science fiction on its screen, but the hall itself was a kind of science fiction, ultramodern of 1932, and I must have visited it fifty times to see whatever was there to see: my first color film (*Becky Sharp*); Will Rogers comedies; my first, and almost only, 3-D (a short subject; you wore red and green celluloid goggles to make it work); above all, the Fred Astaire and Ginger Rogers musicals, on which I doted. The Music Hall gave you more than a film. There was a stage show with the Rockettes and the Corps de Ballet, and a symphonic overture and an organ interlude, hopefully planned to empty out the house between shows. I had a fixed itinerary at the Music Hall. Up in one of the balconies for the film, so I could smoke. Down in the front rows, far left, to watch Jesse Crawford play the organ at microscopically close range. Middle aisles of the orchestra, two-thirds of the way back, to watch the Rockettes.

But there was a growing amount of science fiction, too, if not in the music hall, then at some other theater, even the "nabes." The original *King Kong* (only film I have ever seen that gave me nightmares). Claude Rains in *The Invisible Man*. Boris Karloff in *Frankenstein*. The very first sf film I saw was *Just Imagine*, produced in 1930, about the incredibly distant future world of 1980 (autogyro traffic cops, Martians, babies out of a slot machine): it was a slapstick comedy starring El Brendel, notable now mostly because it was the first American film made by lovely Maureen O'Sullivan, later Tarzan's favorite Jane. There were gadgety future-adventure movies like *F P 1 Does Not Reply* (floating airport in the middle of the Atlantic, where planes refueled en route to Europe) and *Transatlantic Tunnel* (marvelous zappy machines boring through the undersea rock). There were semi-satirical spoofs like *It's Great to Be Alive*. What was great about it, for the hero, was that some pestilence had killed every male in the world but him, and he was therefore the object of every girl's affections. It was a musical, and the way the girls courted him was through song and dance numbers.*

Not all of the science-fiction and fantasy films were really much good (as you maybe have already figured out!) but among them there were two that turned me on to a degree no subsequent film has matched.

One of them was *Death Takes a Holiday*. It starred Fredric March. Its theme music was Sibelius's *Valse Triste*, which stayed in my mind for months on end. (After a while I wrote words to it, so I could sing it in the shower.) March played the part of Death, proud anthropomorphic Prince of Darkness, sulkily curious about why mortal beings bother living their brief, tatty little lives. He takes time off to visit a house party in Nice or Graustark (villagers tossing rosebuds into an open car, pergolas, drawing rooms, reflecting pools). His intention is to satisfy his curiosity, but he falls in love. While he is on vacation no one dies. Suffering is prolonged. His fellow guests figure out his identity and beg him to get back on the job, but he won't go without the girl. . . . Well, the plot does

---

* E.g., a troupe of Eastern European lady wrestlers singing:
   We are the girls from Czechoslovakia.
   We are strong, and how we can sock-y-ya.

not bear rational examination, but I loved it. What I
love I love a lot. I saw it twenty-three times.
The other film that blew my mind was *Things to
Come*. I still think it is the finest science-fiction film
ever made, greater than *Metropolis*, more meaningful
than *2001*. I concede that it looks pretty quaint now,
but so will *Star Wars* in another forty years. I saw
Things to Come thirty-three times before I stopped
counting. Quite recently I saw it again—in fact, took
on the chore of organizing a college science-fiction
film festival just to give myself the chance to see it.
It is still *grand*.

Things to Come was the first major film for Ralph
Richardson and Raymond Massey, and I have had an
immense liking for both of them ever since. It wasn't
exactly a story. It was almost a documentary, and
financially speaking it was a bomb. But every frame
is engraved on my mind. So is Arthur Bliss's score.
For years I had the 78-rpm album of the music, until
the winter I unwisely left the wax discs on a radiator.
Now I have an illicit tape dubbed off the radio, and
I still think it's fine. The film was real science fiction,
not papier-mâché Godzillas or carrot-shaped Martians.
It was written by a real science-fiction writer, in fact
the father of us all, old H. G. Wells himself. And it
was handsomely filmed with actors who knew what
they were about.

Let me confess to something. I think a great deal
of *Death Takes a Holiday* and *Things to Come* rubbed
off in the deep-down core of my brain. I have no
particular fear of dying, and I think that one part of
the reason for that lies in some subliminal feeling that
when it happens it will be old Fredric March who
takes me by the hand and says, "Hey Fred, long time
no see." And in spite of all the evidence, I am opti-
mistic about the future of the world. I have a conviction
that bad times and good all pass, and all are endurable,

and that is what *Things to Come* had to say. You can blow up the world as often as you like, but there is a future, there is always a future, and while some of it will be bad, some of it will be better than anyone has ever known.

For the opening of *Things to Come* we fans got up a real theater party—not a very big one (I think about six of us could afford tickets), but there we were, en masse, going to taste this great new experience together. James Blish, kid fan from far-off East Orange, New Jersey, came in to join us. Like all of us, he wanted to be a writer. Like all of us, he was learning how in the fanzines, publishing one of his own and writing for others. And like a lot of us, he got his heart's desire, with books like *Cities in Flight* and *A Case of Conscience* among the long list of first-rate work that only ended with his death, a year or so ago.

Jim Blish from New Jersey, Bob Lowndes from Connecticut—we were becoming quite cosmopolitan. Evidently there were specimens of our own breed in other parts of the world. We had linked up with them through fanzine and letter, but we hungered for the personal contact. And so, one Sunday in 1936, half a dozen of us got on the train for Philadelphia and were met by half a dozen Philadelphia fans, and so the world's very first science-fiction convention took place. Considering the historical significance of the event, it is astonishing how little I remember about what happened there. It's no good looking for the official minutes, either: I was the secretary who took them, and I have no idea where I put them. Philly fan John V. Baltadonis's father owned a bar, and we met in one corner of it for the business part of the session. Robert A. Madle and Oswald Train were part of the Philadelphia contingent, and I still see them pretty regularly at sf conventions; so was Milton A. Rothman, who published a few stories (some of them

with me) under the name of Lee Gregor before de-
ciding to devote his time to nuclear physics. From
New York were Johnny Michel, Don Wollheim, Will
Sykora, Dave Kyle, and myself.

The last convention I went to had four thousand
people in attendance, and it was by no means the
biggest sf convention ever. There must be a hundred
of them a year in the United States, and maybe another hundred here and there in the rest of the world.
But that was the first.

By 1937 the ISA had served its function and was
off to join the dodo and the diplodocus. There was a
change in the scenario, this time. Once we had de-
populated the BSFL and the ILSF, their directors,
Clark and Kirshenblit, dropped out of science fiction
and were seen no more. Willy Sykora was of sterner
stuff. He stayed on, joined a new group called the
Queens Science Fiction League, and formed powerful
alliances with its leaders, Sam Moskowitz and James
V. Taurasi. The three of them before long created a
whole new wide-ranging group called New Fandom,
of which more will be heard later.

What we others did was equally new. Previously
we had, cuckoolike, laid our eggs in others' nests. Now
we decided to form our own club. Weary of initials,
we selected a name for it that did not need truncation:
The Futurians.

For that we will need another chapter, but before
we get to it there is something else that needs to be
spelled out. It was not only science fiction that held
some of us together any more. A few of us had found
an interest in politics—politics of the left; in fact, one
or two of us called ourselves Communists.

4

Boy Bolsheviks

Kings Highway has been a major thoroughfare for three centuries. It cuts clear through Brooklyn and picks up again on the other side of the Bay in New Jersey; it was the King's road, and his troops retreated down it after the Battle of Monmouth. In 1936 it was the heart of a prosperous Brooklyn residential district. You got off at the BMT Brighton Line station and walked south along the highway, past restaurants and candy stores, kosher delicatessens and funeral parlors, and after half a dozen blocks you came to a storefront with meeting rooms on its second floor. Usually they were rented to wedding parties or bar mitzvahs, but one night a week they belonged to the Flatbush Branch of the Young Communist League.

Johnny Michel was a YCLer. When he told me that, I was startled and thrilled. It seemed a *very* grown-up thing to be. Elliptically I tried to find out from him what a Communist was, what they did in their meetings, how he had come to be one, why he thought it was worth doing. I didn't get much satisfaction out of him, but after a couple of months of building my curiosity the tip was ready to turn, and he allowed that if I really wanted to know all these things, I could come with him to a meeting and find out for myself. I was sixteen, and quite flattered to be chosen; I think I was also a little scared by it, which made it even more irresistible.

The room was still set up for some sort of party, fake palm trees in pots and hooded band instruments against the wall. There were about a hundred people there, mostly young, but none younger than I. The principal speaker didn't seem young at all to me. I suppose he was around thirty. His name was Mike Saunders (I found out later it was a "Party name"; most YCL leaders used them), and he gave a speech of welcome to all the "new friends" in the audience. (Until that moment I had thought I was the only one.) Probably we had come there with all sorts of misconceptions about the YCL, he said. He reminisced about his own first encounter. It had been that way with him. He hadn't known what to expect: people with bombs and beards, girls walking around with mattresses strapped to their backs. I was a little uncomfortable with that. It seemed to be in bad taste, and besides, it was a little bit of a downer because I had daydreamed about something like that myself. But the YCLers, Mike explained, were not like that. They were really no different from any other American youth, except in good ways: Smarter, more alert. More socially conscious. More politically aware of the real needs of the people, which were jobs, security, democracy, and peace. Communism, he told us, was Twentieth-Century Americanism. The Communists were the chief defenses of the liberty-loving peoples of the world against the Fascist imperialists, Hitler, Mussolini, and Franco. The Communists supported the right of workers to organize in trade unions. The Communists were against race discrimination and in favor of civil rights, and the first thing the Communists had to do, he told us, was to reelect Franklin Delano Roosevelt President of the United States. Not on the ticket of the corrupt Democratic Party! No, but on the ticket of free, socially conscious Americans, the new third party that had just been formed; and we sang a song about it:

> We've got a baby all our own,
> All our own, all our own,
> We've got a baby all our own,
> The Farmer-Labor Party!

A couple of speeches, a few lefty songs (and great old songs they were), and that was the end of the formal part of the evening. For the next hour or so we talked about the club newspaper they wanted to publish and general get-acquainted topics over coffee and cake.

I observed them with the paranoid care of any kid in strange surroundings. They seemed to be pretty nice people. They were the right age. All the leaders were in their twenties or beyond, but the rank and file were teen-agers, a lot of them high-schoolers like me. They appeared to be one hundred percent white and ninety percent Jewish, but that was no surprise. So was the neighborhood. In the late 1920s I had lived just a few blocks away, at 1701 East 14th Street, and I had early learned I was the only Presbyterian on the block. Most of the most interesting science-fiction fans and writers I was meeting were also Jewish, but not working at it, and it was the same in the YCL. And, like the sf community, they were bright and articulate. I have always liked meeting people who know a lot about things that interest me, and I found in the Flatbush YCL a lot of people who knew a great deal about music, theater, art; above all, about politics and history—two areas in which I was all but totally ignorant. One of the disadvantages of going to Brooklyn Tech was that there were no history courses. Another disadvantage was that there were no girls in Brooklyn Tech, nor in the monastically male sf community of the 30s, and the other great attribute of the YCLers was that nearly half of them were demonstrably and attractively female.

I don't think I ever heard Franco's name before I walked into that meeting—his revolt against the Spanish government had only begun a few weeks before. I doubt seriously that I ever gave a thought to the evils of Hitler or Mussolini, or to the virtues of trade unionism or the New Deal. But they sounded like good things to feel strongly about. I liked singing and learning new songs. I foresaw a great career for myself on the proposed chapter newspaper. And before I left the hall that night I was a paid-up member, with a little red card with a hammer and sickle on it.

Johnny and I went back and reported to our fellow fans. We didn't make much of an impression at that time. Don Wollheim listened tolerantly with his usual half-smile, eyes gazing forty-five degrees to starboard. I don't think he minded the parts about Spain and peace, but he couldn't go along with supporting Franklin D. Roosevelt. When the time came a couple of months later, he marched off to the polls and cast his ballot as he had intended all along, for Alfred Mossman Landon.

Words take on the coloration of their times. The word "Communist" has one sound today, had quite another in the 50s, when Joe McCarthy shambled across the land, and probably will sound different still in the year 2000. In 1936 it sounded adventurous, active, and, above all, "progressive."

I'm not sure what the word "progressive" meant to

me, except that it seemed generally forward-looking. The Communists had made sure that it sounded so. They had finally figured out that if they didn't get a revolution in 1932, when the bonus marchers looked like an uprising even to Herbert Hoover and millions wondered where their next month's rent was coming from, they weren't going to get one at all in the forseeable future. So the word had come down to broaden the base. It worked pretty well. The Communist Party and the YCL combined had well over a hundred thousand members in the late 30s, vastly more than ever before or after. They controlled countless other groups—workers' fraternal organizations, trade unions, anti-Fascist leagues—with memberships ten or a hundred times as large.

I carried my YCL card for almost four years. For most of that time I believed in what I was doing and worked hard at it, a regular Jimmy Higgins: president of my own branch, street-corner rabble-rouser, ace recruiter, even a kind of low-level policy maker. Of course, the really important policies were set by levels of leadership so high they disappeared out of sight. But in the implementation of the commandments there was room for interpretation, and I held membership in a dozen county and state committees and in the national conventions. It was all pretty open and aboveboard, except for this curious little custom of "Party names."

From 1940 on the Communist apparatus became a lot less benign and a hell of a lot more conspiratorial, but I was long gone by then. I suppose that even in the 1930s some sort of infrastructure was being laid. But I saw no signs of it, no trace of anything that I could not reconcile with the Pledge of Allegiance and the Boy Scouts' oath. Maybe half a dozen times I was asked to do mildly covert things: attend a Nazi Bund meeting as a potential convert to report back on what they were up to (I chickened out of that one), pretend to be a member of some union to take part in a picket line. That was about it. The YCL was so square it was a disappointment.

What we did was right out in the open. We cruised the five-and-tens looking for Japanese goods, and when we found them we picketed the stores, urging boycott. When the International Catholic Truth Society picketed theaters showing the movie *Blockade,* an ever-so-mildly pro-Loyalist film about the Spanish Civil War, we counterpicketed the International Catholic Truth Society. Several times a year we filled up Madison Square Garden with conventions, rallies, debates, anti-Fascist mass meetings, whatever. Those were glorious fun, twenty thousand clenched fists raised in the last lines of the "Internationale," and afterward streaming out to Times Square to picket Walgreen's drugstore (in the process of a strike at the time) or just to show the flag.

More than anything else, we met. There were meetings all the time. Each branch met once a week. Committees met when they could. Between times there were parties, socials, musicales. Those were fund-raisers, a dozen people paying a quarter apiece to listen to records in someone's apartment. Mostly what we heard was strictly long-hair, Beethoven-Bach-Brahms, rarely even Stravinsky or Prokofiev. Since I didn't own a record player until I was twenty, the most exposure I had to classical music was at YCL musicales.

The actual meetings of the branches were something else, heavily political, with a table of pamphlets always by the door, and wondering hurt in the eyes of the comrade behind the counter if you didn't buy a couple. Yet, politically, what they said made sense. In the social dialogue, the opposition always has all the best lines. Boycott Japanese goods? Why, only a couple years later every human being in America shared those feelings. Practice collective security against the Rome-Berlin Axis? In far less than a decade, that became American national policy; it is what we now call the United Nations. Trade unionism, civil rights, an end to racial and sexual discrimination—no one now thinks of them as revolutionary. What the Communist Party and the YCL stood for in the 1930s, absent Moscow, looks pretty good right now.

But Moscow was never absent. It was the Homeland of the Working Class, the socialist paradise. It could not be criticized. Whatever it did was right. Among the pamphlets for sale at the YCL meetings was a little copy of the new Constitution of the U.S.S.R., a marvelous document whose concern for the rights of individuals and national minorities should be an inspiration for freedom fighters everywhere. Especially in the U.S.S.R. We could see in the Soviet Constitution that the death penalty was abolished. We could see in the daily paper that, nevertheless, an astonishing number of Old Bolsheviks were being systematically stood up against a wall for left-wing, right-wing zigzag deviationism, and what was in those rifles, bottle corks? And yet this astonishing dichotomy not only was not resolved in the endless YCL discussions, it was not even raised. I do not remember a single person in any YCL meeting ever questioning the treason trials, the concentration camps, or the denial of civil rights. Not even me.

We simply closed our eyes to what we did not want to see, and, of course, there are those who still can. Even now. Even after Solzhenitsyn's memoirs and Khrushchev's "secret" speech. Two or three years ago I was standing on the steps of Moscow's Hotel Ukraine, waiting for the embassy driver to pick me up, and I struck up a conversation with an Australian trade unionist. He was on a socialist holiday, he told me. He had been saving up for ten years to do it.

Stars were in his eyes. He had been to a light-industry factory that morning, and wasn't it wonderful, he asked me, to see workers happily engaged in industries that they themselves owned?

My driver came by before I could think of an answer, which is fortunate enough because I didn't have one, or at least one that he would have been willing to hear. Clemenceau said, "A man who is not a socialist at twenty has no heart. A man who still is a socialist at forty has no head." And my Aussie friend was well past forty.

I think I learned something from my four years in the YCL, and most of what I learned was—what shall I call it?—skeptical compassion. I am a lot less sure of my own moral incorruptibility than I might otherwise have been and, maybe, a little less righteous about other people's sins.

Like most teen-agers, I had a general distrust of authority figures; also like most teen-agers, I had a strong need to be part of something larger than myself. The YCL solved those problems for me. I could march while I decried militarism, oppose regimentation in disciplined ranks.

I wonder sometimes what might have happened in some alternative paratime world—say one in which my father's parents had not left Germany and my mother's had somehow wandered there, so that I grew up under Hitler's Third Reich instead of Roosevelt's New Deal. Would I have joined the Hitler Youth as easily as I plunged into the YCL? I hope not. On good days I even think not. I don't see how I could possibly have swallowed that hogwash and joined with the murderers of the innocent. . . . But I comprehend how it is that others did.

Over the next couple of years Johnny Michel and

I succeeded in persuading a few other science-fiction fans to follow us into the YCL.

Everything considered, we were not particularly successful. All YCLers were expected to reproduce themselves by the recruitment of others, and we did what we could; but most of my own tally of souls won for Stalin came from casual contacts at open-air meetings, prospect lists furnished by higher authority, and other sources not connected with science fiction.

I don't think our failure was because Communism was so outrageous an idea for science-fiction fans. It may even have been that it was not outrageous enough. Science-fiction fans, like science-fiction writers, are about the most obstinately individual people alive, and they do get into strange things. Preaching Marxism, we were competing with Technocrats, Esperantists, Single-Taxers, New Dealers, Ham-and-Eggers, and even one or two self-labeled Fascists. None of them were making much headway, either.

Of course, we were quite sure that there was a significant difference between them and us. They were whoring after false gods, and we had the real stuff. So six or eight of us constituted ourselves The Committee for the Political Advancement of Science Fiction, and drew up a manifesto for what we called "Michelism."

The Michelist Manifesto, signed by John B. Michel himself, but written with the help of all us master theoreticians, was syncretic, idiosyncratic, and stylistically derived from an F. Orlin Tremaine thought-variant story. It had a lot of V. I. Lenin in it, and a lot of H. G. Wells. We circulated it like any other fanzine, and it drew about the same kind of response, which is to say, it was treated as an entertainment instead of a revelation.

If we couldn't make Bolsheviks, perhaps we could at least create a few fellow travelers. Some of us copied the names of new fans out of the letter columns in *Astounding* and *Thrilling Wonder* and attempted conversion by mail:

> Dear Jim:
>   I enjoyed your letter in *Brass Tacks*, and I think you are right about Doc Smith. Have you read "Wollheim Speaking for Boskone"? It really shows what a Fascist mentality Smith and John Campbell are trying to foist off on us. A lot of us progressive fans are getting pretty irritated, and if you'd like to join us—

That didn't accomplish very much, giving our political-action efforts a nearly perfect score. I don't really think we expected it to. We knew whom we were dealing with: science-fiction fans. In order to read science fiction with any enjoyment, you have to be willing to make some pretty preposterous assumptions: men from Mars, time machines, invisibility, trips through the fourth dimension, all manner of mind-blowers. You don't have to believe these things are real. But you have to accept them as postulates at least while you are reading the story, or the story won't work. Trained in that school, science-fiction fans will play any game you propose. Just tell them the rules, and they're off . . . and then, ten minutes later, they're playing a quite different game with other rules entirely, and nothing is changed. Right discouraging, it was. Or would have been . . . if we hadn't been playing the same game.

5

The Futurians

By 1937 there were half a dozen science-fiction clubs in New York City, but none was quite satisfactory. Either we weren't particularly welcome in them, or we didn't like them to begin with. So we decided to start our own. We were getting pretty bored with Robert's Rules of Order, and so we limited the number of formal meetings, and even more bored with BSFLs and NYB-ICSCs, so we chose a name that did not lend itself to compression to initials. We called it The Futurians.

The Futurians was not exactly a club, it was a description: The Futurians were us. The Futurians was the air we breathed and the world we moved around in. It was home base. We were all growing and adventuring into new areas of experience. The Futurians was what we came back to.

The Futurians wasn't political, though some of its members surely were: Johnny Michel was, and so was I, and so over the next couple of years were six or eight others. Most of the Futurians were simply not interested. What held us together was science fiction,

70

and a common desire to write it. As near as I can remember, the original Futurians were:

Isaac Asimov
Daniel Burford
Chester Cohen
Jack Gillespie
Cyril Kornbluth
Walter Kubilius
David A. Kyle
Herman Leventman
Robert W. Lowndes
John B. Michel
Frederik Pohl
Jack Rubinson
Richard Wilson
Donald A. Wollheim
Dirk Wylie

Later additions included Hannes Bok, Damon Knight, and Judith Merril, and, as you can see, a fair proportion of Futurians achieved their desire. There are three or four names on that list who, as far as I know, never succeeded in publishing a science-fiction story and getting paid for it, but there are also three or four who are collectively responsible for several hundred books and a number of short stories beyond my counting. To some extent, the winners owe a little of their success to the Futurians, if only for the reciprocal goading-on that we all supplied each other. We were almost all, from time to time, each other's crutch. The only way to learn to write is to write; but there are ways of making the process easier, and one is collaboration, and we collaborated madly: Johnny with Donald, Dick Wilson with Dirk Wylie, Cyril with me, and as time went by, in other permutations and combinations that defy recollection. (I know there was one story on which *seven* of us collaborated. What I can't remember is the story, probably because whatever memorability it had hoped to possess had been beaten flat by the hooves of the herd of collaborators.)

I doubt that we Futurians, taken collectively, were a very likable group. We were too brash for that. More than brash; we were egregious, egotistic, adolescent, highly competitive, and a touch insecure. We were given to put-down jokes, and the one among us who showed a human weakness was savaged about it endlessly. We were pretty damn smart—I'd guess the average IQ somewhere over 125, with peaks past 160—and we knew it. We made sure everyone around us knew it, too.

A little bit, there was justification for our arrogance. Collectively talented we were. Collectively lazy we were not. Nearly all the Futurians supported themselves from late teens on—not so much out of preference as that the Depression was not yet over and there wasn't much choice. Dirk pumped gas at a filling station in Jamaica; Dick Wilson clerked at a bank until he moved on to a genuine publishing job with *Women's Wear Daily.* Johnny Michel worked for his father, silk-screening "Special Today Only" signs for the Woolworth five-and-tens. Danny Burford delivered telegrams for Western Union. (Remember Western Union? Remember telegrams?)

Evenings and weekends were for hobbies and talents. Cyril and Bob Lowndes wrote poetry—I still remember some of it, and still like it. When Isaac Asimov wasn't tending counter at his parents' candy store, he was reading the *Encyclopedia Britannica* through, volume by volume. Jack Gillespie and Jack Rubinson wrote plays—none ever produced, most long lost. Johnny painted funny little proto-PopArt scenes—one was a magenta sperm approaching a lavender ovum on a background of cobalt blue; it was called "Love." Curiously, none of us did much about music except to sing. Probably the voice was the only instrument any of us could afford.

As time passed and we grew a little older, we began experimenting with the standard adolescent vices. There was no such thing as a drug scene, but there was liquor. Isaac, Donald, and one or two other oddballs were next door to teetotal, but the rest of us experimented in varying degrees. Some of us experimented a lot. I think I was more often taken drunk with Dirk Wylie, and later with Cyril, than with all the rest of humanity combined. As far as I know, only one Futurian turned out to be anything you could call an alcoholic (he died of it, decades later), and he was one of the sparser drinkers of Futurian times. Most of us gave it a conscientiously thorough try and tapered off. Since our young male glands were boisterously flowing, there was a lot of interest in sex. But not much action. In the beginning the Futurians were one hundred percent male, and although one or two made regular trips to 125th Street to get their ashes hauled, and a couple of others had outside female interests, most, no doubt, relieved their stresses in the time-honored adolescent way. There was certainly no detectable homosexuality. On the one occasion when a Futurian made some sort of ambiguous approach to another, he was greeted with such revulsion and horror that he cravenly crept back into line; I am not even sure how serious the approach was—I was not present. In the breeze from the opened closets of the 70s that seems odd, if only on statistical grounds. But the climate of the 30s was something else. We were tolerant of diversity, but not *that* much diversity.

Most of our pleasures were innocent. We made up our own games, word games like Djugashvili and La Spectre, variations of the old spelling-out Ghosts;

trickster sports like The Piece of String. (Two Futurians stationed themselves at a dimly lit park path. As a stroller approached, they pretended to be unreeling a piece of string across the way at tripping-up level. The fun lay in the reactions of the strollers.) There was a vogue for the hotfoots, and most of our shoes were scorched for a year or so, and a brief fad of dialing strange numbers on the telephone to strike up conversations.

Although we began to be published for pay more and more frequently, we were still fans, and addicted to fan feuds. Will Sykora, our former ally of the NYB-ISA, had declined to disappear once we walked away. With Sam Moskowitz of Newark and Jimmy Taurasi of the Queens Science Fiction League, he had flanged together another national organization they called New Fandom. No CIA nor KGB ever wrestled so valiantly for the soul of an emerging nation as New Fandom and the Futurians did for science fiction. Pronunciamentos were hurled back and forth. Alliances were formed with empires as far off as Philadelphia and Los Angeles. At a time of uneasy truce, all of us in the New York area had conceived the notion of a World Science Fiction Convention to take place at the time of the New York World's Fair in 1939. Now we were enemies, and the prize we fought for was sponsorship of the convention.

Heavy drinking, foolish games, blood feuds, and escapades—were we all really as bad as that? The head says yes, this is the record of the facts. But the heart says it was not that way at all.

Daniel Patrick Moynihan says that all established societies are destroyed, fertilized, and reborn through the invasions of the barbarians. Sometimes the barbarians come from outside. More often, in fact always, says Moynihan, they are born out of the society itself:

the young men from fourteen to twenty-four, who look at the Establishment from outside, and resolve to take Rome or burn it.

So it was with us. We saw Imperial Earth from outside, and we wanted in. Because we were nicely brought up, we zapped the enemy with words instead of with bicycle chains, but we were out to draw blood. When I first took Cyril Kornbluth up to meet John Campbell—feisty, fresh Cyril and staid, almighty John—Cyril behaved like a boor. Outside I asked him what the hell had been going on, and he said simply, "I wanted him to notice me." We all wanted to be noticed. We would have enjoyed being loved, but next best was to be resented.

With all this activity, fandom, writing, YCL, and general exploration, there were not enough hours in the day. What I gave up was school. I had been getting spotty marks at Brooklyn Tech. Then they all turned bad. After some unhappy hours with my faculty advisor I transferred from Tech to a less demanding, and even less interesting, school called Thomas Jefferson.

Thomas Jefferson was a bad school, the building crumbling, the students unruly. The teachers were an oddly assorted lot, a few saints who were there because their conscience drove them, a larger number of incompetents who simply did not deserve a better job. It didn't matter much to me, because I didn't spend much time there. I played hooky most of the time for three or four months, and as soon as I had reached the legal dropout age of seventeen I was gone. I didn't graduate, and I never attended any college, though I've taught in a few; as John Brunner says, I had to quit school because it was interfering with my education.

Still, I did learn one thing from Thomas Jefferson

High. One of my courses was in touch-typing. I didn't learn it there, because I didn't show up that often for classes, but I took the textbook home, spread the keyboard chart out before me, and plugged away on my lavender portable. It took about ten days to master. It is probably the most valuable single skill I have ever acquired.

Do you hear me, would-be writers?

There are some questions that I get a hundred times each a year. They come by mail, in rap sessions after college lecture dates, in chance encounters of all sorts with people who would like to be writers but don't know quite how to go about it. The third most frequent question is: What courses should I take to become a writer? *

Most questions imply some sort of expectation about the answer, and usually what is implied in that one is whether to choose courses in journalism, short-story writing, English lit. But none of those are particularly important. They may not do any active harm—I know a few good writers who have exposed themselves to them. But they surely are not necessary, because most writers have never gone near them.

A few years ago I was allowed to sit in on a meeting of the faculty of a Western university, rethinking its mission in life, and one of the deans said, "We have to get away from the concept of the university as a place where you learn to make a living, and approach

* You may want to know what the first and second most frequent questions are. The first is, "How do I become a writer?" The answer is, you write. There is no other way. Intending to write, talking about writing, studying how to write, do not do the job; you actually have to keep on putting words down on paper. The second is, "How do I get published?" The answer is, you take what you have written and you send it to someone who might conceivably publish it—the editor of a magazine, a book publisher, whatever. There are other ways, but that's the best one.

the task of making it a place where you learn to live."
That makes sense to me, for anyone. For a writer, the
two objectives come out in the same place. A writer
is in the business of interpreting life to an audience,
and the more he knows about living the better he will
write. In my own brief school career I am grateful for
early music-appreciation classes, for the exposure to
physical science and technology in Brooklyn Tech, for
a reasonable competence in mathematics, and for very
little else. What I regret is that I did not learn foreign
languages in school, when I was young enough to
assimilate them fairly easily, but had to pick up smat-
terings out of books, tape cassettes, and travels. (I also
regret that I didn't learn to play an instrument or
dance, but not too many schools offered those courses
then.)

But if you confine yourself to the view of education
as a kind of vocational training, then the courses you
want are in spelling, punctuation, grammar, and touch-
typing. They are fundamental.

They are not quite indispensable. There are a number of fine writers who can't spell K-A-T *cat*, or punctu-
ate the sentence, "Help!" But their lives are harder
for that reason. A lot of writing is in bold strokes, and
you can dictate that sort of thing into a machine if
you like. But a lot is in nuance, too, and if you don't
know what is conventional, you are clumsy and less
effective at doing what is unconventional.

Sure, when you are rich and famous you can hire
little people to correct your mistakes and type your
scripts. You can go further than that. You can buy
plot ideas out of the ads in *The Writer's Digest*. You
can hire a ghostwriter to finish them off. You can send
the scripts off to a reading-fee critic for evaluation and
revision, and then if you want to, and you probably
won't have much choice, you can pay a vanity press to
print them for you. But, my God, why bother?

A year or two ago I met a lovely young Italian countess, or something of the sort, beautiful, sweet, smart, well brought up, loaded. Her sister was a science-fiction fan. The *contesa* invited me and a couple of Italian science-fiction writers up to her hotel room for a drink. The "room" turned out to be an immense suite in a Milan hotel so posh and exclusive that I had never heard its name. Servants brought hors d'oeuvres and cocktails—not those yard-tall fruit-punch things that the Milanese call "coctel," but authentic Beefeater martinis, double dry. A few jet-set friends had dropped in, and the conversation was poly-lingual, like in a Maugham or early Huxley drawing room. The *contesa* invited my advice. Her sister wanted to become a science-fiction writer. Who, Mr. Pohl, should she hire to do the actual writing for her? I said, well, I personally would not be in a position to do that. She nodded, gracefully respecting my wishes, and asked if I had any other recommendations: Asimov, Clarke, Heinlein, who?

She was too nice a person to play jokes on. So I didn't suggest she make her offer to one of them. But it would have been interesting to see the reaction, from a safe distance.

Out of school, into fandom, writing, and the YCL, the next step in my growing-up was to get myself a girl. On May 11, 1937, an ex-classmate with whom I had kept in touch, Teddy Hill, invited me to meet the girl he had eyes for. Her name was Doris Marie Claire Baumgardt, and I approved highly of Teddy's good taste. Doë was strikingly beautiful, and strikingly intelligent, too, in a sulky, humorous, deprecatory way that matched well with most of the other people I admired. She could paint some, and write some, and she liked me. Having found my way to the girl-fields of the YCL only a few months earlier, I now decided to settle down. Doë and I dated steadily for three years, and then we got married. The marriage didn't last quite as long as the courtship, and that was a great pity, because she was a nice person. Doë tolerated my YCL activities without showing much desire to share them. My science-fiction life seemed a little more promising to her. She had never read the stuff, but as time went on she began writing and drawing it and wound up with a catalog of published works of her own. And she liked my friends. More important, her friends, all girls, liked my friends in the Futurians, one hundred percent boys. It was marrying time, I suppose. Over the next few years her friend Rosalind married my friend Dirk, her friend Jessica married my friend Dick Wilson, her friend Elsie married my friend Don Wollheim, not to mention any number of less formal involvements. We did everything collectively, as you see.

The Depression was lightening a little, though a long way from over. Money was a little more plentiful than it had been. Even in our house. I had pretended to a job that did not exist in order to get permission to leave school, but after a while of that my mother made it clear that it was time I brought in a little money, and I went to work for a firm of insurance underwriters called W. L. Perrin and Son, on Maiden Lane in downtown New York.

Apart from requiring me to get up early in the morning, which I have never liked, the job was not without charm. Without dignity, yes. It was *totally* without dignity. What Perrin hired me to do was to deliver letters for them. I was competing with the Post Office. It was cheaper for Perrin to pay me ten dollars a week to schlep the letters around than to put two-cent stamps on them and leave it to the mailman. The best part of it was the chance to explore the old New Amsterdam part of the city—my route stopped north of City Hall. I learned what an intricate marvel New York City is, from the old Customs House and Bowling Green to Brooklyn Bridge and the Woolworth Building. In nice weather it was a pleasant ramble. In bad I learned to dodge through buildings and secret underground warrens, avoiding the inclement open air. I made friends with other insurance runners—we debated dividing our routes, but never dared risk the anger of our bosses—and with elevator girls, starters, receptionists, even policemen. The central five-and-ten where Johnny Michel worked was only a few blocks from the Perrin office. Two or three times a week we would have a quick lunch together and then prowl the immense Goldsmith stationery store on Nassau Street, coveting the typewriters and the automatic mimeograph machines. A block in the other direction was the Federal Reserve Building, and every once in a while you could see an army of guards sweating pallets of genuine gold bricks across the sidewalk.

For a writer, there is a lot to be said for a job that makes no demands on the intellect and does not carry over past quitting time. Washau the chimp could have been trained to do what Perrin paid me for. The forebrain was not involved. I carried a notebook and a pencil with me, and while I was waiting for an elevator, or sneaking a cup of coffee in some underground cafeteria where no one from Perrin was likely to come, I scribbled story ideas or wrote poetry.*

---

* I wrote a lot of poetry in those years. Cyril had a book on the various forms of poetry, and between us we tried most of the formal varieties: haiku, villanelle, chant royal, and all. I found out that a sonnet had some interior laws of its own, and after experimenting with the forms of Shakespeare and Petrarch, I tried evolving my own. Here is a sample.

SHAFT
Through a die one-sixteenth of an inch in diameter drawn,

Perrin's wasn't the first job I had ever held. I had been a busboy in a restaurant on Times Square one summer, twelve hours a day, six days a week, for twelve dollars a week. I had worked part-time after school now and then—mostly running errands for Mrs. Bradley's boarding house on Dean Street. (Strange old anachronism! The cooking was on a coal stove and the illumination from gas, Welsbach mantles and all, this in 1931! The best part of that job was a buying trip down the street to the Bond's Bakery day-old shop, where you could get nickel package cakes to feed the boarders for two cents each. True, they were a little stale, but that did not much impair their quality. That would not have been easy to do.) But Perrin's was full-time, and I held it nearly a year. I was almost sorry when it came to an end. I told my boss, in a rare conversational exchange, that sooner or later I was planning to leave, and he took umbrage. If I was that disloyal to the firm, I should be fired right then, he said, and so I was.

By that time I was beginning to earn a few dollars here and there from writing.

You must understand that when I say a "few" dol-

Cold when drawn, emerging smoke-hot, a metal strand.
This and a thousand others, woven tight together,
Attached to an electric winch and to a car.
A hole is bored through sheets of blueprint cap.
Created then, a steel and stonework frame to fit.
Straight up and down three hundred feet,
    the pit,
The womb of emptiness, becomes a fact.

Then blindly humans enter, wary men, yet blind.
Ascending viciously, they viciously go down,
To rise, to fall, on vicious errands.
Iron cord in iron-bound vacuum.
Iron consciousness, inflexible and dull.
Iron all (vicious), iron (vicious) all.

lars, I mean so few that each separate one was an event. There were many people who were earning pitifully small incomes in the late 30s, but not very many who earned less than I. The next step below my annual income was zero.

But the difference between "nothing" and "almost nothing" is very large. And it got bigger as I went along, jumping almost an order of magnitude a year. A few dollars in 1937, a few tens of dollars in 1938, a few hundred in 1939—well, boy! If that rate of economic growth had only continued, I would now be earning, let me see, something like 10^{40} this year, or roughly 10,000,000,000,000,000,000,000,000 times the gross global product.

It has not worked out that way. But I had established the principle that money could somehow be earned out of the writing business; it was only necessary to increase the flow. Writing was unreliable, and I had not yet aspired to editing, but I had heard of the existence of such a thing as a literary agent.

I had never seen one, and had no very clear idea of what anybody needed one of these creatures for, but the theory seemed simple. You persuaded writers to give you their stories, and you sent them out to editors. When an editor bought one, you then sent the check to the writer, deducting ten percent for your trouble.

That seemed as if it should be easier work for the dollar than writing. I calculated that if I had nine clients and sold an aggregate of a thousand dollars' worth of their work, they would each have averaged one hundred dollars net. And so would I! That was a fascinating revelation. It meant that if I had nine writers as clients, I would be earning as much as if I were a writer myself. (I have always been good at figures.*)

---

* Less good, maybe, at making them come out in the black.

I knew that a literary agency was a business, and a business needed printed letterheads and cards. That was no problem. Johnny Michel's father had remarried and the new wife sort of preferred Johnny out of the house, so he had come to live in the spare room of our apartment and brought his Kelsey 3 x 5 flatbed printing press along. He taught me how to set type, and so I set up and printed my own letterheads and even business cards. I was all set, except for the lack of any clients.

My first client was myself. I could see that it didn't look good for an agent to be peddling the work of only one writer, especially if he was the writer, but I devised a way around that. I had always thought it a romantic notion to write under pseudonyms, and I could have ten instant clients simply by signing ten of my stories with different names. It didn't matter particularly that I did that. None of them sold, anyway, in those years.

Then there were the Futurians. They didn't like wasting money on postage stamps any more than W. L. Perrin and Son, and most of them were willing to let me risk my efforts on the problematical results. Out of their collective resources I made one or two tiny sales. At the time of the first "convention" in Philadelphia, I had met a young fan named Milton A. Rothman, just out of high school and torn between colleges. He had won a science scholarship to Penn and a music scholarship to Juilliard: did he want to be a physicist or a pianist? He finally settled for physics, but what he really wanted to be was a science-fiction writer. He gave me a couple of his stories. I didn't just market them, I actually rewrote them (we had agreed on a twenty-percent share for me in the event of sale, somewhere between agent's fee and collaborator's half), and, my God, I sold them both. And to *Astound-*

ing, at that.* By then I had begun to meet a few pros, and I wheedled rejects out of them.

It made a certain amount of sense for the pros, because the science-fiction market was in one of its recurrent flare-star periods, and you really needed to be on the scene to find out who was hungry for manuscripts. *Wonder Stories* had been taken over by the Thrilling Group. It had developed some distressing comic-book aspects (the letter column was conducted by a "Sergeant Saturn"), but it was solvent, and they had even added a couple of companion magazines, *Startling Stories* and *Captain Future*. F. Orlin Tremaine, having left *Astounding* and all of Street & Smith, was starting a new magazine called *Comet*. Malcolm Reiss had entered the field with *Planet Stories*; a new fellow named Robert O. Erisman had a couple of titles, *Marvel* and *Dynamic*; even Hugo Gernsback was coming back into the field for the third time. (After the war, he went for number four.) With all these customers I found homes for an occasional script. Put them all together, and they added up to—

Well, not very much. In actual dollars and cents I had earned more running errands for W. L. Perrin and Son. But it was more interesting work, and it gave me entry into the offices of real flesh-and-blood editors.

When you speak of science-fiction editors in the later 1930s, you are really talking about one man, and his name was John W. Campbell, Jr.

Science fiction has had a great many idiosyncratic editors. Some have wound up on the funny farm. One or two have landed in jail. A few have been very good, many have been competent, and a *lot* have brought to

* "Heavyplanet" and "Shawn's Sword," both appearing under the pseudonym of Lee Gregor.

their craft the creativity of a toad and the intelligence of a flatworm. John stands above them all. By any measure you can name, he was the greatest editor science fiction has ever had.

He was also quirky, gullible, susceptible to attacks of bigotry, and given to long stretches of apathy. First and last, John edited *Astounding/Analog* for thirty-four straight years. That's too long. No one can hold a job like that without at least an occasional sabbatical year to renew one's perceptions of the world and repair one's soul. John showed the strain. Sometimes for years on end he would edit the magazine with a maximum of twenty-five percent of his attention, maybe less than that. John swallowed whole such magnolious nonsense as dianetics, the Hieronymous machine, and the John Birch Society. There were a lot of things about him that were funny: his private under-the-counter bottle of ketchup at the branch of Chock full o' Nuts where he was accustomed to take his lunch. None of that matters. You can't be better than the best, and John was the best there was.

When John became editor of *Astounding* in 1937, he had already been well established as a writer, with at first a keen sense of gadgetry and no clue as to what went on inside a human being. He began while still an undergraduate at MIT and rapidly took over the Number Two position, behind Doc Smith, as the leading spot-weld-me-another-busbar space-opera author. There was no living in that, of course—remember what writers were getting in the 1930s. So John sold second-hand cars, or did whatever he had to do, to supplement his half cent a word, promptly on lawsuit, from Hugo Gernsback.

To me, in 1936, Campbell was a hero, in the sense that every science-fiction writer was a hero, but not a *big* hero like Doc Smith, say, or Stanton A. Coblentz. His space operas were fine fun, but Smith had been there first. His shorter works were not particularly distinguished.*

Then, all of a sudden, upheaval. There was a high-level tremor at Street & Smith. Tremaine was kicked upstairs, and John Campbell was hired to succeed him.

I didn't like that much, because I had been getting along very well with Tremaine and doubted I would do any better with the new boy.† But it was worth a try, so I trotted up to the familiar decrepit office building, a few blocks from the women's prison, and was admitted to The Presence. As I came into the office John rolled down his desk top, swiveled around in his chair, pointed to a seat, fitted a cigarette into his holder, and said, "Television will never replace radio in the home. I'll bet you don't know why."

That set the pattern. Over the next few years, and intermittently for much longer, I made the pilgrimage to John's office and was greeted each time with some such opening remark. The conversation always went the same way:

Gee, no, Mr. Campbell, I never thought of that.

Right, Pohl, and no one else did, either. But what is the audience for radio?

Uh—

(Rueful shake of the head.) The *primary* audience is bored housewives. They turn the radio on to keep them company while they do the dishes.

Yeah, I guess that's right, all r—

And the point (warming up, jabbing the ciga-

---

* Later on, yes; he wrote some of the finest sf novelettes ever: *Who Goes There? The Cloak of Aesir*, and many others. But they were published under his pseudonym, Don A. Stuart (= Doña Stuart, his wife's maiden name).

† And, in fact, I didn't. In all of John's thirty-four years I never sold him a story that was all my own. Fair mortified my feelings, he did.

rette toward me) is, you can't *ignore* television!
You have to *look* at it!

After a few such conversations, and after reading
the editorials in *Astounding* a month or two after
each of them, I figured out what was happening. That
was how John Campbell wrote the editorials. On the
first of every month he would choose a polemical
notion. For three weeks he would spring it on everyone who walked in. Arguments were dealt with, ob-
jections overcome, weak points shored up—and by the
end of each month he had a mighty blast proof-tested
against a dozen critics.

I didn't mind that. Actually, I admired it a lot. I
filed it away in my mind as one of the smart things
editors did, and very quickly it appeared that there
were a lot of smart things John did.

Every word he said I memorized:

On atmosphere: "I *hate* a story that begins with
atmosphere. Get right into the story, never mind the
atmosphere."

On motivating writers: "The trouble with Bob Heinlein is that he doesn't need to write. When I want a
story from him, the first thing I have to do is think
up something he would like to have, like a swimming
pool. The second thing is to sell him on the idea of
having it. The third thing is to convince him he should
write a story to get the money to pay for it, instead
of building it himself."

On rejection letters: "When there's something wrong
with a story, I can tell you how to fix it. When it just
doesn't come across, there's nothing I can say."

On plot ideas: "When I think of a story idea, I
give it to six different writers. It doesn't matter if all
six of them write it. They'll all be different stories,
anyway, and I'll publish all six of them."

On the archetypal sf story: "I want the kind of story

that could be printed in a magazine of the year two thousand A.D. as a contemporary adventure story. No gee-whiz, just take the technology for granted."

He was also a fount of information on the technological infrastructure of publishing: line engraving, halftones, four-color separations, binding machines. I had never known anyone else who knew about these things, and I learned from him as from Jesus on the Mount. He was a great teacher. Later I figured out why. He was learning the same things, too, maybe forty-eight hours ahead of me on the track, rehearsing his own learning by teaching it to me. When John took over *Astounding* he was around twenty-seven, very junior to every other editor at Street & Smith. He must have got, and must have needed, the reassurance he found in people like me, like Isaac Asimov, like the dozens of other writers and would-be writers who took the subway to 79 Seventh Avenue and were even more junior than he.

Even at seventeen I perceived that he was not wholly without seam or flaw. I had a nice little racket going with Street & Smith, because my friend Pudna Abbot worked in the circulation department there. She could bring home the newest copy of *Astounding* as soon as it came off the press, a full three weeks before the official release date. Not only did I get my copies before any other kid on the block, but I got them free.* Unfortunately I made the mistake of bragging about it to John. He put a stop to it. That was the first time I was ever disappointed in him. *I* wouldn't have done that. It showed a lack of class.

John's tackier side has had a lot of exposure in the last few years. I sat with him all through a banquet in California, two or three years ago, while the prin-

---

* Or almost free. There was the little matter of an hour's subway and bus ride each way from my home in Brooklyn to the Abbots' house in Flushing, but who counted things like that?

cipal speaker denounced John for anti-semitism. John took it imperturbably enough, but I didn't think that showed much class on the part of the speaker, either.

Was John a bigot?

I have no doubt that he was always a little embarrassed by people who didn't have the sense to be born white, male, and Protestant. Like most WASPs of his generation, he was brought up to believe that blacks were shiftless and Jews kind of comical. But I do not believe that he ever in his life withheld any obligation or courtesy on the grounds of race or religion. But he wasn't sure that his readership (who he assumed were also largely WASPs) were as tolerant as he. So he invited his Jewish writers to conceal that blemish. When I sold him Milt Rothman's first story, he laid it on the line. "The best names," John declared, "are Scottish or English. That's true for characters and for bylines. It has nothing to do with prejudice. They *sound* better." It was not just for Milt that he insisted on that. It is only because Isaac Asimov and Stanley G. Weinbaum were first published elsewhere that we don't know them now as, maybe, Tam MacIsaacs and S. G. Macbeth.

John was not, of course, the only editor who thought that. There are few Jews or blacks in the science-fiction stories of that period; the entire Doc Smith Skylark-Lensman canon contains only a handful of Jewish names, and almost every one is either petty racketeer or pitiful victim. I now think that John and the others underrated their audience. As time passed and blacks, Jews, Orientals, and females began to appear both as sympathetic characters and as authors, the readers showed no serious concern. But that's hindsight. In 1937 the evidence was on John's side, as far as it went.

John was a bull dinosaur, roaring his challenge across the swamps, and maybe a really good editor has to be like that. I was a pretty cocky kid, and he was a supremely self-confident young adult, and there were times when we fought like wombats. I would come charging into his office full of the latest exposés of the wickedness of the capitalist system from yesterday's *Daily Worker*, and John would fit a cigarette into its holder, squirt a little decongestant into his sinuses, and tell me where I was wrong. He was a hundred percent behind the capitalist system, was John Campbell. He was getting a fast thirty-five dollars a week, and punching a time clock to get it, but he was a *boss*. If I told him that in a decent socialist society we Creative Literary Artists would be state-subsidized and wouldn't have to work on trivial jobs to eat, he would tell me that his own odd jobs had been a more important part of his education than MIT. If I informed him that Big Corporations were buying up and suppressing inventions that would make everything cheap, beautiful, and streamlined, he told me I was crazy and took me to meet his father, a senior executive with Ma Bell, to prove it.*

My feelings about John Campbell have to be colored by the fact that throughout my later career as a science-fiction magazine editor I was competing with him. Sometimes it was no contest. In the 1940s I didn't have the maturity, the experience, or the money. I caused him no concern at all. In the 1960s it was different. I won as many rounds as I lost, and maybe a few more, but I was at the peak of my form and John just wasn't very interested any more. I could pay almost as much as he did. And I had learned from him.

* There's a funny thing. Years later I found myself debating some of these questions with him again, only we had switched sides. I was in favor of writers working in other areas while they learned, and John had come to believe the corporations were withholding technology. This shows how inconsistent John was.

But he was, and remains, over all, the best science-fiction magazine editor there ever was.

A quarter of a century after we first met, it happened that we were on the same bill at a scientific seminar, the American Astronautical Society's annual Goddard Memorial Lectures. I gave the keynote address. That year's theme was announced as "Technology and Social Progress: Synergy or Conflict?" I took it seriously, and spread myself with a quantitative approach of my own devising to the question of what "progress" really was. On the way home John turned up in the same Eastern Airlines shuttle to Newark. He patted my shoulder and said, "Fred, you did real good for science fiction." And all of a sudden I was seventeen again, and I blushed like a fool.

At the age of eighteen or nineteen I was sampling for the first time the mixed diet of a free-lance writer. Your time is your own. But it is the *only* thing that you own that you can sell, and how you portion it out is reflected in how well you do.

I devised a system for making my time more useful to me. I slept sixteen hours at a stretch, every other day.

That worked out well. The time when I was sleeping, on even-numbered days, was disposable time, when there were no social demands on me: the eight hours when the rest of the world was sleeping, and the eight hours when most of the rest of the world was at work. When I was awake for thirty-two hours at a stretch, it was really fine.* There is a special kindness about the middle of the night for a writer. The phone doesn't ring, no one comes to the door, the kids (when you get to the point of having kids) are asleep; long consecutive thoughts are possible. I did a lot of writing in

---

* But I think you have to be nineteen yeas old to survive it.

those prolonged stretches. Not much of it was any good, and hardly any of it survives, but I was learning my trade.*

So in every forty-eight hours I had a sleep day and a workday, and all my evenings free for business. The YCL took up a couple of evenings a week. The Futurians took up a couple more. Doë occupied most of what was left. It was a cheap time to be dating a girl. Even on my budget of nothing much we could see Broadway shows, go to the ballet, wander in the park. Those were the days of the WPA Theater Project, when half the theaters on Broadway were lighted only by make-work projects paid for by the federal government. For thirty-five cents you could see Orson Welles do *Doctor Faustus*, operatic Elizabethan voices rolling out Marlowe's thundering lines, shocking-fantastic makeup and costumes, puppets acting out the Seven Deadly Sins from a box. There were dance drama and Living Theater. The parks were full of free band concerts in warm weather; lounging on the lawn to Edwin Franko Goldman playing "Poet and Peasant." The New School ran a film series, free or near enough to free not to matter: quaint old science-fiction pictures like *The Crazy Ray*, flaky Cocteau like *The Blood of a Poet*. Even Real Broadway itself was not inaccessible. Most shows stayed open by papering the house with twofers: buy one ticket, get one free. Or Leblang-Gray's ticket agency always had cut-rate specials. An evening's relaxation started out with eating something at home (restaurant meals were still pricey; no way you could get out under a dollar for two people), picking Doë up at her home on Glenwood Road, taking the subway to Times Square for a show. Sometimes we went by ourselves, sometimes with other Futurians

* One story which does survive I like pretty well: "A Gentle Dying," a collaboration with Cyril Kornbluth. We misplaced the rough draft for years, and it only turned up after his death.

or friends; and afterward a leisurely snack in the 42nd Street Cafeteria, where coffee was a nickel, sandwiches started at a dime, and no one ever asked you to move on. The 42nd Street was "our" place, but there were a dozen like it in the Times Square area and a thousand around the city. They never closed. They tolerated indefinite loitering for minimal purchases, even none at all. Now the world is all different, and even the 42nd Street Cafeteria closed a couple of years ago, battered out of existence by pimps, prostitutes, muggers, holdup men, and general crazies who made a lot more trouble than we ever did. We never bothered anybody. The worst we ever did was eat the flowers out of the vases on the table, and they put in new ones every morning, anyway.

And then, along about two or three or later, we would break it up. If I didn't have to take Doë home, and if one of my walking friends was present we might stroll home. It didn't take more than three or four hours, and by then the quiet streets would become all different and rosy in the dawn. I almost got it on one of those same streets a couple of years ago, when four young things approached me with mugging in mind, but in the late 30s there was nothing to fear.

In spite of our competing arrogances and differing interests, the Futurians hung together for years, and one of the reasons was the appearance of a common enemy. We were engaged in a titanic intrafan struggle over the possession of that glamorous dream, the First World Science Fiction Convention.

It was Don Wollheim's idea to begin with. It struck us all as fantastic, but we were used to thinking galactically big. The more we thought about it the more feasible it seemed. The coming New York World's Fair would draw people to the city, that's what World's Fairs are for, and surely among them would be fans and writers. We were not confident we could get anyone from Outside just to talk about science fiction. But if they were coming to New York, anyway—

It all came to pass just as we had planned, with one tiny difference. We lost control of the committee. When the event happened, half a dozen of us Futurians weren't allowed in. There had been a falling-out with Willy Sykora, genius of the NYB-ISA, who had then allied himself with Jimmy Taurasi from Flushing and Sam Moskowitz of Newark; and the three of them combined took the convention away from us. They had persuaded the professional editors to cooperate. They had secured professional writers to speak. They had hired a hall. They had pledges of attendance from fans as far off as Chicago and California. And there we were, out in the cold.

To be truthful, we pretty nearly had it coming. Not quite. The punishment exceeded the crime. But we Futurians were, as you must have observed by now, a fairly snotty lot. Politics had something to do with the struggle, but not actually very much. Although we Communist Futurians maintained a high profile, we were never a majority in the Futurians (and actually, there were one or two lefties on the other side). What we Futurians made very clear to the rest of New York fandom was that we thought we were better than they were. For some reason that annoyed them.

We were, to be sure, a good deal more literary than the New Fandom group. Apart from that, not that much difference. Jimmy Taurasi was a good-natured guy who worked for Consolidated Edison or something of the sort. Sam had made a few abortive attempts at writing science-fiction stories, but quickly realized that his future lay in some other area of the publishing field and has, in fact, scored major successes in more than one way. Will Sykora was something else. He was a hard person to like. I was used to cynics, even wanted to be one myself when I grew up, but there was something about Sykora that outdid even Wollheim and Michel. They cut up writers and editors as individuals; Willy derogated the whole profession of writing. Sf writers were no better than anyone else, he said. If he wanted to, he could write a story in three weeks and have it published in any magazine in the field. His confidence impressed me; why didn't he do it, then? Because it would just be more trouble than it was worth, he said. That struck me as more than cynical, it was close to a sin against the Holy Ghost. Especially as I came to recognize a grain of truth in what he said. To get a story published wasn't then (and isn't now) a particularly impressive feat; all it takes is luck, determination, and a few monkey tricks of style and plot. (To write a *good* story is something else, but there are a hundred bags of monkey tricks in print for every really good piece of work.)

Regardless of the merits, in any case they had the muscle. When we came to Bahai Hall, Don Wollheim, Johnny Michel, Bob Lowndes, Jack Gillespie, and I were turned away. Other Futurians were let in, and ran courier between us excludees and the action inside, but we were Out.

I didn't personally mind that a whole lot. It was kind of exciting. I've never really enjoyed what goes on in the formal sessions of any convention as much as the socializing that surrounds it, and we had plenty of that. To the cafeteria down the block or the bar next door the writ of New Fandom did not extend. When the conventionees found the going tedious and stepped out for refreshment, we were there. We met Californians like Forrest J. Ackerman and his feminine sidekick Morojo,* both of them stylishly dressed in fashions of the Twenty-fifth Century and turning heads in every cafeteria they entered. Kid fan Ray Bradbury was there, two years away from his first professional sale and anxious to display the art of his young friend Hannes Bok. We met Jack Williamson, a slow-spoken New Mexican who looked as if he should be wearing a .45 and a star, and L. Sprague de Camp, hottest and newest star in John Campbell's powerhouse stable. We even ran our own counterconvention, at the headquarters of the Flatbush III Branch of the YCL in Brooklyn. (We had no trouble getting the use of the hall; I was the president of the chapter.) A dozen of the out-of-towners made the long subway trip to Brooklyn, curiously observing the posters and slogans on the wall. Our convention was smaller than Theirs, but more fun, I think, and so the Futurian Exclusion Act failed of its purpose.

There was an interesting postscript, long later. In 1950 the Hydra Club decided to put on a convention of its own in New York, and Sykora came roaring out of the Long Island City swamps to challenge us, I have forgotten over what. The Futurians had decayed away by then, in propria persona, but enough of the Hydras accepted the heritage of the blood feud to debate excluding Sykora from our con. I voted against it. It was more fun to turn the other cheek. In the event, Will showed up, and leafleted some of the chairs in the ballroom with handbills against "the nine phony heads of Hydra," and then was gone, to be seen no more.

One thing the Futurians lacked was a headquarters, and so we decided to go for broke. We found a house and signed a lease—or at least Doë and I did. Un-

* Acronym, in the Esperanto alphabet, for Myrtle R. Jones.

fortunately we couldn't handle the rent, and after some stressful times with the lawyer for the landlord we got out of it unscathed. But Wollheim, Michel, Lowndes, and Dirk Wylie had had enough of a taste for sf-commune living to want more, and so they found an apartment at 2754 Bedford Avenue in Brooklyn. They called it The Ivory Tower, and it was solar plexus for the Futurian nerve network for the next couple of years. They four remained the main tenants, but there was a floating population of whatever other Futurians chose to crash for a while, and all of us used it as an operating base. We had parties there, we published fanzines there, we sat around and talked endlessly there.

Quietest and gentlest of the Futurians was Jack Rubinson, so quiet that mostly we didn't know he was around. One day he surprised us by turning up with a full-length play he had written, all by himself, without announcing what he was going to do—quite contrary to Futurian custom—and, even more surprising, I thought it astonishingly good.* He gave all of us speaking parts, but the starring part—the character in the play had no name but "Hero"—was obviously himself. He gave me a line which I thought summed up quite neatly what we were all about:

Hero: Then what is "The Ivory Tower"?

Pohl: It is nothing more nor less than a shell or an attitude built up by several people to separate their group from the general mass of people. It is a method for keeping the group intact at the expense of everything else. The group tries to deny the existence of anybody except its members.†

* He surprised us again, somewhat later, by going on to get a doctoral degree. The only other Futurian who stayed in school that long was Isaac Asimov, and we all knew about *him*.

† From *The Ivory Tower*, a play by Jack Rubinson. March, 1940. (Unpublished.)

Trouble was, we couldn't deny the existence of the rest of the world. The rest of the world was closing in on us. That summer Joe Stalin and Adolf Hitler signed their nonaggression pact. Consternation in the left wing. Argument and confusion among the political Futurians. And a few weeks later the panzer divisions were loping through Poland.

If Chamberlain and Daladier had stood up to Hitler in Munich in 1938, would the Nazis have collapsed? If the Czechs and the Poles had accepted Stalin's treaty offer of aid, would they have survived as independent states? Or would it have meant going directly to Soviet tanks on the street corners of Prague and Warsaw half a decade earlier? What is Truth? I am tempted to write science-fiction scenarios, but they go in a dozen different directions, some toward a later but worse World War II and some to permanent peace and brotherhood. I doubt they are any of them realistic.

I can only say what I perceived in 1939, colored by science fiction, politics, and my own raunchy young-male glands. Like most young males, I thought the idea of fighting in a war was scary but exciting, by no means without appeal. A year or two before, I had volunteered to join the Abraham Lincoln Brigade in Spain.* Being a soldier was only an adventure. Being a citizen of a country at war was something else. America in the 20s and 30s seemed to be exempt from that sort of European folly. Oh, now and then our Marines went down and beat the hell out of somebody in Nicaragua, but I had no idea of what it would be like to have an organized enemy bombing our cities and sinking our ships. When I observed that my

---

* They would have none of me. They needed fund-raisers in America a lot more than eighteen-year-old bodies in Teruel.

science-fiction friends and pen pals in London and Paris, Ted Carnell and Georges Gallet, were now in that precise position, reason recoiled. World War? *We* knew what it meant. H. G. Wells had explained it to us in *Things to Come*. And here was the Luftwaffe pounding Warsaw as flat as Wells had smashed London in the film. It looked like the end of Western civilization, and science fiction's nightmares were coming true.

It was a stressful and perplexing time. The Communist Party expressed no doubts. They made a 180-degree flip-flop overnight. On one day the slogans were "Quarantine the Aggressor" and "Death to the Nazis." On the next it was "Keep America Out of the Imperialist War."

It hurt. It was like being awakened from a pleasing dream by a kick in the gut. I could not change my head to keep pace with the slogans. I had grown up to hate Fascists. They had not changed. Neither had my feelings toward them. I found it more and more difficult to function as a YCL leader, or even to sit through a meeting. I knew what words I was supposed to say, but I couldn't stand the taste of them on my tongue.

So the YCL was in trouble with me, but I was also in trouble with the YCL. In the angrier, harsher climate that fell over the YCL after the Stalin-Hitler pact, there was a new and inquisitorial attitude toward deviationism. Who were all these science-fiction people I had invited to come into the Flatbush III YCL headquarters? At a meeting of the executive committee, an Irish youth named Marty O'Shaughnessy (my own recruit!) furiously hissed the damning question: Were any of them *Trotskyites?* I couldn't help it. I laughed. And then there was the problem of Cyril Kornbluth's morals. Cyril was only about sixteen or seventeen at the time, looked like thirty, drank like a retired railroad switchman; and he and I stayed behind at some

YCL party with what was left of a bottle of wine and sang and giggled for hours. Did I not realize, the comrades asked judgmentally, that I had involved the YCL in impairing the morals of a minor?

That was even funnier, but there was no one in the branch to share the joke. The comedy had gone out of the YCL personality. I began to miss meetings now and then. When the next branch elections came along, I was not reelected president; I wasn't even nominated, nor expected to be.

A year earlier that would have hurt a lot. I had *started* that branch. But under the circumstances at least a trial separation was indicated, if not actually a divorce; and besides, I had found something a good deal more exciting that used up all the time and attention I had.

The great advantage of constituting myself a literary agent specializing in science fiction was not in the sparse commissions. It was in the entry it gave me to the offices of real professional editors. I could see at once that they came in all shapes and sizes. Some were wise and grizzled, some almost as young as I. Some had backgrounds stretching back before I was born; others were learning before my eyes.

I did not hope to compete with someone like John Campbell in diligence or inventiveness, but few of the other editors I saw impressed me. To the extent that their jobs involved knowing a good science-fiction story from a bad one, I was pretty sure that I knew more than they. So I took my courage in my hands and began to shop around for a job. One of the friendliest of the editors was a man named Robert O. Erisman, veteran of many pulp titles, now experimenting for the first time with this newfangled thing of science fiction. Did he, I asked him very tentatively, think he could use an assistant with a solid background in the field, namely me?

No, he said, gently and pointedly, he couldn't; the budget didn't allow that sort of thing. But maybe there was a chance somewhere else. He had heard that Popular Publications, down at the other end of 42nd Street, was adding a cheap line of pulps, half a cent a word tops. If I put it to them right, maybe they'd find a place for a science-fiction magazine on the list. Why not go talk to the boss there, Rogers Terrill?

So I did; and Rogers hired me; and there I was, nineteen years old, and the full-fledged editor of not one but two professional science-fiction magazines.

6

Nineteen Years Old, and God

The office of Popular Publications was on the twentieth floor of the Bartholomew Building, at 205 East 42nd Street in New York City. The building cornered on Third Avenue, tatty street of bars and one-man barbershops, shadowed and dirtied by the El. At the other end of the block was Second Avenue, even tattier and dirtier because the Second Avenue elevated trains were older and rattlier and the whole thing was just that much farther from the real part of the city. A block farther still, just at the river, was a sudden eruption of elegance: Tudor City, luxury apartments inhabited, so my mother told me, by KWs—which is to say, Kept Women. Just north of Tudor City on the East River was a slaughterhouse.* Sometimes on a lunch hour I would walk down to watch the river, and would see the flats come in with their cargo of sheep, and the Judas ram leading them up the ramp to the killing place. Across 42nd Street from us was the Daily News Building, with the biggest globe of

* The site is now occupied by the United Nations buildings. No jokes, please.

the earth I have ever seen turning ponderously in its lobby. We were a block or so from the Chrysler Building and the Grand Central complex. We were, boy, in the *heart* of things.

Not only was I at the very core of the Big Red Apple, but I commanded a network that stretched across the continent. Even the world. Linotype operators in Chicago were waiting to turn my words into metal. Newsdealers in Winnipeg and Albuquerque were going to display my magazines to their customers. Writers in California would tailor their prose to my wishes, artists would paint what I ordered, fans from India and South Africa would send me letters. It was a heady dose for a nineteen-year-old. I had aimed my whole life to this moment, and here I was.

Of course, the reality was not quite so glamorous. Even then I was aware that my two little science-fiction magazines were hardly a pimple on the mammoth corpus of the pulp magazine industry. With one part of my head I knew it. With the rest of me I was just floating in joy.

I met my colleagues with awe. To me at nineteen they seemed pretty impressive. The other editors were mostly young, if not quite as young as I; I doubt the average age was as much as thirty, even if you leave out the giggling girls from Accounting, where I never trod. But some were very old, and very wise. Just down the short hall from my own little office was Ken White, editor of *Black Mask*. Ken had inherited directly from Cap Shaw, who with Dashiell Hammett had shaped the modern detective story only a few years before. On the longer hallway, toward the 42nd Street side, was Janie Littell with her love pulps; heavyset ex-circus performer (so she said), she wrote a lot of the contents herself under a dozen pen names, all intensely moral tales in which there was never any touching below the neck, gobbled by an avid audience of young girls. In the other direction along the long hall were most of the other editors: Alden H. Norton (later my boss) with his sports pulps; Rogers Terrill, genially overseeing all at a salary reported to be as much as Fif Teen Thous And a Year; the myriad Westerns, the dozens of detectives, the horrors, the air-wars, with their editors Loren Dowst, Willard Crosby, Mike Tilden; Aleck Portegal and his Art Department; and The Two Houses of Heaven. They were the two largest offices on the floor, and they belonged to the two men who owned the company, Harry Steeger and Harold S. Goldsmith. Rog Terrill was the fellow I had applied to, but Steeger was the one who actually hired me: courtly, youngish Princeton millionaire, who liked to yacht and to ski. He carried my typewriter into my new office, and when I said I'd rather do my own typing than have a secretary, did not burst out laughing. Secretaries got easily eighteen or twenty dollars a week. I was getting ten.

1939 was mid-autumn in the long, glorious season of the pulps. Popular wasn't the biggest pulp chain, or the best, but it was up there. We had more than fifty titles going at one time. The Thrilling Group had about as many. Street & Smith had fewer titles, but generally much bigger sales: they had original titles, like *Love Story*, *Detective Story*, and *Western Story*, not to mention the series books like *Doc Savage* and *The Shadow*. We were about Number Two to Thrilling in number of titles, and Number Three behind them and Street & Smith in aggregate sales; but there were at least a dozen other sizable pulp houses, and any number of small ones and transients. Put them all together and there were close to five hundred pulp magazines, with aggregate annual sales of around a hundred million copies.

I learned a great deal about the pulps, but one thing I never quite figured out was who read them. There were hundreds of titles on the stands. *Somebody* bought them, because that's where the money came from that paid our salaries. But you never saw a person reading one on the subway or carrying one on the street, so where did they all go? A lot of the readership, I knew, was in the small towns and on the farms, where the local movie house wasn't as handy as in New York. But New York dealers sold a lot of copies, too.

What was clear about the general pulp audience was that it was not finicky about literary quality, because, my God, most of the stories were *awful*. Even the science-fiction magazines of the time showed an awful lot of leaden prose and tone-deaf style, and they were the class of the field. The worst of modern television is not quite as brainless as the average pulp story of the 20s and 30s. And yet most of the people who edited them, and even most of the people who wrote them, were cultured and refined, as much so, at least, as their opposite numbers in the major book publishers of today. The guys who were editing *Sinister Stories* and *G-8 and His Battle* sometimes talked about Dos Passos and Alban Berg in the coffee breaks and then went back to shrieking, swooning females and the rattle of twin Vickers sluicing destruction into the Baron's Fokker triplane. Popular was not the classiest of the pulp houses. It was a me-too operation; when Westerns were selling, we did lots of Westerns; when they stopped, we stopped. But it wasn't the worst, by a long way. Ken White did fine things with *Black Mask* almost always, and there were individual writers —Joel Townsley Rogers was one—who always wrote with an understanding of the sound of the language and a care for its structure, whichever pulp they were aiming at. It was not all trash. But trash was the way to bet it.

One reason the stories were so bad was the patheti-

cally low rates. A penny a word is not lavish. I am
a reasonably productive writer, but my lifetime average
is not much more than a hundred thousand words a
year (and that includes a lot of early years when I
was more interested in volume than in quality, and it
showed). That's higher than most writers. It's even
higher than most pulpsters of the 1930s; but, as you
can see, a pulp writer in 1939 who wrote a hundred
thousand words, and sold every word of it at a penny
a word, would have been blessed each week with just
a touch less than twenty dollars.

The result was that good writers got out of the pulps
if they could, or, if they stayed, drove themselves to
such heavy production schedules that quality disappeared.

If you want to think of a successful pulp writer in
the late 30s, imagine a man with a forty-dollar typewriter on a kitchen table. By his right hand is an
ashtray with a cigarette burning in it and a cup of
coffee or a bottle of beer within easy reach. Stacked
just past his typewriter are white sheets, carbons, and
second sheets. Stacked to his left are finished pages,
complete with carbon copies. He has taught himself to
type reasonably neatly because he can't afford a sten-
ographer, and above all he has taught himself to type
fast. A prolific pulpster could keep up a steady forty
or fifty words a minute for long periods; there were
a few writers who wrote *ten thousand words a day*
and kept it up for years on end. Some writers contracted to write the entire contents of some magazines
on a flat per-issue fee, under a dozen pseudonyms;
two of our air-war magazines were done that way,
by a young fellow named David Goodis. Series-character magazines like *The Spider* or *The Shadow* were
written by single authors; Robert J. Hogan did G-8 for
us that way. At Popular most of those writers didn't
get a penny a word. Some didn't get half that; some-

times the fee for a whole magazine was as little as $150, for as much as sixty thousand words.

The key to survival in the pulps, the old-timers kept telling us, was *volume.* I schooled myself to write and sell first drafts. I would put clean white paper, carbon, and second sheet in the typewriter one time through, and when I came to "The End," that was the last I saw of the story. It went directly to the editor. If I was lucky, a month or two later it was in print. If not, it bounced around until I had used up all the possible markets, and maybe then, and only then, I considered revising it.

You see, it didn't matter. The customers were not critical, and there were no rewards for virtue. Not with the readers—they were not consulted—and not even with the editors. Dependability, personal contact, and adherence to policy, those were the important considerations; literary quality came a poor fourth. And what the readers wanted—as far as I know, which is not very far—was vicarious adventure. If they could buy half an hour's anodyne, they would not raise questions of style. Oh, I am sure that there were stories they liked better than other stories. I am even sure— it is an article of faith with me—that they could distinguish between good style and bad. But the distinction was not reflected in the cash register.

All those magazines are gone now. The paper shortages of World War II mowed them down like standing wheat. There was a flickering resurgence after the war, but television, paperbound books, and the increased costs of publishing finished what the war had started. Even science fiction, runt of the litter that survived its bigger brothers, is now limited to a handful of magazines, though it is an immense factor in the paperbound book market; and as to Westerns, air-wars, sports pulps, even detectives, they just don't exist.

Said Harry Steeger to me: "What kind of a budget do you need?"

Said I to Harry Steeger, stalling for time: "Well, let's see, I need to buy stories, departments, art—"

"Right," he said. "Two hundred seventy-five dollars for stories. A hundred dollars for black and white art. Thirty dollars for a cover. That's four hundred and five dollars an issue for *Astonishing Stories*. On the other one—what do you want to call it?"

"*Super Science Stories.*"

"Whatever. That's going to be sixteen pages longer, so we'll make it fifty dollars more on the budget. See Aleck about cover logos. Anything else, see Peggy Graves."

The smaller of the two magazines, *Astonishing Stories*, held 112 pages an issue and sold for a dime. I counted a lot of pages and discovered that a full page of type amounted to 620 words. Subtracting the pages that would be filled by advertising, illustrations, and front matter, I found I would need about sixty thousand words an issue. I didn't quite have half a cent a word, but close enough, close enough.

Art was something else. When I brought my budget to Aleck Portegal, the art director, he looked at me with compassion and disgust. Where the hell was I going to get artists to work for that kind of money? Writers, sure. Everybody knew what writers were like. But artists did a job of work for a dollar, and they wouldn't take less. That didn't worry me, because I had a secret weapon. In fact, two of them. There were the fan artists, as eager as the fan writers for publication in a science-fiction magazine. And besides, my girlfriend, Doë, was an art student at Cooper Union. She had at her fingertips a whole school of striving newcomers to whom five dollars would look like a hell of a price for something they would gladly have bribed us to print.

In the event, the art students were a disappointment, and most of the fans were worse. But there were a couple who were competent, and one—Hannes Bok, whom Ray Bradbury had been touting at the World Convention not long before—who was superb. We got the art, anyway. Aleck found, to his mild surprise, that a fair number of his regular professionals would be willing to take a little less for the extra work, and as I learned how to juggle my budget I found a few extra dollars. I didn't really need to buy sixty thousand words an issue. I could write long editorials, use big house ads, run a letter column; I could save six or eight pages of paid stories that way. And some writers couldn't count very well; the story that they said was six thousand words would actually turn out, when Peggy Graves checked it, to run seven thousand, maybe even more. The house rule was that if the official count was lower than the author's count, we paid off on the official count. But if the author's was lower, we paid on his. Altogether I could scrounge as much as forty or fifty dollars an issue on text, and Aleck taught me how to save a little on the art, too. If there was a nice-looking spaceship or an all-purpose alien-planet scene in a piece of art, we marked the line cut to hold, trimmed off the specific detail, and used it over and over again as a spot illustration. After a while Harry Steeger asked me if I thought an extra fifty dollars an issue would help. I assured him it would. . . . But, you know, I think I lied to the man. In my experience, the money a market pays for stories has only the roughest congruence with how good the stories are. Some writers will stretch themselves when the money is good. Some won't. Some react the other way: the more they get paid, the worse they write; probably a kind of stage fright is involved. It seems to me to be an editor's bounden duty to get as much money for his writers as he can, but once he gets it, what is he to do with it? Divide it equally between them all? But the harsh fact is that not all stories are of equal merit. Some you print with joy and thanksgiving. Some because the alternative is to put out a magazine with some of the pages blank. There is neither justice nor morality in paying the same price for both. So when I told Harry Steeger that a few more dollars in the budget would make a difference in the quality of the stories, I was hallucinating. What it did do, though, was make me feel good.

I did not understand all this at the time, but I quickly found out that the best stories were not necessarily the ones that cost the most. My principal instructor in this area was a Grand Old Man named Ray Cummings. He was tall, skinny, wore a stock instead of the conventional collar and tie, and was unimaginably old to me—he had actually been too old for World War I, which had ended before I was born. I suppose he must have been around sixty when we met. I respected Ray as a writer very much. He had never been a great writer, but he had been a prolific one, and sf was his specialty. He had a fascinating background— had even worked for Thomas Edison in his youth— and was a personally engaging, roguish human being. What he was not was a source of good stories. I don't think his talent had left him, I think he just didn't care any more. In the beginning I am sure that he cared about science fiction, but his typewriter was his living and he used it to produce whatever would sell; by and by it must all have seemed the same to him. Before I came to work at Popular, he had been selling them quantities of mystery and horror stories, under a variety of pen names. Horror stories were the dregs of the pulp market, cheap thrill-and-sadism stuff to a precise formula: the buildup involved a fear of the supernatural, but in the end it always had to turn out to be a hoax perpetrated by some criminal, spy, or

madman.* When I started there and Ray discovered
I was a fan, it was a great day for Ray. Not only could
he get back to science fiction, but he quickly perceived
that I was his pigeon. I had no way of saying no to so
great a man. Worse than that. He would not write
for less than a penny a word, and I missed my chance
to tell him that that was beyond the limits ordained
for me by God and Harry Steeger, because the day he
first walked into my office was the day I discovered I
had a few extra dollars to play with. So for months
he would turn up regularly as clockwork and sell me
a new story; I hated them all, and bought them all.

I had at least the wit to keep them short, and so although Ray depleted my disposable surplus, he didn't
quite wipe it out. I had always kept one eye on John
Campbell's magazine. What I saw there I coveted, and
with a little extra money I had hopes of acquiring
some of his writers. The new Titans in my eyes were
A. E. Van Vogt, L. Sprague de Camp, and Robert A.
Heinlein. They are still Titans, to be sure, but in 1939
and 1940 they were not only great, they defined what
was great in science fiction. I wanted them a lot. I
never did get a Van Vogt, but one of John's weaknesses
as an editor (he didn't have many) was his conviction
that readers got tired of any byline after a while. He
urged his writers to use pen names from time to time;
and now and then he rejected a story by even the best
of them.

In this, as far as de Camp and Heinlein were concerned, he was wrong. Both of them were at the peak
of their form, trotting ahead of the rest of the field
without a misstep. The Heinleins and de Camps I got
—"Lost Legacy" and "Let There Be Light" in particular

---

* Although they were even more awful than I have said, I
wrote a few myself. So did even so fine a writer as Henry Kuttner. One likes to flex one's muscles on a new form, and also one
likes to eat.

from Heinlein, and from de Camp especially his fine
collaboration with P. Schuyler Miller, "Genus Homo"
—would have looked good anywhere.

John's other weakness as an editor was that he just
didn't want to talk about sexuality. All the characters
in *Astounding* were as featureless around the groin as
a Barbie doll, and one reason he didn't want the Heinleins was that they contained what he thought pretty
raunchy language. (Sample: "I suggest you follow the
ancient Chinese advice to young women about to
undergo criminal assault." "What's that?" " 'Relax.' ")
This blatant filth did not go unreproached in *Super
Science Stories,* either. One reader wrote in:

> ". . . the vulgarity of the language is such as to
> make me look thrice before buying the magazine
> again."

And another:

> "Frankly, I'm disgusted. If you are going to con-
> tinue to print such pseudosophisticated, pre-prep-
> school tripe as 'Let There Be Light,' you should
> change the name of the mag to *Naughty Future
> Funnies.*"

I met other writers at the Thursday Afternoon
Luncheon Club, the back room of a kosher restaurant
just off Times Square where Manly Wade Wellman,
Malcolm Jameson, Henry Kuttner, and others got together to talk shop once a week. Other editors were
grazing in that same pasture. Mort Weisinger would
show up from the Thrilling Group now and then, and
Dave Vern was a regular. *Amazing Stories* was still in
New York, no longer owned by Teck and no longer
edited by T. O'Conor Sloane. The new people had
made it bigger and richer, but not better. Under

Sloane it had developed fine pale mold around the edges; under the new people it had turned cheap pulp. But Dave Vern, the new editor, was a decent guy, and generous to a kid competitor.

I enjoyed the Thursday Afternoons, and from them I got some good stories. One I particularly liked, and rued, was Malcolm Jameson's "Quicksands of Youthwardness." I liked it because it was a great idea for a science-fiction story. It wasn't original with Jamie, or at least it had been suggested a decade before by no less than Sir James Jeans. He had written, in one of his popularizing books, that Time was probably the Fourth Dimension. H. G. Wells, he said, had written a science-fiction story in which a man went through some sort of transdimensional reversal and came back with his left and right sides interchanged, but how much more exciting, Jeans said, if he had come back with his past and future interchanged. Jamie had picked up the hint and made a nice twenty-seven-thousand-worder out of it. What I rued was that I had read the same book and had written the same story, not nearly as well, and I could see I had been outclassed. Sadly I bought Jamie's story and shelved my own.

But what to do with twenty-seven thousand words in my two rather small magazines? I decided to run it as a three-part serial. The readers quickly pointed out to me that they hated that; both magazines were bimonthly, which made it worse, but in any event nine-thousand-word installments were pretty skimpy. That was a mistake . . . and, I'm afraid, only one of a great many.

I wasn't really a very good editor. I was learning as fast as I could—I had Harry Steeger and Peggy Graves standing over me with circulation figures, a powerful spur. But being an editor requires kinds of maturity and resourcefulness you do not find in your average

nineteen-year-old. An editor doesn't have to be always
wise and authoritative. But he has to make most of his
writers think he is, most of the time, and that is not
easy when you don't yet need to shave more than
once a week.

Editors as a class are not highly respected. Very few
of them become famous. From an editor's point of
view, it is the writer who gets all the breaks. Writers
make more money. Writers get their names known.
They do, even when the editor has at least as much
to do with the success of the story as the writer himself. Does that seem unlikely? But there are some very
famous stories that began as slop, until some editor
worked painfully with the writer, over a long time,
coaxing him through revisions, cajoling him into
changes, hewing out of the shapeless fat of the first
draft a work of art. Then, years later, when the story
is a classic, no one but the writer knows that it was the
editor who made it so.*

On the other hand, from where the writer sits, the
editor looks like the boss. The editor makes the decision to buy or to bounce. At the end of the year the
writer may have twice as much money to pay taxes on
as the editor. But on that day in February when he
needs that thousand-dollar check to get his kid's teeth
fixed, it is the editor who says whether he gets it or
not. This conflict is not helped by the known fact that
most editors are failed writers, and most writers are
sure they could edit anything better than the incum-
bent—and are often right.

The editor is always in the middle. His job is to
harvest the basic exudations of writers, as ants lick the

* I am not speaking out of private pain (or, anyway, not *just*
out of private pain). The particular science-fiction editors who
come instantly to my mind in this connection are John Campbell of *Astounding*, Horace Gold of *Galaxy*, and Gene Roddenberry of *Star Trek*.

sweat off their dairy aphids, to pick them over to find the ones that will stimulate the readers' pleasure glands, process them in the most attractive way, and place them on the market.

How does he know which ones will please the readers?

Ah, that's the problem, isn't it? He doesn't. He can only guess. If he is any good at his job, it is an informed guess, with experience and insights to help it, but it is a guess all the same.

If an editor is a systematic professional (translation: hack), he probably makes a study of all the successful magazines in his area, observes what they have done that has seemed to work, and does the same. If he is a genius, he looks for what *isn't* being done by anybody else. Then sometimes he does it, and sometimes he doesn't. Most of the things that aren't being done aren't worth doing, so you can't count on novelty alone for success. You make a series of those informed guesses, rejecting the ideas that won't work, as God gives you the gift to perceive them, and trying out the ones that might. Editorial skill lies in knowing what has worked. Editorial genius lies in taking a chance on what hasn't worked yet, but will when someone summons up the nerve to try.

All this I understood pretty well at the time, but between the understanding and the execution was a wide, wide gap.

I look at those old magazines now and my fingers itch; I want to pick up the telephone and dial 1-9-4-0 and tell that kid what to do. It was an easy time to be an editor. With what I know now I could have made those magazines sing, but as it was they just lay there.

But my, I had fun! First kid on the block to be a

professional editor! The rest of the Futurians were jealous as hell.

When I say the "rest" I mean mostly the leaders, myself and others, a feisty lot, given to competing for the sake of game-playing even when no stakes were involved. Among the Futurians there was clear-cut distinction between the leaders and the led. Whatever our politics (and by then most of the top considered themselves at least cosmetically Marxist), none of this nonsense about a classless society was allowed to interfere with how we ran our own group. The People Who Decided were Don Wollheim, John Michel, Bob Lowndes, and I. We called ourselves "the Quadrumvirate," and we lived in and among each other's lives almost inextricably. In fan and science-fiction affairs we operated under a unit rule. The decisions we wrangled out in private we presented to the world as monoliths. But even among ourselves there was a fine structure of interlocking relationships and power positions—and yes, by gosh, of friendship. Johnny and I joined the YCL together and went camping in pup tents at Lake Tiorati. Donald and I went to amateur-press conventions together. Bob Lowndes and I shared an obsessive interest in popular songs, and in the more flamboyantly decadent writers: Huysmans, Mallarmé, James Branch Cabell.

We also competed with each other, never more strenuously than between Donald and myself. I don't know what Donald thought was going on—someday I would like to ask him—but I know where I stood. Donald represented something to me. At a parlor game, in the early Futurian days, among non-Futurian people, I had been asked to name my hero, and the name that popped out was "Donald A. Wollheim." I was maybe sixteen then, and Donald had a towering advantage over me in years and experience. But I was catching up. I was *working* at catching up; not only to

catch up but to surpass; and, of course, no one knew
that better than Donald.

It is a marvel that that four-way directorate survived
as well as it did, but when I got to be an editor it began to shred. The other three Quads began to write
for me for pay. Friendship could have survived that
(that sort of strain has been placed on most of my
friendships, one time or another, over the years). But
the temporary armistice among young bulls each confident of his destiny as herd leader was more fragile, and
a space developed between the rest of the Quadrumvirate and me.

But I needed the Futurians, needed them in my job.
If writers think of editors as empowered to pollinate
whatever blossoms they choose, over acres of flowers,
editors quickly perceive that those acres are not very
broad, and most of the blossoms are duds. An editor
has to scratch to find good stuff—particularly with the
pitiful money I had to offer—and one of the best
places for me to scratch was among the Futurians.
There was a wonder of talent there. Most of it was
still new and growing, and some never really lived up
to early promise; but first and last I bought stories not
only from the other three Who Counted but also from
Cyril Kornbluth, Dirk Wylie, Isaac Asimov, Richard
Wilson, David A. Kyle, Jack Gillespie, Walter Kubilius, and others. They would work for very little, and
sometimes they worked very well. Cyril Kornbluth was
born with a trenchant phrase in his mouth. He was
terribly young and inexperienced—around fifteen when
I published his first story. But he was learning very
fast the technical skills of story construction, and he
had never needed to learn to shape a sentence. Isaac
Asimov was growing visibly with every story. He carefully numbered them in series; I can still see the shape
of his manuscripts, the title double-spaced, the first
page almost entirely blank, but with the serial number

of the story up in the corner to keep his records systematic. (He was always a horribly well organized person, Isaac was, and a standing reproach to the rest of us.) Unfortunately (for me, not for Isaac), he had already made the Campbell Connection. I had to content myself mostly with John's leavings. Hannes Bok, Doë, Dave Kyle, and others did illustrations for me, and I farmed out departments and columns to those who wanted to do them—for nothing, of course; the lure of possible free books or movie tickets was enough reward. The "perks" that went with being a professional editor were scarce (no such thing as an expense account, of course) but enjoyable, and some of them I was able to share. Both Dick the Drama Critic and I had passes to the New York World's Fair, and so one or two nights a week he and I would wander past Trylon and Perisphere, dine economically at the Mayflower Doughnut Pavilion (our passes did not include anything to eat), visit Salvador Dali's Dream of Venus (big goldfish tank of mildly nude girls swimming in underwater ballet) or whatever else looked exciting.

The space that was growing between me and the other Futurian leaders left room for new associations. Some came along with the job. I began to meet the Old Pros of the field, or at least nearly all who came through New York in those early years of the 1940s. Manly Wade Wellman was a regular at the Thursday Afternoon Luncheon Club, a courtly, heavyset Virginia gentleman who wrote several useful, workmanlike stories for me. So was Malcolm Jameson, an ex-naval officer who had had part of his larynx removed, smoked like a chimney, and spoke only in a harsh whisper. Henry Kuttner turned up, a slim, dark young man, humorous and surprisingly gentle, considering the terrifying words he was pouring into *Weird Tales* and the horror pulps. At a dinner party at the Jamesons' I met a flamboyant character who had just returned from being shipwrecked off the coast of Alaska and was on his way to some equally jock exploit in some equally improbable part of the world. His name was L. Ron Hubbard. He was the kind of person who expects, and without fail gets, the instant, total attention of everyone in any room he enters. If his later destiny as guru of world Scientology was anywhere in his thoughts at that time, he gave no sign of it. Lester del Rey came up to my office one day with a couple of manuscripts John Campbell had been unwilling to buy. I was unwilling to buy them, too (and it is possible John and I were right, because those stories, long lost, have never been published anywhere), but Lester himself I was willing to buy. Scrappy little kid with the face of an unseamed angel, he was then and has been for all of the forty years since one of the most rewarding human beings I have ever known.

All of us live at the centers of our own individual universes, most visibly so when we reminisce. But that is palpably unfair. Collectively all of these people were creating a literature. Individually they were loving, hating, marrying, learning, failing, and now and again most brilliantly succeeding, and to kiss any one of them off with a casual line is not only a disservice but a disrespect. So I leave this catalog dissatisfied, but I do not know how to make it complete.

It was not only males that I met. I encountered, and marked with one eye, Malcolm Jameson's pretty young daughter, Vida. Jamie was not the only writer with a pretty young daughter; Ray Cummings had one whom I also met and admired. But along about that time things became serious between Doë and me, and so I took myself out of competition in at least one area by marrying Doris Baumgardt in August of 1940. I was still under the legal age of consent. I had to get my parents' permission, and so my mother and father were required to show up at the Municipal Hall of

Records to sign my marriage license. It was the first time they had seen each other in years, and it turned out to be the last.

We were married by a minister I had never met before (I have been married a lot, but never by anyone I knew) and took off for a sort of honeymoon in Allentown, Pennsylvania. Why Allentown? Both Doë and I were pretty parochial people. Allentown was the only nearby place we had ever heard of.

The other thing that happened in 1940 was that I finally and for good severed my connection with the Young Communist League.

Paris fell that spring. The next day one of my YCL friends turned up at my office for lunch. He bought us wine, held up his glass, and proposed a toast: "To the liberation of the bourgeois capital by the people's forces of socialism."

I drank his lousy wine. But it lay sour in my stomach while I brooded in my office all that afternoon. The YCL was very close to the core of my existence as a social person; what structure of belief I had managed to erect followed its blueprints, as I had perceived them. I don't think my belief-structure has changed much. The evils that the YCL had called my attention to (Fascism, militarism, the persecution of helpless people) are still evils. The Marxist interpretation of history no longer seems quite right, but it is not much more wrong than most others. But the YCL changed with the Stalin-Hitler pact, and my friend's toast to the panzers grinding up the Champs Élysées made me confront that change in a way I could not escape. It was not easy to separate myself cold turkey from the YCL. I had dear friends, and commitments made. But I couldn't hack it, and over the next few months I phased out, not without reproaches and by no means without pain.

Most of the friends I left behind ultimately drifted away, too. The Party line flip-flopped again in June of 1941, when the Germans attacked the Soviets. But by then I no longer cared.

After our marriage Doë and I moved into an apartment in Knickerbocker Village. The rent was $42.75 a month, which was reasonable enough, even in 1940. The problem was that the salary Popular Publications was paying me was ten dollars a week, which comes to $43.33 a month. I have always been good at arithmetic. It took me no time at all to do in my head the simple calculation

$$
\begin{array}{r}
\$43.33 \\
-42.75 \\
\hline
\$\ 0.58
\end{array}
$$

and deduce that my salary might pay the rent but would do little about meeting our expenses for food, clothes, entertainment, or even an occasional pack of cigarettes.

Well, I didn't expect to keep house on fifty-eight cents a month. Popular Publications didn't expect me to, either, but it took me a while to figure out that what they expected me to do was what all the pulp editors did: to supplement my salary by writing for myself and for the other magazines in the chain.

Because I was slow in catching on to this, my 1940 total of sales amounted to only $281.42 (and that represented eleven stories and a poem!). But by the end of the year I had learned the ropes, and besides, Popular Publications had doubled my salary. It looked as if 1941 would—with a little luck—give me a cash income of nearly two thousand dollars. Not luxury, no. But enough for even a little comfort.

There were about six good months in there, the first half of 1941, when everything went pretty much as I had expected and the world seemed almost worrisomely easy to cope with. Doë and I were nest-building, and Knickerbocker Village was a fun place to live in. It was the first of the giant New York apartment developments. It took up a whole city block, hard up against the Manhattan Bridge on one side, a few blocks from Chinatown and the Five Points on the other. Architecturally it seemed something from the future, two separate structures, each a hollow square surrounding a grassy little park, a children's playground dividing the two. Under the building was a warren of passages and chambers, so that you could go from any building in the complex indoors to any other, and even to any of the built-in ground-floor commercial establishments—drugstore, candy store, co-op supermarket, restaurants, bars. Most of what one needed for life was right there in Knickerbocker Village, including friends.

A few months after us, my friend Dick Wilson married Doë's friend Jessica Gould and at once moved into a KV apartment the mirror image of ours, across the central court and a few stories lower down. We could see each other's windows, and arranged signals for when we wanted company to save on phone bills. On the penthouse floor of our own building were Willard and Eleanor Crosby. Bill was one of my colleagues at Popular, a marvelously witty and urbane man who ultimately wound up on *The New York Times* until his death in the 1960s. Another Popular editor, Loren Dowst, had an apartment in the complex, and two Brooklyn friends, Ben and Felice Leshner, turned up a few tunnels away. Our own neighbors across the hall were named Hoke and Cara Smith—Hoke a librarian, Cara a student. We got along well, especially in the hot weather, when we learned that if we and they kept our hall doors open, we could get a straight-through ventilation almost as good as (wild fantasy of luxury!) air conditioning.

Knickerbocker Village had been built in part as a sort of primeval urban redevelopment plan. The neighborhood was tatty, and a lot of it was pure slum. It was the old Five Points neighborhood, in the middle of the nineteenth century the armpits of hell, ridden with crime and violence far worse than anything in East Harlem or Bed-Stuy today. The ghetto people then were Irish, rather than black or Puerto Rican, and that whole area was where the Civil War draft riots started, where police dared go only in pairs, and then only walking down the middle of the street. That was 1850 and thereabouts. Now, in the 1970s and thereabouts, it is—New York. It is like any other part of New York. If you walk the streets late at night you are reasonably likely to be mugged.

But in 1941 and 1942 it was gentler and more colorful. The neighborhood was a mosaic. Here was an Italian street fair, there a Greek kaffeineon; Jewish pushcart peddlers were all over, and Chinatown was just a few blocks away. North of Chinatown was the Bowery, solid ranks of missions, quarter-a-night flophouses, and dime-a-shot bars. Derelicts were sprawled sodden in every doorway at night and lurched down the sidewalks all of every day. Each morning I took the Second Avenue El from Chatham Square to 42nd Street on my way to work, and you could look right into the windows of the flophouses to see the ranks of cots in the dormitories, and the shoulder-high partitions that defined the "private" rooms for the more affluent. New Yorkers had not yet learned to be afraid. It did not occur to us that any of *them* would harm any of *us*, and none of them ever did.

In among all these warehouses and old-law tenements Knickerbocker Village stood tall and self-contained, gates open, playground unlocked, like the keep of a particularly prosperous baron in a particularly tranquil decade of medieval Europe.

We weren't even isolated. We went out into the bigger world to theaters, to friends, to work. Friends came to see us. We seemed to have a lot of parties (bless those thick, quiet Knickerbocker Village walls), and people were in and out of the apartment every day and night. On Sundays Isaac Asimov came clear across the river from Brooklyn to visit. Doë wasn't terribly fond of him, and so we would go out and walk around Chinatown while he told me the plot of the newest Foundation story he was writing for John Campbell, and I would try to interest him in writing something else for me. Willy Ley had come to America a few years earlier out of pure loathing for Hitler and the Nazis. He was writing articles and the odd story for science-fiction magazines, and he brought his pretty wife, Olga, down for dinner once or twice, a lovely, slim, dark girl with a ballerina's figure. (She acquired it dancing with the St. Petersburg Corps, and as of a few weeks ago has it still.)

But Europe was at war. The United States was still a year and more from Pearl Harbor, but the handwriting was on the wall. The Army had begun to draft men. Dirk Wylie had signed up in the reserve, and they took him away to become an MP. Dave Kyle went off, and reappeared a few months later in the uniform of a staff sergeant of the Armored Corps. Jack Gillespie didn't much care for wearing a uniform. That was what the cards spelled out if he didn't do something to prevent it, so he got himself into the Merchant Marine as a deckhand, and came back from time to time to report on what life was like in the Caribbean and the Med. My own draft situation was reasonably comfortable (Doë qualified as a dependent because we had married before the cutoff date), but all young males understood well that the rules could change any time if the war went badly; and badly it was going. After creaming France, the Nazis had sat tight for a time, flexing their muscles and organizing their conquests. Then, in a series of lightning strokes, they occupied Denmark and Norway, moved into the Balkans, and in the summer of 1941 attacked the Soviet Union. If I had had any faith at all left in Joe Stalin as wise all-father to the proletarian republic, it would have been destroyed by his handling of that invasion—if, of course, I had known what was really going on. He blew it badly, disastrously badly. What saved him was the toughness of the Russian people and the almost equal foolishness of Adolf Hitler. Even so, within a few weeks the Germans were deep inside the Soviet Union, and Stalin was in nervous collapse.

There was, to be sure, a certain amount of sardonic fun in the situation. As soon as Hitler struck at Stalin, the Communist Party line flopped back, from "The Yanks Are Not Coming" to "Victory for the Freedom-loving Peoples of the World." And not just the Communist Party. All at once Stalin was our friend, the Russians our allies and protégés. Hollywood began churning out a series of films showing how the heroic Russian masses were outsmarting and outfighting the invader. Chicago meatpackers began manufacturing kielbasa for lend-lease. And one ludicrous evening in the Radio City Music Hall I heard their symphony orchestra playing, for God's sake, the "Internationale."

It was not only a bad time in the war, it was suddenly a very bad time for me. About that time I became unemployed.

I have never been sure whether I quit or got fired. I hung at Harry Steeger's doorway one morning until I got to see him. My intention was to ask for a raise, meaning to quit and free-lance if he turned me down.

But Steeger had complaints of his own. When I walked out of his office I didn't have the raise, and didn't have the job, either.

From the early summer of 1941 to the beginning of 1942, seven months in all, I was a free-lance writer. That wasn't the first time I had been a free-lance writer. What else was I to call myself in 1938? But it was the first time that it mattered much whether I made a living or not. Knickerbocker Village wanted its rent every month. We ate. We burned electricity. The landlord called, and twelve o'clock arrived too often.

In that seven-month period I wrote quite a lot. I actually finished five stories which sold, for a collective price of not much less than a thousand dollars—for the first-serial sale, that is; over the years, they've earned quite a lot more than that. If you divide seven months into a thousand dollars, you find that my weekly earnings came to around thirty dollars, or almost, not even counting what long-subsequent reprints brought in. That was just about what I had been earning in salaries and free-lance checks while I was at Popular.

But it was not the same thing at all, at all.

There is a vast difference between earning a thousand dollars at the boiler factory and earning that same thousand as a free-lance writer. At the boiler works you get a check every Friday. If you write for a living, you get your check when you get it, and not a moment before. Maybe you get it when you finish your story. Maybe you get it a few months later, after a few editors have had the unwisdom to reject it. Maybe you get it never.

This is a terrible trauma for many writers, not just the effect on their credit of the slapdash arrival of checks, but the effect on their writing itself. Jim Blish was one of the more successful, and also one of the more deservedly successful, writers I have known. For more than twenty years he alternated between periods of holding a job and writing on the side, and periods of full-time writing as a free-lancer. And for all those years the best and most successful writing he did was when it was in his spare time; when he took his courage in his hands and set out to be Pure Writer, he froze. Not just Jim. Many of us. To some degree, at some time, all of us. Including me. (But always excepting Isaac Asimov, who is not like mortal man.)

The good thing about writing as a career is if you are any good at it, the paychecks keep coming long after the work is done. Nearly half my income usually comes from residual rights on work done anywhere up to forty years ago, including a share from those stories written in the fall of 1941. (If those subsequent earnings are added in, my actual income from those seven months must come to well over a hundred a week, at least twice as much as I then deemed affluence.)

The bad thing is that the money doesn't come when you need it. The normal curve of a writer's income is steadily up. But the point from which the curve starts is zero.

Doë and I weren't desperately poor. We certainly weren't being hounded by creditors; we had never bought anything on credit. Although we had no appreciable savings, and the cash inflow for that seven-month period was meager, I don't recall needing any tangible thing that we didn't have. What I personally needed very much was quite intangible: a touch more self-respect.

The funny thing is that I am sure I could have found another editorial job if I had looked. Young male editors were disappearing into uniform every week, and a draft-deferred specimen like me could easily have found a home. I am astonished to say that, as far as I can recall, the thought never crossed my mind. If I couldn't edit *Astonishing* and *Super Science*

I would write, and if I couldn't write I would do nothing.

And nothing is what I did a lot of the time, or at least nothing very productive in terms of bringing cash into the domestic economy. What I did a great deal of the time was play chess. I had never been any good at it, but I wanted to be, and now, with time to spare, I lived on the chessboard for seven months. I learned all the end games, and puzzled for weeks over the fact that a knight and a bishop could checkmate a king but two knights could not. I bought a book of famous games and played them out. And I challenged any player I could catch.

The player I could catch most frequently was Dick Wilson, handily right across the court in Building E. By the time he got home from work I would already have the light impatiently in the window, and as soon as he was through dinner he would come up to BH8, or I would come down to EE2, and we would play until he had to go to sleep. I don't remember what Jessica and Doë did while we played chess. I don't know if I cared.

When I wasn't playing chess, I read. When I wasn't reading, I listened to music. Doë and I had discovered ballet a little earlier, and as often as we could afford we were off to the old Metropolitan Opera House to see the Ballet Russe de Monte Carlo, Fredric Franklin taking a hundred and twenty-eight bars to die as the slave in *Scheherazade*, the astringent excellence of *Les Sylphides*, *Swan Lake*'s heart-meltingly sweet cygnets. Once I had seen the ballets, the music meant a great deal more to me than it had before, and I began listening in earnest. Somehow I had reached the age of twenty with only the sketchiest acquaintance with classical music. I hadn't owned a record player and had not fully realized that WQXR and WNYC were broadcasting all the concerts one would want to hear every day on the radio. The ballet *Petrouchka* opened up Stravinsky to me; *Gala Performance*, Prokofiev. I bought the fragile, ponderous 78-rpm albums—*The Song of the Nightingale, Firebird, Sacre*—and played the grooves right off them. From *Les Sylphides* I discovered Chopin, and just about that time Alexander Brailowsky began a concert series that included the entire Chopin oeuvre, even the seldom-played ones that seem to need twelve fingers on each hand; I went to Town Hall for some of them and marveled. When I wasn't playing chess or reading or listening to music, I was visiting with friends; and when I wasn't doing any of those things, and *only* when I wasn't doing any of those things, I wrote.

There are well-organized writers in the world, but I haven't known many of them. (Just one, I think—and you know who you are, Isaac.) I do know what a well-organized writer is like. He gets up in the morning, washes the sleep out of his eyes, sits down at his typewriter, and picks up where he left off at five the evening before. For three hours he types, and then he breaks for lunch. After a pleasant meal and a stroll in the garden, it's back to the typewriter for three more hours. Then, virtuous and complacent, he covers the typewriter and revels all the evening long.

It is not like that for me, and isn't for most of the writers I have known—all the hundreds, maybe thousands, of them. What we mostly do is sweat, stall, worry, and convulse.

I have subsequently learned how to be somewhat systematic. It doesn't come naturally, but I couldn't function without it. Now I have formal quotas and projections, and I often know fairly well in February what work I will have finished by the end of the year. Even so . . . even so, not long ago I found myself totally unable to write for nearly six months; a few years before that, I was convinced I would never write again; and it was only this week, even this day, that I sat and stared at the typewriter for an hour or more without putting a word on paper. As far as I can tell, from my own experience and that of many others, that is how the game is played.

At twenty-one I was far less well organized than (even!) I am now. Writing was scary. The stakes were high, my confidence was shaky, I put it off when I could. When I wrote it was in bursts: an eighteen-thousand-word novelette all one night long, taking the last page out of the typewriter at noon and falling exhausted to sleep. It was not a bad novelette,* but the way I wrote it was very bad. To produce so much so quickly and so exhaustingly makes it that much harder to sit down to produce again. The experience gives you the confidence that a great deal can be done in a short time, which encourages delay. The memory of the exhaustion gives you the knowledge that it won't be any fun, which discourages getting started.

I now think that everything I did at that time—in fact, everything I was doing in all those years, and almost everything I've done through my life—carried its own justification of a sort. What a writer has to sell is his own perspective on the universe. The way to make that perspective significant is to learn all one can learn about—everything. What I was doing was informal, disorganized, spasmodic, but it was all learning. All of it helped to unravel that central mystery which is what writing is all about,† and so all of it contributed to my career. I don't regret a minute of it

---

* At least, I don't think it was bad. It was "Wings of the Lightning Land." It has been reprinted since, and is in *The Early Pohl* (Doubleday, 1976), but I've never had the courage to reread it.

† That "central mystery" can be defined in many ways, but most of them revolve around a single central question: "Who am I?"

. . . now. But at the time it didn't feel good at all. It felt as if I were washed up at twenty-one.

I have sat staring at this page, trying to remember and to understand, so that I can say just what was happening in those seven months. I think I do understand. I don't like my understanding of that time in my life very much, and I have buried so much of it so deeply inside the layers of my head that it is difficult to exhume fact out of the strata of rationalization.

But whether I like it or not, I think I know what happened. I was not feeling happy about myself, and for that reason I was not happy with those around me. The principal person around me was Doë. We were two raw children, Doë and I. We married very young; even the marriage ceremony only ratified a commitment that had been implicit almost since we first started dating at seventeen. The growing-up process that most adolescents experience through transient dates and relationships, we worked out only on each other, and we carried a lot of adolescent role-playing into our marriage. I more than she. I had made a model of myself in my head, and I acted it out. The model was mature, authoritative, a genu-wine leader type, capable of command decision and never at a loss. And the tide went out and the sand washed away and the foundations crumbled, and I had to learn a new model for myself. The father-bear role would not play any more.

Where did I learn the father-bear role? Why, I think we all learned it. It came out of the sexist society that taught us role-playing, out of a dozen Astaire-Rogers movies, out of the stereotypes of the stories we wrote and read, out of all the conventional wisdom of the age. We were all a little crippled. Some of us still limp when the rain wind blows from the east. Prickly Women's-Lib ladies, you can have anything you want of me. Your fight is my fight, but you come a little late; I wish you had been around forty years ago, when *I* needed liberating. Because we were taught that women were dependent, it followed that there was no one for them to depend on but men. Among others, my own father had taught me to play that role, but I think he had also taught me to fail at it.

I don't want to give the impression that Doë and I suffered through months of misery, because it wasn't like that at all. We had a lot of fun. We did productive things. We were so young that we knew, fundamentally and surely, that there would always be other chances and new experiences without end, and in fact there were. But we blew that one. Not "we." I. Having married Doë as part of a scenario I had written for myself, and then having found out that the scenario didn't work, I was restive. I had signed a run-of-the-play contract, but I wanted to quit the part.

It was a gritty personal time, and made grittier and more confusing by the world scene. In December the Japanese bombed Pearl Harbor, and my country was at war.

Early in 1942 Alden H. Norton sent me a telegram, asking me to come back to Popular Publications as his assistant. To make it sweeter, he offered me more as an assistant than I had been paid as a full-fledged editor. I felt around my pride to see if it was injured, and when it did not seem to hurt anywhere, I accepted at once.

Al Norton was a boss editor, a department head. He had fifteen or sixteen pulp magazines to look after and four people to help him do it: a secretary and three assistant editors, including myself. The staff had been depleted by the draft and other turmoils, and when I came aboard there was only one surviving assistant, Olga Mae Quadland, tall, dark, good-looking, and good-humored. Ollie had the curious attribute of being a female deacon in the Episcopal Church, but I was big enough not to hold that against her, and she was very good at her job. A little later another assistant signed on to complete the roster, Dorothy LesTina. She was a pretty, brown-haired recent divorcée from San Diego. Tina was a year or two older than I, wore her hair in coronet braids, and was new enough in New York that she didn't know a soul.

The war had begun to change publishing, even in seven months. There were new things, real or on the horizon, called "price controls" and "rationing." Paper was going to run short. The Canadian forests were still there, and the mills were ready to grind the trees into magazine pages, but to get the trees to the mills and the paper rolls to the printing presses involved trains and trucks, and they were suddenly heavily committed to troop movements and shipments of airplane parts. There was even, without warning, censorship. None of us knew how that was meant to work. But one day I wrote an editorial for one of the air-war magazines, full of pulpy fantasy about the terrible vengeance our Air Force was about to work on the Axis, and laid it on Alden's desk. He came in an hour later, looking worried, and said Harry Steeger had told him he would have to clear it with Air Force Intelligence. We phoned around, and got a name, and sent it off, and a few days later it came back, heavily red-lined and amended. "Night fighters parachuting agents into the heart of Occupied Europe" had been changed to "support of ground operations, covert and otherwise." Bragging about the invulnerability of the B-17 "Flying Fortress" had been revised to a recitation of the published official performance figures on rate of fire and armor. It was apparent at once that the censors hadn't yet figured out how they were supposed to work, either.

But we got along fine, all of us corralled into the long, narrow room at the end of the hall. We slashed

the Western and sports stories into English, took fair
turns at editing the worst of them, lunched together
more often than not, went bowling at the alleys down
the block once or twice a week. After the fretful ten-
sion of trying to free-lance, coming into the Bartholomew Building every morning was like a vacation with
pay. Alden made it easy for me to be his assistant,
decent man, careful to consider the feelings of the
people who worked for him. Apart from the growing
alienation in my marriage, it was an easy time. I liked
the work, relished the abdication from decision-
making, had enough money to meet our needs; it was
clear that it could not last forever—the Red Death
was stalking the world, and the cracks were spreading
at the foundation of my personal universe—but that
was something that could be worried about at a later
time. I was not Prince Hamlet. But it was pleasant to
be an attendant lord while my glands caught up with
my ambitions.

I had almost lost touch with the Futurians. Most I
still saw on a one-to-one basis, but I was no longer
part of the group. Partly it was my own vanity—having
thrown my weight around as a boy editor, it was quite
a comedown to be one more faceless aspiring writer
in the mob—but it was also that I had had all the in-
jokes and scurrility I wanted for a while. Individually
the Futurians contained some of the brightest and best
people I have ever known, but collectively they—no,
we—were often kind of awful.

They were also changing. Old Futurians were vanish-
ing, new blood was flowing in. The center of gravity
had moved from the Ivory Tower in Brooklyn to a
West 103rd Street walk-up called Prime Base. There
was a pentacle painted on the tatty linoleum of the
living room, and murals on the wall (the figures were
the Unholy Trinity: Stinky, Shorty, and the Holy

Ghost). The artwork was due to a new boy in town named Damon Knight, skinny, callow, with a pear-shaped head and a lot on the ball in his idiosyncratic way. Damon had been a fan since he was old enough to read, and his intention in coming to New York was to become a professional science-fiction artist. He might well have succeeded, in spite of having no discernible talent at art, if the example of the other Futurians had not suggested to him that writing was easier. A few editors bought his illustrations, but then they began to buy his stories as well, and he put away his sketch pad for good. Jim Blish had been a fringe Futurian for some time and now became more active in the group; a little later Judy Merril came in, first female Futurian accepted in her own right rather than as a ladies'-day guest of some male.

But by then I was long gone.

The pleasure had begun to diminish, and the cracks to widen. By the end of 1942 Doë and I came to the parting of the ways. When the lease ran out on our Knickerbocker Village apartment, she went back to her parents' home, and I took a room in a hotel on West 45th Street. I had begun to get very interested in that hazel-eyed girl with the coronet braids, Dorothy LesTina. But the dynamics of the situation were more than I could handle, and I decided to go for to be a soldier.

Unfortunately, Uncle Sam did not seem in any particular hurry to acquire my young flesh. The draft machine was in high gear, and voluntary enlistments had been suspended while they figured things out. And they didn't draft me.

This displeased me, and so I went down to Local Board 1 to complain. Take me, I said. Go away, they said; we'll come to you when we come to you. How come you didn't come to me already? I asked. And they said: Because, first, you are deferred because of dependency; second, because we have been assigned a quota, and our quota is overfulfilled. All the young fellows in Chinatown signed up long ago to fight the Japanese. When we finish with them, maybe we'll get to you, so go away.

Well, that bugged me. I had been talking anti-Fascist so long that I was beginning to feel guilty about doing nothing more tangible in the war than writing editorials in *Fighting Aces*. And when you come right down to it, I have this special unalterable love for the United States of America. Bumbling, sometimes blundering, it is still my country, right or wrong, and I take much pride in the fact that over its two hundred years it has been right a lot more than it has been wrong. (God preserve us all from the exceptions!) So I wanted in. A lot.

There was some fun to be had in the situation because I appointed myself spokesman for all the unwilling draftees in the country. I wrote my local board, I telephoned them, I went down and pounded on the table. The dependency depended on the marriage, I said, and the marriage was over. We'll make a note of that, they said, and don't call us, we'll call you. I'm not really in Local Board 1's territory any more, because I moved to West 45th Street, I said. We'll make a note of that, too, they said, but go away.

In the long run they did grant me my wish, but it took some four months of doing. They inducted me on April Fool's Day, 1943.

7

My Life as a Cardinal Man

In writing about this period I don't feel as if I am writing about myself; in fact, not about any real person at all. I think I know why. I was not a person. I was an enlisted man in the Army. An EM has no more individuality than the seventh egg in a box of a dozen. He is a unit quantity. He is not just a number, he is less than a number, because he does not even have that limited identity we sometimes give to certain numbers, like Third Base or the Year 1492. He has cardinality: if he is missing from a formation, the tally is one short. But he does not have ordinality: it does not matter (except perhaps to him, but who cares what a cardinal number thinks?) whether he is the fifth or the fifty-fifth in the muster roll, any more than it matters whether the sheet of paper I take out of a ream was the first or the last to go in.

If a soldier were not a cardinal man, armies would not be possible. No *person* would allow himself to be restricted to his barracks because a quarter will not bounce off his bed, or would tolerate being refused admission to an "officers only" bar, or would stroll down to the Venetian Causeway, as I did on many evenings during basic training in Miami Beach, and gaze hungrily at the city lights across the bay, accepting the prohibition against walking across the bridge. A cardinal man in the uniform of the other side can be killed or maimed without penalty. A cardinal man on your own side can be ordered to storm a pillbox, or be shot for falling asleep, without consideration. A *person* would not put up with any of this crap for a minute.*

Since I was born a white male Protestant, and thus competitively advantaged in the American society in ways that kikes, niggers, girls, gooks, and wogs were not, it would be hard for me to understand all the passions that lie behind the liberation movements . . . if I had not been an enlisted man in the Army. Aw, sure, I know it's not the *same*. I knew it was only a game, and that when I got my discharge all the rules would change back again. But it was close enough while it lasted. An EM knows what it is like to be treated like a piece of meat. And he knows, too, the delicious advantages of accepting the status quo. You can let someone else do the worrying. Uncle Toms and cuddly girls learned this long before I did.

Since the game rules called for me to be a cuddly Tom, I played that game and, my God, I actually enjoyed it. All of it. Even the utterly revolting parts, like cleaning grease traps on KP and getting up at a quarter to five in the morning, with the stars still out. Basic training (at least for the Air Force, at least in Miami Beach at that time) was a lot like going back to Camp Fire Place Lodge and the age of twelve.

In 1943 the Miami Beach hotels were clustered south of Lincoln Road. They were relatively small and nearly vacant. The hotel owners had been torpedoed

---

* There are a lot of cardinal people in the world, and not all of them are in armies. But that's a whole other discussion.

by the war as surely as the tankers whose oil washed up on the sand now and then, and so they struck a deal with the government. Almost all their hotels were used to house Air Force basic trainees. The owners were happy enough, and for us rookies it beat the hell out of sleeping in tents.

I drove through that part of Miami Beach a few weeks ago, and it is all shabby and down at the heel. Collins Avenue, which used to resound with the cadence count and singing of our marching platoons, is now filled with elderly retirees trying to get along on Social Security, sunshine, and canned pet food. The signs on the little hotels I barracked in are in Cuban Spanish. The beach itself has almost disappeared. But in 1943 it was a whole new thing to me. I had never been in Florida before, had never tasted a subtropical climate except when I was too tiny to notice it. I found the smell of rotting palm trees fascinating, was astonished at the luminous clarity of Biscayne Bay, observed with interest the number of GIs who fell over with heat prostration at the daily retreat ceremony. I quickly made friends, first and most permanently with WINTERS Joseph S, ASN 32879797. Joe and I, as the two tallest men in Flight O, were almost always together leading the files as we marched. In the quick swap of autobiographies we discovered we also had the two tallest IQs, but of course the Army didn't care much about *that*.

Joe and I spent a lot of time together. When we could make our own decisions we swam, or drank a little beer in the blacked-out bars, or listened to Sunday-afternoon record concerts on the lawn of the public library. What we mostly did was what the Army told us to do, sitting around in the sun while someone explained one more time the nomenclature of the carbine, or watching films on venereal disease, or going through the obstacle course. We fired a lot of guns. My summers in camp and on my uncle's farm paid off with a lot of marksmanship medals, and by and by they told us we were finished killers and sent us off in a thirty-car troop train to Chanute Field, Illinois, to become Air Force weathermen. Joe shipped out in the same batch. We snaked through every by-pass in Georgia, Alabama, and Tennessee, following the land-grant lines because that was the cheapest way for troops to go. At every siding there were Gray Ladies with coffee and cake, and on one short jump the engineer let me in the cab to drive the train for an omnipotent instant.

Chanute Field was more like *real* Army. You could smoke in the mess halls ("You're at an Air Base now, soldier!"), you could get weekend passes to go as far away as Chicago; I even think there was no bed check, although that seems more wildly indulgent than I can believe. As a special bonus particularly for me, Jack Williamson turned up at the weather school. Jack was a year or so ahead of me on the track. He had already done his basic, become a weather observer, and gone out for a year or two in the field; now he was back at Chanute for advanced training as a fore-caster. He was a most welcome sight, and reminded me that ordinality was still not permanently beyond reach. Joe Winters's wife, Dorothy, came out from New York to spend the summer in the tiny town of Rantoul; they took a room, Joe got an off-base pass, and they introduced me to square dancing and the delights of string quartets. Tina stopped by on her way from her own basic training to a commission as a second lieutenant in the WACs. When I finally came in season for a weekend pass to Chicago, I spent it with the new editor of *Amazing Stories*, Raymond A. Palmer. I had read Ray's own stories as a kid, and his magazine (though under a prior editor) had actually printed the first words of mine that anyone

paid money for. But we had never met. His appearance
was a great surprise. Ray had suffered some sort of
spinal damage and carried a conspicuous hump on his
shoulders. He was twisted and tiny, not much more
than four feet tall. I had not known! It was impossible
not to notice it. I had often discussed him with mutual
friends, and yet no one had ever mentioned that about
him. I am sure the reason was Ray himself—bright,
warmhearted, willing to put himself to immense
trouble for a stray GI like me.

All this mingling with writers and other human
beings made my typing fingers itch again.

I had asked my mother to ship down my lavender
portable while still in basic training, as soon as I was
sure there wasn't any rule against having it. But I
had used it only for letters. Now I wanted to try a
story.

The problem was finding a place to work. There
were thirty thousand GIs in Chanute Field, and they
occupied all the holes. I knew *when* I could write.
Saturday nights were my own, and there was no reveille
on Sunday mornings, so I could write until I couldn't
stay awake any more and sleep late the next day. But
where? The day rooms closed at midnight. The barracks
lights went out at ten-thirty. The classrooms were
locked.

But in all of Chanute Field there was one facility
that never closed, day, night, or Sunday; moreover, it
would disturb no one if I typed there, because there
was no one sleeping there to disturb: the pro station.

So there I sat, rattling away on one story or another,
while the soldiers who had expended their raunchiness
in a doubtful place lurched in and stumbled out. They
didn't bother me. And none of them lingered long
enough for me to bother them.

I think one of the stories I wrote in the Chanute
pro station was a detective short called "The Life of

Riley." Oddly, I don't seem to have made any use of
the surroundings for what I now perceive as interesting local color.

After Chanute I made corporal and shipped out to
an operational air base in Enid, Oklahoma. I had
made private first class as soon as I completed basic.
That came to one rise in grade every sixty days or so,
which meant that the war would only have to last
another two years to see me a brigadier general, if
nothing went wrong with the system.*

Enid's weather station was a real working facility.
Enid was a basic flying school. The kay-dets had to
rely on what we told them about the weather, so there
were real values at stake when we played at spotting
synoptic maps and following pilot balloons through a
theodolite. A nice touch was that several of the
weather observers were WACs, notably a very fine-
looking and highly smart blonde divorcée from Florida
named Zenobia Qualls Grizzard. Zenobia and I were
seriously misgraffed in respect of years, but we had
a lot of fun, golfing together, bowling together, drinking three-point-two beer together in the Passion Pit
of the Hotel Youngblood in town. Zenobia outclassed
me in all those activities. She was a champion golfer,
tournament type; fortunately for my ego, she had
broken her ankle not long before and still couldn't
put much muscle into her swing. So I always lost, but
not always badly.

Our drinking was somewhat affected, if not really
handicapped, by Oklahoma's quaint image of itself as
a dry state. Only three-point-two was legal, but you
could get anything you cared to name from the bell-
boys at the Youngblood. At least they said you could;
I never heard them turn down a request, but every

---

* Something did, and I wound up a buck sergeant.

bottle came with the seal broken, and I have my suspicions about where and how they were filled.

After six months at Enid it 'peared to me that I could hear the step of the Fool-Killer coming up behind me. It seemed time to move on. The trouble with Oklahoma was that there weren't very many Nazis there to fight. I wanted action. My 201 file bulged with applications to be transferred to a combat theater. None of them seemed to move anyone to action, and the war was moving on. Then a circular came through, soliciting volunteers for Arctic training. I signed up at once.

In the fullness of time my orders came through. I was sent to Lowry Field, Colorado, for cold-weather instruction, they pulled all the fillings out of my teeth and replaced them with freezeproof North Pole models, and then they sent me to Italy.

The troopship *Cristobal* steamed into the Bay of Naples and moored, not at your usual New York or London variety of pier, but next to a bombed-out, belly-up freighter. The Bay of Naples had been hit very hard by bombers, everybody's bombers. First the Americans and the British had stamped it bloody; then, when the city changed hands, the Luftwaffe finished up what was left. Nobody cared about bombing the city, but the port was big business; so in order to get ashore we had to march on catwalks across those capsized ships.

I was not quite prepared for the reality of war—I don't mean the fighting itself (I had read all about that, and seen it in a hundred Hollywood movies), but the open wounds that were left behind when a war moved on. We went by truck to a repple-depple on the Caserta Road, and it took me time to realize that those buildings with holes in them had not been marked for urban renewal by a demolition crew but were the inadvertent targets of bombs or shells aimed at something else. In the evenings the women pressed up against the fence of the replacement depot, offering, in their soft, hoarse peasant voices, laundry services, home-cooked meals, and themselves. We spare parts lay in the bin for a week or so while the scoops came through and shoveled us out to our stations. I wound up with the 456th Bomb Group—"Colonel Steed's Flying Colts," for God's sake—in a place called Stornara, surrounded by walnut groves, a few miles from the Adriatic on the Foggia plain.

The 456th flew B-24s, clumsy four-engine bombers that rumbled out to Romanian oil installations and Yugoslavian marshaling yards every day they could fly. They did not always come back. Sometimes they didn't even get out of sight of the field. We lost a few on takeoff—*blam!* and a pillar of smoke at the end of the runway—and one awful night, at the time of the invasion of southern France, two pairs of B-24s collided as they were forming up and another was ignited by a scrap of debris, so that five of them were burning in the air at once over the field. The equation

$$5 \text{ B24} = 50 \text{ } 0 + \text{EM}$$

solved itself in all our minds, and we ground crew stood staring while those fifty human beings died. Some of them jumped, but none of them lived, because the parachutes were on fire.

Shortly after I reached the 456th, I got a lawyer's letter from Florida to tell me that Doë had brought suit for divorce. As I was a soldier and therefore divorce-proof for the duration, I could have stopped it. But I deduced she had something in mind, and so I signed the paper and sent it back. A little while later I heard through mutual friends that she had married Tommy Owens, a neighborhood kid who had known Doë longer than I had, now a B-25 navigator in the States.

And about that time my mother's letters became shorter and less frequent. I knew she was ill. She never talked about her illness in her letters, but when two weeks went by with no mail at all, I realized she was sicker than I had thought.

Well, I knew what to do about that. It was in all the magazines. When our brave soldier boys at the fighting fronts had a problem, the Red Cross was always there. *They* would know how to help.

So I went looking for the 456th's own Red Cross man. The Red Cross had communications facilities denied to the rest of us; he could send a cable to the hospital in Allentown, Pennsylvania, and get an answer back in hours. He could even arrange compassionate leave, a quick trip back to the States on a courier plane via Dakar and Natal. He could do a lot. And I really think he might have, at that. If I had ever been able to find him. Unfortunately his schedule did not permit him to be in his little office very often, and for a solid week, every time I went looking for him, he was out playing golf. And then I did get a cable and the issue became moot. My mother had died of bone cancer in Allentown.

The headquarters squadron facilities at Stornara had been improvised out of tents, barns, and wineries, but there was one building that was solid and new: the enlisted men's club down the hill. Square, empty cinder-block building, it had been someone's fantasy of Red Cross dances and film showings, but in practice it seldom held anything more than the all-weather, all-group crap games. I claimed a corner of it and set up my typewriter.

Because I was a little homesick about New York, I decided to write about it. A novel—why not? I meditated on the plot and decided that the most interesting thing in New York was the advertising business, and so, page by page, I began to hammer out a long, complicated, and very bad novel called *For Some We Loved.** The Italian civilian who cleaned up the EM club respected what I was doing immensely, guarded my privacy, and gave me a picture of himself which I still have, taken while he was in Mussolini's army in Ethiopia. It shows him brandishing an immense revolver and looking exactly like the reason the Italians lost the war: a gentle man with a great sense of humor; it is impossible to imagine him ever firing that gun at a human being.

There wasn't really a lot to do. For a few hours before the group took off on a mission we were all busy; the rest of the time we played chess or wrote letters or talked during our duty hours. Donovan Bess was there, perhaps the best chess player I've ever encountered; he had the curious idiosyncrasy of calling a knight a horse, but his country-boy dialogue covered up grand-master play. The station commander was an apple-cheeked second lieutenant named Jack Adler, who had just discovered T. S. Eliot, and for a solid week we went over the imagery in *Prufrock* to make sure we knew what the man was talking about.

The weather wing picked up all the high-IQ oddballs in the Air Force, and we had among us a tithing fundamentalist from Ohio, a Polish halfback from Hamtramck and the first admitted homosexual I had ever known on a social basis; he was out of action for the duration, he said, because that was grounds for court-martial and a dishonorable discharge, but he enjoyed telling everyone who would listen what his preferences and plans were.

* The novel was never published and no longer exists, because one night years later I burned it. But it wasn't a total waste. *For Some We Loved* led directly to writing *The Space Merchants.*

When the resources of the air base ran thin, I borrowed a jeep and went to visit Foggia, Cerignola, or Barletta. There wasn't much in Foggia, because it had been bombed flat. There wasn't a lot in Cerignola, either, because there never had been; sleepy farm town with a huge new cathedral that smelled like a latrine, it was the kind of community that the Italians used to say Christ never bothered to visit. But Barletta lay on the lovely, limpid Adriatic, not yet a septic tank, and you could swim and lie on the beach and gaze speculatively at the beautiful fifteen-year-old Whore of Barletta, rejecting commercial offers in the afternoon for the sake of improving her suntan, and even meet civilians of a different kind. One was a former Italian Army artillery captain named Ugo Vittorini, whose brother, Elio, was one of Italy's finest novelists. Ugo had served in Yugoslavia. A fierce anti-Fascist, he had managed to persuade his entire battery to desert to the partisans there, while his wife, Maria, was operating a "safe house" for *partigiani* between the lines in northern Italy. Now they were a quiet professorial couple with children and a pleasant apartment on a courtyard, and they impressed me very much.

Twenty-two years after the war my wife, Carol, and I attended the Science Fiction Film Festival in Trieste and arranged to meet our two older daughters (then at school in England) in Naples as soon as their term ended. We had a week to spare, and we spent it driving a rented Fiat through my war. I don't know what it did for Carol, except a little heat prostration here and there, but I found it fascinating. Foggia! In 1944 there had been almost nothing standing except the beat-up tower of the church; in 1967 it was all pastel stucco high-rises, and I couldn't even find the church in the towers around it. Barletta, too, was all high-rise pink and blue apartment buildings and a whole new battery of hotels and restaurants. But in

Cerignola time had stopped. Not a building had been added, none taken away, and the church still smelled like a latrine, while all the rest of the area had risen from the grave and turned into Miami Beach.

Around the same time I found the solution to a minor mystery that dated back to Stornara. A bomb wing was made up of four groups, but our wing had only three: the 455th, 456th, and 458th. I always wondered where that last group had got to, and then in a casual conversation with Hal Clement, he supplied the answer. The 457th had been detached to fill a hole in the AAF in England, and he had been in it. Pity it worked out like that. I would have been thrilled to meet Hal Clement in Italy.

An observed fact of my life is that I have almost always gotten everything I wanted, sooner or later. Another observed fact is that sometimes by the time I get it I don't want it any more. For Christmas the Army gave me that thing I had been scheming and contriving for, for a year and a half, a chance to transfer to the Infantry, go to OCS, and become an expendable second lieutenant with the Fifth Army as it crawled up the mountains toward the Po.

Catch-22 was that in order to take advantage of this boon, one had to re-up for two more years, and it was clear to everyone who looked at a map that the war wouldn't stretch that long. It was annoying that the Germans didn't seem to perceive this fact. Indeed, they had just launched the Ardennes attack, perplexingly as if they thought they were still a viable military force. But the Russians were grinding bloodily west, and the Fifth Army was creeping north up the Apennines; even the Japanese were being pushed off one island after another, and there was no doubt in my mind that the European part of the war would run out in a few months and the rest of it not long after.

But still—

A third of a century later, with Vietnam so huge in the recent past, it is hard for me to remember how righteously most of us viewed our cause. But we did. The Nazis had done terrible things. How terrible we were being reminded every day, as the Americans and British liberated one concentration camp after another. It was a moral obligation to stop them, even at risk— maybe especially if at risk, to prove, well, *something* to, well, somebody.

So I stewed over this problem for a while, doing arithmetic in my head. Allow a month for the papers to be processed; that brings us into January. Add ten weeks for the OCS course, and say another two to hang around a replacement depot waiting for an assignment. That brought us to early April at best before I would be handed my platoon to lead into combat, and where would the combat be? Surely not in Europe any more. And the war against Japan seemed mostly a matter of Air Force and Navy, even if it managed to stay in business long enough to get me there.

As it turned out, my arithmetic was a little wrong. The Germans managed to hold out until May, plenty of time for me to get my head blown off if I had really wanted it. But in the event it was taken out of my hands, anyway. Someone in AAF/MTO headquarters in Caserta had his eye on me. They had discovered that I had been a writer and an editor as a civilian, and decided I would be more use with words than with weapons or weather instruments. So in January, 1945, I packed up and headed west across the peninsula.

U.S. Army Air Forces/Mediterranean Theater of

Operations was headquartered in the King's Palace in
the town of Caserta, a few miles inland from Naples:
immense rectangular tenement of a building that reminded me a lot of Knickerbocker Village. It wasn't
just Air Force, or even just Americans. The whole
allied Mediterranean war effort was directed from
there. People like Eisenhower and Churchill passed
through from time to time, causing much pain to the
headquarters troops who were required to shine themselves up for ceremonial parades. (We Weather
Squadron people were never involved in that sort of
thing, fortunately for the good name of the service.)
The place was full of foreigners. There was a big RAF
unit, and I became friendly with some of them on a
bridge-playing and beer-drinking basis. There were
French troops, including black colonials; co-belligerent
Italians; and quite a few former members of the
Wehrmacht, now working in the mess halls as KPs
to feed us conquerors. There I met my longtime friend
Eddie Cope, the sage of Houston, Texas, who passed
on to me all he had learned at the University of
Texas's drama department. ("There are only three
reasons for any line: to show character, advance the
action, or get a laugh." "If you show a gun on the
stage, you have to fire it." Etc. They are all good rules,
tolerant about being broken when necessary.)

What I was supposed to be doing was public relations and editing the squadron newspaper. Public
relations wasn't hard. I prepared a standard form, and
was given a clerk-typist to pound them out and mail
them off to local newspapers whenever any of our
number did anything interesting, like getting promoted
from Pfc to Corporal. Editing the newspaper was a
little less straightforward, since I didn't know anything about newspapers. I solved it by converting it
to a magazine, borrowed a mimeograph, found a

civilian printer to do the covers, and put out one of the nicest fanzines you ever saw.

It was an undemanding way to spend time in Italy, but in the familiar environment of typewriters and layouts ordinality was seeping back. I didn't seem to be *doing* much, and I began to hear the step of the Fool-Killer catching up behind me.

I was also in love. Dorothy LesTina and I had been heating up the Army Postal Service with an awful lot of correspondence. Now she was in Germany, a first lieutenant, whose principal job was to stand up on a platform in front of ten thousand troops while some GI crooner sang "Darling, je vous aime beaucoup" to her. (Of many odd individual contributions is a war effort made.) Germany was on the same side of the Atlantic as I was, which was tantalizing, and it was my deep belief that if any GI was going to sing love songs to my girl, it should be me. I could not see any way to arrange that, and frankly, the war was beginning to seem a bore. The Germans had been pushed back out of the Bulge, and it was all just mopping up. And not very interesting.

What I didn't know about the Bulge was that two of my best friends were receiving their death sentences there. Neither of them was wounded. But Dirk Wylie hurt his back jumping out of an Army truck; it got worse, turned into tuberculosis of the spine, and he died of it in 1948. While Cyril Kornbluth strained his heart lugging a .50-caliber machine gun around the Ardennes Forest, and died of essential hypertension a few years later.

What I did know was that the Bulge was the last real effort the Germans could possibly make, and the war was winding down. So I cast about for some more interesting way to spend the time until I would get back to civilian reality, and found it on Mount Vesuvius.

The 12th Weather Squadron had requisitioned a former Cook's Tours hotel there. It was called the Eremo, which means "hermit," and it was isolated enough for the name to fit.

As a headquarters flunky, I had the use of it any time I could borrow a jeep to get there, which was often. The Eremo made it quite a comfortable war. We had kept on the civilian staff—not all of them, and without spit and polish; but they cooked much more interesting meals than I had had anywhere else in Italy at that time, trading Army Spam for civilian fresh vegetables, and they were perfectly willing to make our beds and shine our shoes and bring us drinks on the terrace. It was a quiet place to write, I perceived at once. There was also a writing job which needed to be done—preparing the Squadron History—and I began to scheme to transfer myself to the Hill. About the time the war in Europe ground to an end, I got my druthers.

Living on the side of a volcano is not like being in your average Mamaroneck split-level. This was the same mountain that had creamed Pompeii in A.D. 79. It hadn't done anything quite that spectacular since. But you never knew. It had voided some pretty substantial lava flows a year or so before I arrived, while the Eremo was the pleasant fringe benefit of some Luftwaffe unit. You could still feel the warmth of the rock, just inches below the surface, and now and then there would be a little shudder.

What mashed Pompeii, of course, was not lava but airborne ash. When time permitted, I drove to the excavations and poked around in the interrupted life of the Roman city, and it was quite a contrast to look up from the yards-high ash-fall to the peaceful top of the mountain, gently steaming a couple of miles away, and realize that *that* came from *that*. But in the hotel we were safe enough. Ash would be windblown away.

**The Author at Four
Brooklyn, N.Y., ca 1924**

We had been living in hotel suites and luxury apartments,
but my father's fortunes dipped and we moved to a walkup on
Fourth Avenue, near Atlantic Avenue. It was not a desirable
neighborhood, but no one told me that and I liked it.

**The Author at ease in his loggia
Il Vomero, Naples, 1945**

The 12th Weather Squadron appropriated a mansion in the most exclusive Neapolitan residential area, and I was billeted there for my last few months in Italy during World War II.

**Dorothy LesTina and
the Author
Enid, Oklahoma, 1944**

I was a corporal when this was taken, and Tina was a first lieutenant. By the time we were married, a year later, I was a sergeant, but she was a captain. I was gaining three grades to her two, and might have caught up around brigadier-general, but the war ended too soon for that.

Opposite:
**Mother, Father and the Author
Niagara Falls, ca 1927**

We really were at the Falls—I remember my mother making me practice the multiplication tables all the long drive up—but what is behind us in the photo looks very much like a painted backdrop.

**8/9ths of total attendance at world's
very first science-fiction convention
Philadelphia, 1936**

From left to right: Ossie Train, Don Wollheim, Milton A. Rothman, the Author, Johnny Michel, Will Sykora, David A. Kyle and Robert A. Madle. The other 1/9th of the assembly is taking the picture. His name was John Baltadonis.

The Futurians, 1938

First row: Dirk Wylie, John B. Michel, Isaac Asimov, Donald A. Wollheim, Herman Leventman. *Second row:* Chester Cohen, Walter Kubilius, the Author, Richard Wilson. *Top row:* Cyril Kornbluth, Jack Gillespie, Jack Robins. This was taken in my apartment, around Christmas, and the painting above us is by Johnny Michel.

The Big Name Pros: 1940
Chicago

Seated: Russ Hodgkins, Arthur K. Barnes, Edward E. Smith, Ed Hamilton, T. Bruce Yerke. *Standing:* Robert A. Heinlein, Jack Williamson, Forrest J. Ackerman, Walt Daugherty, Charles D. Hornig.

This was taken at the Second World Science Fiction Convention (of which fans Hodgkins, Yerke and Daugherty were organizers). I'm not in the picture, or even in Chicago. I couldn't afford it.

At the New York Metrocon, 1950

Lester del Rey, Evelyn Harrison, Harry Harrison, Isaac Asimov, Judith Merril, the Author, Poul Anderson, L. Sprague de Camp, P. Schuyler Miller.

The Agent
1951

In the year 1951 I sold more to the leading science-fiction book and magazine publishers than they bought from all other sources combined. Under conditions like that, it was not easy to go broke.

Washington, 1963

Carol Pohl is wearing her costume from *The Reefs of Space.* Isaac Asimov is explaining his philosophy to her while Peg Campbell, overhearing, considers calling the police.

In the Ackermansion
Los Angeles, 1961

L-R the Author, Ray Bradbury, Forest J. Ackerman.
4e's collection is the despair of all rivals and should be declared a national treasure. So should Forry.

**With Jack Williamson
Portales, New Mexico, ca 1966**

Most of our collaboration was done through the mail, because our homes are 2,000 miles apart. This was perhaps the only occasion when we worked on a story in physical proximity.

**On the Long John Show
1965**

Long John Nebel ran the world's longest and best-rated radio talk show. Man and boy, I appeared on his show nearly 400 times, second only to the record run up by The Magnificent Lester del Rey, who got me into it in the first place.

Opposite, above:
In the Art Exhibit, Cleveland Worldcon 1966

John Campbell and I take a break from hitting on authors we want to contribute by hitting on each other.

Opposite, below:
Who Gets the Hugo?

I'm supposed to be receiving the Hugo for Best Editor in Cleveland, 1966, from Isaac Asimov. But Isaac doesn't want to give it up.

In 1966, the year after Doc Smith's death, the Boston fans began the E. E. Smith Memorial Award, the "Skylark", and gave me the first one. No award has ever pleased me more. Harry (Hal Clement) Stubbs presented it.

Opposite, above:
Betty Ballantine and the Author
At the New York Worldcon in 1967.

Opposite, below:
Star Trek
Hollywood, 1967

L-R the Author, unidentified flying alien, Gene Roddenberry.

When I visited the *Star Trek* set shortly after the 1967 World Convention in New York, Gene and I had both won Hugos and amused ourselves by passing them back and forth for the photographers.

Lunacon 1967, New York City
Judith Merril, Arthur C. Clarke, L. Sprague de Camp, Hal Clement.

Opposite, above:
Toronto Worldcon 1973

Lester del Rey is giving me the Hugo for *The Meeting,* the last
collaboration published with C. M. Kornbluth. It may not *look* like a
Hugo, but it is—the rocket-ship topping wasn't delivered in time,
and all we got was the base.

Opposite, below:

Theodore Sturgeon, the Author, A. Bertram Chandler, Norman
Spinrad, Alfred J. Bester. A huge science-fiction exposition was
planned for New York in 1976. It collapsed, leaving only a party,
where we were drowning our sorrows.

What Robert A. Heinlein and I are celebrating is his honorary
doctorate from Eastern Michigan University in 1977,
and we celebrated it well.

International Science Fiction Symposium
Nagoya, Japan, 1970

L-R the Author, Carol Pohl, unknown press photographer,
Brian Aldiss, Arthur Clarke. At this press conference the Japanese
had thoughtfully provided cans of Coke for the Westerners and
cans of kvass for the Soviet delegation.

Soviet Spacemen
Moscow, 1974

The Author, Vitaly Sevastianov, Vassili Zakharchenko.

Sevastianov is the only Soviet cosmonaut I ever met, and a marvelous man. The photograph was taken at the publishing office of MIR. Zakharchenko, an old friend from the 1970 Tokyo symposium, is the editor of *Molodya-Technika,* a boy's popular-science magazine which prints occasional science-fiction stories.

The Pohl Family

Seated: the Author, Emily Pohl-Weary, Kathy, Carol.
Standing: Ann, Karen, Rick.

**The Author as Guest of Honor
World Science Fiction Convention
Los Angeles, 1972**

All those Hugos, and not one for me.

Lava would come down the side of the mountain, in unpredictable directions and possibly very fast, but the Eremo was on a little bulge, with the Italian government volcanological observatory just above it. One felt a certain reassurance from that. Any likely lava flow would probably divide around the bulge, and anyway, the volcanologists would know what was happening. Until they started running, there was no need to worry.

The most adventurous thing about the Eremo was the drive up the narrow, winding mountain road that led to it. I learned to drive a truck on that road, the night of V-E Day. We had to get back to Caserta. We were all drunk, but I was less so than the others, so I drove the six-by-six down those hairpin, guard-rail-less curves, over the shifting pumice roadway, and somehow survived. But that was a small price to pay for living on the Hill, among the beautiful slopes where Spartacus held off all the Roman legions, looking out over Capri. Living on the Hill entitled one to a few little extras, such as Red Cross girls. Normally they were officers' issue and knew it, but a private hotel halfway up a volcano was a powerful inducement to some.

Most of all, the Eremo was a peaceful place for writing—not necessarily on the history of the 12th Weather Squadron. I did do a little of that, from time to time. But I also wrote the first draft of "Donovan Had a Dream" * there, still one of my favorite early action-adventure stories. I also wrote a large number of perfectly lousy *New Yorker*ish stories about Army life, some of which still survive in my sin file and none of which have ever been published. I was beginning to feel like a writer again.

Altogether, I was in Italy less than two years. It

* Published in *Thrilling Wonder Stories*, October, 1947.

does not now seem very far away—it is a trip I've made over a long weekend since—but it seemed like voyaging to intergalactic space then. It stays in my mind as an unending flicker of kaleidoscopic impressions. Playing ping-pong among Roman ruins, strolling in the Borghese Gardens. Italian music, the *canzone* they sang in the streets. The opera. An afternoon in Milan, just after the war was over. La Scala had been bombed out and the opera was being performed in a movie theater a few blocks away, and there I saw the most tenderly comic performance of *La Bohème* I had ever seen or ever hope to see; the mind-blowing Mimi turned out to be Renata Tebaldi, dewily fresh at the beginning of her astonishing career. And at the other end of a career, a few weeks later in Naples, Toti del Monte singing the same role, the voice still beautiful but the weight of ages in the way she moved and looked.

Hitchhiking in a British truck in Barletta, and finding myself surrounded by soldiers in a uniform I had never seen, speaking a language I could not recognize; they were Yugoslav partisans, wounded out of the gorges, recuperating in an Italian hospital before being smuggled back to fight again. Giving a lift to a Rothschild baron, from Naples to Rome; he was of the Parisian branch of the family, sent to ride out the war in the lesser holocaust of Italy. Racing a Mercedes in my jeep all the way up the Apennines. Standing in the ruins of Catullus's summer home, at the tip of the Sirmione peninsula in Lake Garda, with defeated Germans blowing up their ammunition dumps and preparing to surrender all around the shores of the lake. Drinking cherry liqueur *con selz* in Naples's *galleria* (and, years later, finding John Horne Burns's magnificent, tortured novel about that wartime Stew). The stench of Neapolitan alleys. The warm salt idleness of Adriatic beaches. The rotting hemp all along the road to Caserta. *Lacrimae Cristi* and raw wartime *grappa* with, it was said, one hundred-octane gasoline added to give it authority. The streams of tracers over the Bay of Naples as a Luftwaffe photo-reccy pilot tried to steal a shot of the harbor. The curate who led me through the Roman catacombs with a skinny taper timed to burn out just before the end of the tour, so that we walked the last ten yards among the walls of bones in darkness. American jeeps and German *feldwagens* waiting in the same mile-long line for their turn at the one surviving brewery in the foothills of the Alps. RAF sergeants, their eyes streaming with tears, on the day that FDR died. In memory it is all one bright flash after another.

And yet I remember very well that what I mostly felt at the time was boredom. Especially after the war in Europe ended, there was very little reason for me to be there that I could see.

And I was still in love, and Tina was in Paris.

I wanted to see her. I knew there had to be a way to cross that invisible barrier between her T/O and mine, and I looked for it. And I found, surprise! there *was* a way. Somewhere in the regulations it said that if what we wanted to do was get married, permission to cross the theater boundaries could be obtained.

We were married in Paris on the third of August, 1945.

The ceremony was conducted in French. I didn't understand a word of it. My "best man" was a French WAC lieutenant, and she nudged me when it was time to say *oui*.

The Army gave us a room in a very Parisian honeymoon hotel just a block or two from the Place de l'Étoile. They also gave us *tsoris*. Tina was a first lieutenant, and I was an enlisted man. As we were not supposed to "fraternize," except presumably in

bed, we were not allowed to eat in either the officers'
or the enlisted men's mess. Since there were no civilian
restaurants, except for the scarce and high-priced black-
market establishments, it seemed we were not meant
to take any meals together. But Tina had a friend,
and the friend had both intelligence and influence. We
wound up in a private dining room of the mess for
major generals and up. The generals ate very well,
and we ate better than they.

And on the last day of our week together I went
to get a haircut in a little barbershop just off the
Champs Élysées and, waiting my turn, tried to puzzle
out the headline in the newspaper of the man next
to me. It said something about *le bombe atomique*.
I laughed to myself, careful not to offend my neighbor.
These crazy French and their crazy, sensation-seeking
newspapers, I told myself. What won't they print
next?

But it was all true, and a couple of days later the
Japanese surrendered.

Six months later Tina and I were back in New
York, looking at each other in our hotel room off
Times Square. Not only were we civilians again, but
that lark in Paris had taken effect and we were married.

8

Ten Percent of a Writer

When I get up before an audience to speak, there is usually someone to introduce me, and that person almost always mentions, among other tidbits of biography, that at one time I was a literary agent.

That part of my life is a quarter-century past, and besides, it ended badly for me. Everything considered, I would just as soon forget it, but it still fascinates the introducers and the blurb copywriters, and I think I know why. Everyone at all involved with writing has heard of agents. Hardly anyone knows what they do or who they are. They are shadowy figures who seem to wield great power, but who do they wield it on? and how?

I'll tell you all that, never fear. But I didn't actually get into the agency business until 1947, so there is a little chronology I'd like to catch up on first.

The Army gave me my freedom on my birthday, 26 November 1945. I spent most of the next couple of months waiting for my new wife to get out to join me, and I spent them with my father.

He was at the height of his prosperity just then.

There was big money in war. He had made a lot of it.

He would have made even more if the war had been kind enough to keep going another year or two. The Japanese surrender was a body blow. If they had only had the consideration to keep fighting as advertised until every island of the homeland was overrun, he could have soaked away a million or two, easy.

He had already begun the soaking-away process, and one of the soaking places was a thousand-acre farm abutting Camp Upton, Long Island. I spent a couple of solitary weeks there that winter, listening to the farmhouse turn itself on and off—the refrigerator, the oil burner, the water pump in the basement, all sorts of friendly little machines keeping themselves busy just for me. I did a little writing, and a lot of loafing, and experimented with the idea of being the son of a gentleman farmer. It was going to be quite a farm, one day. Pop had had two hundred acres cleared and planted in apple seedlings, put a few hundred more into cauliflower, a few hundred into potatoes, and a small but very expensive patch of a few acres into strawberry vines. He had bought a riding horse for his friend Lillian's daughter. I tried to ride the beast to keep him sweet, but it was too late; he was already so hog-fat and lazy that my best summer-camp horsemanship could not get him to move in any direction except toward the barn. I regret the absence of that farm. If it were still in the family we would be multimillionaires for the land alone, but it's the farm itself that I miss. In the event, it went down the tube because my father had soaked too much money into too many different ventures, and the Army's niggardly way with contract cancellations caught him short.

I watched some of that money seep into the ground, leaving nothing but a stain, one night at his apartment. He was entertaining some financial friends at a dinner party, and they sang him the siren song of Cosmopolitan Records. Cosmo was a tiny war-born competitor to such biggies as RCA and Columbia, but it had lucked out in a big way with an oddball disk called "Tubby the Tuba." All America was mad for "Tubby the Tuba." The orders poured in. Cosmo could not press the records fast enough. What Cosmo needed, the sirens sang, was a manufacturing genius like my father, someone who could rev up the antique machinery and get production up to demand . . . and, oh, yes, of course he would be expected to bring in some couple of dollars to help pay for the expansion.

My father's eyes were aglow. I recognized the signs. I kicked him under the table as hard as I could, but he was firmly on the hook and with no interest at all in wriggling free.

So he signed aboard Cosmopolitan Records, and it was a disaster. We went out to the plant to study the production process, lumps of black biscuit tossed into a steam-heated press that squeezed them and molded them and cured them and baked the labels onto them. My father mastered that easily enough and got the rate of production up to competitive levels. But then what would we do with all that production once the madness for "Tubby" died? Obviously there was a need to diversify. So they recorded some hot new prospects and put some of the presses to making the new ones, and "Tubby"'s production figures slipped back. The capricious American public despised the new records. "Tubby," contrarily, kept blossoming, but as we were shipping so few we lost the exclusive rights, and my father lost his shirt.

He still had plenty left. Remained the machine shops: But the War Department was being unexpectedly hard-nosed about paying off for contract cancellations, and what had looked like millions of dollars in income materialized at barely enough to pay the notes.

Remained the farm.

That was blue-chip, gilt-edged; my father had thought it out carefully, and he had done everything exactly right, with one little mistake. He had planned for the long haul. The haul turned out short, and so did he. The apple trees would not produce a crop for four years. The strawberries not for two. It was a bad cauliflower year; a cold snap froze it in the ground, a total loss. Potatoes—ah, they were superb! Tens of thousands of bushels, plump and perfect. But so were everybody else's potatoes that year, and they were hardly worth the trouble of carting to the market to sell. The government stepped in for Long Island potato growers, bought them in the field, chopped them up, dyed them purple, and sold them for hog feed. He made a few bucks on that, but the rest was all ashes. Within a year he was broke again.

I really think my father was some sort of financial genius. He took risks, cut corners, laid it all on the fall of dice; in his life he earned more than a dozen ordinary men, but he lost more, too. He made a couple more modest coups in the remaining decade of his life, but when he died his estate did not cover the price of the funeral.

I think this fiscal idiocy runs in the family. The one talent I am certain I do not have in any measure at all is the orderly cultivation of assets. I know a lot about the theory of money management; what I don't know is how to apply it to real money.

This must be so. How else can one account for the fact that over the next six or seven years I managed to repeat my father's feat by going broke as a literary agent?

Consider the facts. Running a literary agency is about as low-capital, low-overhead as a business enterprise can get. I was really very good at it. I managed to establish a near-monopoly position in science fiction, then the fastest-growing area of the publishing business. Of all the writers who were any good at sf, I represented probably two out of three: John Wyndham and Isaac Asimov and Cliff Simak and Bob Sheckley and Frank Robinson and Jack Williamson and Cyril Kornbluth and Jim Blish and Fritz Leiber and William Tenn and H. Beam Piper and—oh, hell; of the top fifty sf writers of the early 50s, I represented at least thirty-five. The biggest markets in the field, *Galaxy* and *Analog* and Doubleday and Ballantine, all bought more from me than from all other agents and individual writers combined. Not just sf; I had successful clients in half a dozen other fields as well, Westerns and mysteries, regional novels and how-to-do-it books; I sold to film and to the fledgling TV markets, and I had a network of foreign representatives abroad. And after seven industrious years I had managed to lose thirty thousand dollars I didn't have.

I didn't set out to be a literary agent after World War II. I set out to be a novelist. In order to do that, I decided to become an advertising copywriter.

Tina got out of the service in February of 1946. We stayed for a short time in a hotel near Times Square, and then Dave Kyle came along with an idea. He had also just got his civilian clothes back, and his brother had a brand-new postwar car he was willing to lend Dave for a while. So the three of us drove down to Florida, Dave to look up an old girlfriend in Lakeland, Tina and I to visit her parents in Orlando, then a comfortably lazy community of lovely warm orange groves and avocado farms surrounding about a million tiny lakes. We lived on lotus for a restorative month and then came back to New York to find an apartment in (where else?) Greenwich

Village. There didn't seem to be any great pressure. We were young, and pleased with ourselves as honorable veterans of the last of the just wars, and we had plenty of money. Neither of us had spent much during the war. We had pay accumulated, and my mother had left me a little when she died. We could have lived frugally without working at all for at least a year or two.

I didn't much want to live frugally, and the apartment was far from frugal. It cost $175 a month. That doesn't seem like a lot after thirty years of inflation, but it was rather more than my monthly income had ever been in my life up until then. And it was really a nice apartment, modly furnished top floor in an old building on Grove Street, just down the block from where Tom Paine had written one of his *Crisis* feuilletons and around the corner from several of the favorite hangouts of the Mafia. A roof garden went with it. Tina and I carried brown-paper bags of topsoil all the way in from my father's farm to fatten the garden up, and on summer nights it was a marvelous place to sit and observe the world below. Our building was owned by a prosperous and art-loving dentist. He encouraged talent, especially musical, and one of his protégés was a young pianist named Constantine Stronghilos. Tina and I were invited to his first recital, and there was no doubt that he had the touch for Chopin and Liszt. For years afterward I kept watching the pages of the Sunday *Times* to see when he would make his breakthrough into fame, but he never did.* Tina was as gregarious as a pretty puppy and we

---

* Connie Stronghilos turned up in my life again twenty-five years later, when he joined the New Jersey Unitarian Church of which I was then a trustee. I found out what had gone wrong with his career: arthritis. The mind understood the music, but the fingers would not obey his will. (It really is quite a small world.)

quickly made friends—notably Kathleen and Joe Skelly, in the building across the back yards from us, and through them we met people like Ayn Rand and others who floated through their cocktail parties. Tina began taking courses at the New School, in subjects like theater and paranormal psychology. We built mazes and tried to telepathically command mice to follow one path rather than another—it never worked; and she wrote endless scripts for plays and musical reviews, which didn't work very well, either. (She subsequently published half a dozen good books, but the theater never opened its doors to her.) It was a fine way to live, but I could see that our resources were not going to survive it indefinitely without replenishment. Besides, I was about ready to go back to work. I hauled out the novel I had written in the tufa-block EM club in Stornara. It was evident at once that it had a great flaw. It was about the advertising business. I didn't *know* anything about the advertising business, and it showed.

That was a problem, but for that problem there was an easy solution. I bought a Sunday *Times,* looked under the help-wanted ads for advertising copywriters, and answered three of them. And on April Fool's Day of 1946 David Altman put me to work in his little Madison Avenue agency as chief (and only) copywriter.

Advertising writing should be under constant surveillance by the narcs; it is addictive, and it rots the mind. When you spend your days persuading Consumers to Consume articles they would never in their lives dream of wanting if you didn't tickle them into it, you develop fantasies of power. No, not fantasies. Power. Each sale is a conquest, and it is your silver tongue that has made them roll over and obey. If you do not end your day with a certain contempt for your fellow human beings, then you are just not paying attention to what it is that you do.

Most of the advertising I did in my three years in the business was mail-order, and most of the commodities I sold were books and magazines. Book clubs were the specialty of the Thwing & Altman agency, and after six months there I moved over to Popular Science Publishing Company, pushing magazine subscriptions and our line of how-to-do-it books.

One of the characteristics of the advertising business that rots the brain and destroys the disposition is that most people in it hardly ever know whether what they are doing is any good. You can see whether your product sells well or poorly, yes. But what did it? Is it the TV spots, the jingles, the billboards, the space ads, the point-of-sale displays . . . or maybe just the fact that the weather suddenly turned warm, so people are drinking more of your soda pop or acquiring more of your air conditioners? And even if you know that your ads are working, is it because of your copy, or the art department's layout, or none of the above?

My kind of advertising was not like that. If you were good at what you were doing, it showed. No argument. You printed the space ads or sent out the mailings, and either the orders came in or they didn't.

The first things I wrote were big full-page display ads for the best sellers of the Dollar Book Club. David Altman had hired me in the first place because there was not a lot of difference between the kinds of words I had strung together as pulp-magazine blurbs and the kinds that made good headlines for best-seller ads. I think the first one I did on my own was for Frank Yerby's *The Foxes of Harrow*:

> In the wickedest city in the world
> this copper-haired giant built an empire out
> of gunplay, gambling and the eager hearts of women.

That one sold a zillion copies of the book—I really don't know how many, but it filled full-page space in at least fifty of the top circulation media in the country. Another—I have forgotten the name of the book —was:

> He knew the whole town's secrets
> but he had one secret of his own:
> the huge white bride's bed
> that he kept for the wife of another man.

We also did copy for the Junior Literary Guild, and for the G. & C. Merriam line of dictionaries, among other accounts. On all of the ads David Altman stood over me, guiding, revising, editing. Some of the ads, like the two above, survived almost intact; most were heavily changed. I liked and respected him, but I didn't much like being rewritten; and besides, he was paying me only fifty dollars a week. In a month with four Fridays I took home, after deductions, only a dollar more than my monthly rent for the apartment on Grove Street, and it seemed to me that another job would give me both more money and more independence.

Popular Science gave me both, under a grand, tall, gentlemanly man named George Spoerer. Of all the people I have ever worked for, George was about the kindest and most decent. He was a science-fiction fan, which was a big bond. He should have been a science-fiction writer. His apartment in Greenwich Village was just a few blocks from mine, and on halfway decent days we would walk home together, an hour's stroll, enjoying each other's company.* George was very good

---

* On one of those strolls George told me the plot of a science-fiction story he had made up the night before. I told him he ought to write it, but he didn't want to do that; what he wanted was for me to write it. It's called "Let the Ants Try," and I

at mail-order advertising, and at letting his junior
assistant, namely me, be good at it in my own way
rather than in his. He sometimes made suggestions.
Usually he just presented problems: Here's what we
need to do; how do you want to go about doing it?

Almost the first problem George laid on me was a
big coffee-table picture book called *Outdoor Life's
Gallery of North American Game*. Mostly it was full-
color reproductions of the cover paintings from *Outdoor Life* itself, and it was really quite handsome, if
you like that sort of thing. But in the market it was
no wily white-tailed deer or battling steelhead salmon.
What it was in the marketplace was a dog. The company had printed fifty thousand copies of it, and
forty-nine thousand-plus were still in the warehouse.
They had tried everything: buckeye four-color circulars
the size of a bedsheet and personalized we're-all-art-
connoisseurs-together letters on embossed stationery.
And nothing worked.

I decided to test some new copy appeals. At the
time, penny postcards still cost only a penny, so I
wrote up a dozen or so sample appeals for postcard
testing and we sent out thousand-piece mailings to
test them out. I tried all the angles I could think of—

> *The book is beautiful and will impress your
> friends. . . .*
> *With this book you will be better able to kill,
> crush, mutilate and destroy these beloved game
> beasts. . . .*

---

wrote it just as he said it, and all he would ever accept for the
free gift of a story I like a lot was a bottle of Scotch. There are
only about two stories in my whole catalog which were suggested by someone else (the other is "The Midas Plague,"
which I owe to Horace Gold), and it is a source of some
chagrin to me that I like them better than most.

*This book will teach your children the secrets of
wildcraft and keep them from turning into
perverts and drug addicts. . . .*

And then I tried one more card, which said:

HAVE YOU GOT A BIG BOOKCASE?
Because if you have, we have a BIG BOOK for you. . . .

and that was the winner. We didn't bother transmuting
the copy appeal to a circular, we just mailed out those
cards. Nearly a million of them, and the only reason
we didn't mail more was that we ran out of books.

That was the fun part, and the addictive part, and
the part that makes advertising people cynical about
the wisdom of their customers—which is to say, you,
and me, and all of us. Advertising reaches out to touch
the fantasy part of people's lives. And, you know, most
people's fantasies are pretty sad.

But still it was fun. We used our ingenuity particularly in the subscription efforts for the magazines,
most doggedly of all in the renewal series. Because
the money in the magazines came from advertising, and
advertising rates were tied to circulation, we were glad
to spend three or four times the subscription price to
get you to subscribe. And if you once subscribed, boy,
we hung on to you. You would stay on our list, one
way or another, until you died. If you let your subscription lapse, we would send *seventeen* separate
renewal efforts to get you back. First we would bill you.
Then we would remind you. Then we would coax you.
Then we would start to bribe you: two free issues,
three free issues, a year at half price. If you still held
out, we began to get desperate. Kidding letters. Bel-
ligerent letters. Pathetic letters. I wrote one that
purported to be from Diane, the girl who had cut
your Addressograph stencil: "Dear Friend. my boss

just told me I had to take your subscription stencil out of our file. To me, every name on those plates is a friend, and I hate to see yours go—" They all worked, exactly like the osmotic diffusion barriers in a uranium-isotope separation plant. Ten percent responded to the first appeal. Ten percent of what was left to the second. Ten percent of the remainder to the third. We got a perfectly satisfactory return on every mailing at every stage in the cascade, and if you managed to get away unrenewed after receiving all seventeen, my hat, sir, is off to your determination. (Wow, why didn't I think of that then? "My hat, sir, is off to your determination, and as determined readers like you are our favorite subscribers, I am going to extend this one more chance—")

Popular Science was a great success story as a publishing company, and a good place to work. Gene Watson was the VP in charge of our department, wise, sharp, highly competent. Harry Walton, old sf-writing friend, was one of the editors on the magazine side, and now and again we would get together for lunch or coffee. I kept getting promoted, with added duties and added assistants: book editor, manager of subscription agents, executive in charge of book fulfillment; and I was always allowed to try whatever crazy ideas I thought might work. They didn't, always, but the "big bookcase" had bought me a license to experiment, and I used it. Most of what I did was fairly orthodox, four-color circulars, letters, order forms, return envelopes. But each of those presented its own opportunities for varying style, size, and format. I have never been able to draw well, but I could lay out a circular, showing where the art would go and where the type, picking out type faces and indicating the color masses, and have an artist make from it a handsome-looking piece of advertising. I found that I could dictate selling copy as well as I could write it, often better. When I see words on paper I pause and try to mold them into a certain balanced sonority,* but advertising copy doesn't want to be artistic. It wants to be crude and ragged enough to catch hold of the customer's calloused reflexes as it goes down. And sometimes I tried nonverbal communications. Tricks with color, tricks with typography —even tricks with scent. We published a book, experimentally outside our regular hairy-chested-men's area, called *How to Make Paper Flowers and Party Decorations.* I designed some nice feminine mailing pieces, and then it occurred to me that all the women I knew wore perfume. Why not try perfuming? So I went down to the five-and-ten for a gallon jug of their best rose cologne and a flit gun, and a warehouseman and I spent one whole afternoon riffling through sheaves of letters and spraying them with the cologne. First he riffled and I sprayed, then out of compassion I riffled and he sprayed. On my way home that night people turned to stare at me from half a block away.

On the test, the perfumed letters outperformed the others almost two to one, so we went for broke.

We almost made it. Testing is the key to mail-order selling, but you have to understand what it is you're testing. We established that Woolworth's rose cologne would bring in extra sales right enough. But no one was about to riffle through half a million mailing pieces. We had to automate. So for the big mailing we arranged with the printer to add rose perfume to the ink, and the chemical combination produced something that did not in the least smell like Woolworth's best. It smelled a little bit like rotting hibiscus, and a lot like nothing you ever smelled before in your life. It wasn't total disaster; even that unearthly aroma did help the sales a little, as we verified from the test

* You mean you couldn't tell?

mailings we had included with the big one. But not anywhere near what we had expected.

All this was fun. But I had managed to lose track of why it was that I had got into advertising in the first place—*i.e.*, to research my novel. After a year or two it began to penetrate that I was letting a lot of time go past.

Time was passing in the other parts of my life, too. Tina and I had a pretty good year's marriage, but in the second year it stopped being quite as good. We got along well enough. But she had her interests, largely in the theater, and I had mine; and we also had some basic differences about what marriage should be. Tina was quite sure she didn't ever want to have children. I had no burning urgency in that area, but I wasn't ready to foreclose my options permanently. And so in the summer of 1947 Tina went off to visit her mother in California, and dropped me a note to say that her mother was fine, the weather was nice, and, oh, yes, she had filed for a divorce.

I hadn't expected that. I hated it. I had a good night's drunk on it, and when I woke up the next morning I perceived through the hangover that, all in all, it might well be for the best.

Perhaps as a consequence of the divorce, I dropped out of orbit to reenter the world of organized science fiction.

I had not been neglecting science fiction. I had been writing the occasional story all along, and most of them were getting published. Not all were science fiction. I made my first sale outside the pulps in 1946, a sort of domestic mystery that the Toronto *Star Weekly* retitled "Stolen Tires," and I invented a series-character detective named Josh Healey and sold a few stories about him to Street & Smith's *Detective Story*. But most were in the good old sf groove. *Thrill-*

ing Wonder published "Donovan Had a Dream" and "A Hitch in Time" in 1947. *Planet* printed "Let the Ants Try," the story George Spoerer had given me. *Five Novels* used a sort of science-fiction article called "Trip to the Moon." * I still kept in touch with my old friends now and then, but there was no systematic relationship. If the Futurians still continued some sort of shadow life—and I understood they did—I was not involved in it.

But on Labor Day weekend of 1947 there was a World Science Fiction Convention in Philadelphia.

I had never actually managed to attend a worldcon. As you remember, I *almost* made it to the first one of all, in New York in 1939. In 1940 it was in Chicago; in 1941, Denver. I couldn't afford to attend either. The war had imposed a hiatus until 1946, when there was a convention in California; I couldn't afford that either, but Philadelphia I could afford. Everything considered, I doubt that I have ever made a better investment.

From time to time people come to me, skeptical or wistful, to ask, "What's a worldcon like?" It's like— well, it's like the Zen fable of the blind men and the elephant. Gordie Dickson says it's his childhood fantasy of a gentlemen's club; you come back from ten months on the Amazon, measuring the spots of jungle butterflies, and you compare notes with colleagues who have been studying wind velocities in the Antarctic or mating patterns in Haight-Ashbury, and then you go off to further adventures. I think of it more as a family reunion. I have heard it described as a chaos, a madhouse, and a crashing bore; and I think it is all those things.

The thing about science-fiction conventions in general, and worldcons in particular, is that they are made

---

* I *wonder* what I said in it! Haven't seen it in thirty years.

up of science-fiction writers and fans,* as well as agents, editors, artists, teachers, and general hangers-on. This quality separates them from most of humanity in that, by and large, they are in the habit of using their brains for abstract thought.

I hate to say that about science fiction out loud. It puts people off. And, of course, it isn't *absolutely* essential to possess an informed or analytical mind to read science fiction. There's plenty of junk for the junk addicts, and it's even possible to read, say, "Who Goes There?" for the adventure or "Against the Fall of Night" for the lovely color without troubling one's head much about complexities and implications. But you miss the best parts. Sf encourages thought and curiosity, and requires both to appreciate it fully. Your average *Newsweek* reader or game-show viewer can't handle this sort of thing, and responds to sf with hostility or scorn. Sf readers can handle *anything*.

This does not guarantee that in each individual case they will be intelligent, or admirable, or even housebroken. Some of the worst people I have ever met have turned up at worldcons, as well as some of the best. Nevertheless, I cannot imagine any topic on which I could not find someone to carry on a rewarding conversation at a science-fiction convention. I can't think of many subjects that haven't been programmed. I am not all that fond of formal programs, having long since participated in enough of them for one lifetime, but even the formal programs contain jewels: scientists coming to tell the science-fiction world what they have been doing in space communications, or sociometrics, or the structures of the brain; advocates preaching alternate life-styles; writers rapping about their work; editors in give-and-take with the readers.

---

* Who are essentially the same people. Nearly every writer is an ex- or present fan, and I've seldom met a fan who didn't think of trying his luck as a writer sooner or later.

And in and around the program items are the informal
get-togethers, in room parties or bars, with side trips
to points of local interest and reunions with long-lost
friends.

As part of the world's hypertrophy syndrome, sf
conventions have grown uncomfortably huge. Three
or four thousand persons is not rare; sometimes they
are even worse. That's a pity. Too much of a good
thing reduces the possibilities for personal interaction;
it is a confusion rather than a coming together. But
thirty years ago there were only a few hundred of us
band of brothers at Philadelphia. Most of us had not
seen each other since the far side of a war and were
glad to meet again, even gladder to meet people we
had known only through letters or the printed page.
Willy Ley, John Campbell, Lester del Rey were all
there. Ted Sturgeon accompanied a lovely girl named
Mary Mair on his guitar as she sang his song "Thunder
and Roses." William Tenn—brand-newest of the Big
Name Writers—his "Child's Play" just out—gave an
uproariously funny comic lecture on writers' correspondence. And Judith Merril was there. I had met
her briefly a year or two earlier. We had both been
married at the time; now neither of us were. Judy
had just published "That Only a Mother," a brilliant
twisty-dismaying short story about a woman who gives
birth to a radiation-damaged child, the sort of story
that gets right in among the glands and squeezes
pretty basic parts of the psyche, so she was a writer
to be respected. She was also a person to be known
better, in her mid-twenties, with a small, incredibly
beautiful blonde daughter. Judy herself was not pretty.
She was something quite different. My friend Jacques
LeCroix, arguably the best portrait photographer in
Paris at the time, described her as having "the capacity
for great beauty."

Philcon '47 left such a delicious aftertaste in all our

mouths that Lester del Rey and I decided to revive it
on a semipermanent basis in New York. So one night a
few weeks later Lester brought a few of his friends
down to my apartment on Grove Street, where a few
of mine were already gathered, and the nine of us
r'ared back and passed a miracle. We called it the
Hydra Club.

Over the next few years the Hydra Club came to
include nearly every science-fiction writer in the New
York area, plus a lot of others: Fletcher Pratt, Willy
Ley, L. Jerome Stanton (associate editor of *Astound-
ing*), William Tenn, Judith Merril, George O. Smith,
Jack Gillespie, Basil Davenport, Dave Kyle, Sam
Merwin, Harry Harrison, as well as Lester and myself.
It was the place where sf writers met. When Arthur
Clarke turned up from London, Hydra was where he
came. When visiting firemen from California or the
Midwest passed by New York, we laid on special meet-
ings. Hans Stefan Santesson was the general coordi-
nator, in charge of letting us know when to meet;
Debbie Crawford, with a comfortable little apartment
in the North Village, was our usual hostess. At
Christmas we rented a hotel ballroom to revel in.
Betweentimes we met and drank a few and enjoyed
each other's company.

Hydra was a fine place for establishing and cement-
ing relationships, not all of them literary. Lester found
his wife, Evelyn, there. Jack Gillespie met and married
Lois Miles. And I married Judy Merril. By that time
she had become an editor at Bantam Books, and I
was turning into a literary agent.

Q. What is an agent?
A. An agent is a person who acts for another person.
Q. What kind of an agent is a "literary" agent?
A. A literary agent is a person who acts for a writer
in literary matters.

Q. What do you have to be in order to become a literary agent?
A. Willing.

Literary agents come in all shapes and sizes. Some are Big Business. Some are cottage industry. Some are only a kind of hobby, scratching out a piece of a living from the odd reading fee or commission while holding a job, or free-lancing editorial work, or even collecting welfare. There are no professional standards. It is a little trickier to get started now than it was thirty years ago, but only because *everything* is a little trickier now, since a larger proportion of everything is taxed and/or registered with the government. It still isn't hard to set up shop. And in 1947 there was nothing to it.

Dirk Wylie came back from the wars with a bad back, acquired jumping out of that truck in the Ardennes. Army hospitals did what they could for him, and he emerged a civilian in 1946. But he wasn't well enough to get a job, and he was looking for something he could do at his own pace, preferably in his own home, preferably in the publishing business somewhere. He decided to set up as a literary agent.

In this I encouraged him a lot. The writing market was changing every day in the postwar confusion. I kept hearing about new magazines, new kinds of markets. What I really would have wished in my heart was to write for them all myself, but there was no hope. I'm not a very fast writer. It graveled me to see these opportunities going begging, and so I offered to help Dirk out as a silent partner. So Dirk printed up some letterheads and went looking for clients.

I remembered that when I had worked for Popular Publications, standing orders had been to save the outside envelopes from all slush-pile manuscripts and turn them over to somebody in the business department. They copied off the return addresses, typed up copies, and sold them to purchasers of mail-order lists. I asked a few publishers, found that such lists were still available, and we bought a few. We wrote a letter on Dirk's new stationery:

Dear Writer:
We have a vacancy in our lists for a few additional clients. . . .

And manuscripts began to flow in. Not just manuscripts but checks; we were charging a reading fee.

A lot of agents still do charge reading fees. It's not really an intrinsically evil process, just a schlocky one. Like heroin and beer, reading-fee criticism is a commodity that is wanted very much by some people, and if it were against the law to supply it, there would be bootleggers. I understand the need. If you are a writer, you understand it, too. There are times when you are putting all those words onto those sheets of white paper and you would gladly pay anything to have some competent professional tell you whether they are any good or not.

The person who writes the reading-fee letters usually does know more than the client does, but not necessarily very much more. The big agencies tend to hire anybody who can type neatly, grammatically, and fast. They would hire skilled professionals if they could, provided skilled professionals would work for the kind of money a reading-fee person can command, but that doesn't happen. At least with Dirk all the letters were written by people who had actually written and published stories of their own, mostly by Dirk himself. But still it was not exactly what Dirk wanted to do with his life, and after the first year or so, when there began to be a few commissions from actual sales, Dirk decided to drop the reading fees.

Dirk was a fine, bright man. I think he would have made quite a good agent, but what the war had done to him could not be undone. His spinal injury began to relapse. He was hospitalized and released; hospitalized again, and the stay grew longer and release began to look remote. His wife, Rosalind, carried on with the work of the agency, with help from me. And then Dirk died.

Dirk's death was not the first that had invaded my own life. But he was still in his twenties! And he was my oldest friend. I could not accept it—because so much of my growing up had been shared with him, because it was such a shocking waste. I couldn't make myself go to his funeral.

When we were able to make reasonable plans, Ros and I decided to continue the agency as a partnership, retaining Dirk's name.* I was still working for PopSci, so most of my work for the agency was limited to evenings and weekends. But now and then something productive happened during the working day. My boss, George Spoerer, came back from lunching with an old friend at Doubleday to report that they were about to set up a science-fiction line. In fact, they had already begun buying, when someone in the corporate structure happened to think that they really didn't know much about science fiction. Not to worry, George told his friend; I have this kid assistant who knows something about it, and if you like we'll get you together and you can pick his brains. Did I want to do that? he asked.

I wanted little more; it was the nicest news I had heard in some time.

Science fiction had been growing slowly out of its pulp origins. Big slicks like *Collier's* and *The Saturday*

---

* That lasted about three years; then we broke it up and I continued on my own.

Evening Post were trying their luck with the occasional Bradbury or Heinlein story. The trade book publishers had not yet perceived the existence of a market, but a few amateurs had. In Pennsylvania, Lloyd Eshbach had started Fantasy Press. In Chicago, Erle Korshak had Shasta. In Philadelphia there was Prime Press, and in New York City there was Gnome. None of these were very big or very profitable. But they demonstrated that a market was there, though they didn't have the capital or the knowledge to exploit it.

The one I followed most closely was Gnome Press, because it was closest to hand and because my old buddy Dave Kyle was one of its founders. Dave's elder brother, Arthur C. Kyle, was a newspaper publisher in upstate New York. That meant he had a printing press. It wasn't very well adapted to book work. It could print only eight-page signatures, and not very rapidly at that. But it was an asset of importance to a shoestring operation. Dave's partner was a glass blower and science-fiction fan named Marty Greenberg.* The two of them secured the rights from the author, Fletcher Pratt, and published a fantasy novel called *The Carnelian Cube.*

The partnership did not survive very well, and, for that matter, neither did Gnome Press. It kept going for five or six years and foundered in a mass of lawsuits and unpaid bills. But if you look at one of Gnome Press's old catalogs, you find you are staring at a million dollars. The authors they had! Isaac Asimov. Robert A. Heinlein. Arthur C. Clarke. They had them all. They had the rights to books that have collectively sold tens of millions, perhaps hundreds of millions, of copies since, and they had acquired them at prices that would make a cat weep. Jack William-

* Not to be confused with the anthologist and political-science professor Martin Harry Greenberg, who became active in science fiction a couple of decades later.

son and I wrote three original sf novels for Gnome, and the biggest advance we got was $750. Edd Cartier designed Gnome's colophon and did their covers. The finest talents that science fiction owned were lined up and knocking on Gnome's door, hungry for the book publication that all of them wanted and every one of them had been denied.

What went wrong with the semipro publishers was that they could not bridge the distribution gap. The commodity was there, the marvelous stories that had been silting up for decades in the sf magazines. The market was there, hundreds of thousands of readers thrilled by the idea of owning their favorite stories in permanent form. Or, for that matter, in any form, because for some of the newer readers novels like *The Skylark of Space* and *Slan!* were only legends. Unless they could find tattered second-hand copies of the magazines they had been published in, there was no way for them to read the books themselves.

But between publisher and reader lies a wide space, and the best way to bridge it is with salesmen, distributors, jobbers, and a whole network of promotion, billing, and service departments. The semipro publishers had none of these things. They could print the books, and they could sell them a single copy at a time, mostly direct-by-mail, to individual customers; that way they could get rid of an edition of two or three thousand copies, enough to show a theoretical profit. But there was no way for Marty Greenberg in his little office on West 10th Street to reach ten thousand bookstore proprietors and persuade them to stock his books. Worse. The profits were only theoretical. To make them real required the investment of real capital, which none of the semipros had.

Nevertheless, the big trade houses began to notice what was going on. Random House, Crown, and one or two others tested the waters with sf anthologies, and they moved nicely. Simon and Schuster began to sign up an occasional novel—I had already sold them Jack Williamson's *The Humanoids*, for instance.

Doubleday's act of faith went beyond that. They were not talking about an isolated title here and there, they were planning for a category—six books a year, maybe twelve, maybe more than that! It was the Promised Land.

So we met for lunch, George Spoerer and I trekking up to Mad Ave's restaurant of the week, a place called Cherio's. The Doubleday people we lunched with were Jerry Hardy, an advertising-promotion type, very quick to comprehend and full of ideas, and the managing editor of the corporation, Walter Bradbury. Brad was and is one of the great gentlemen of the publishing business, never forgetting a favor, never remembering a slight. He impressed me at once as a good person to work with.

Between the very, very dry martinis and the second cup of coffee I told them all I could fit in about science fiction. Brad's big immediate problem was the first book they had bought for the new series, Max Ehrlich's *The Big Eye*. Ehrlich was a highly competent and successful writer (and still is, as witness *The Reincarnation of Peter Proud*), but he had not previously written any science fiction. No one at Doubleday was sure that *The Big Eye* met the canons of the field. They had sent a copy of the manuscript to a Harvard astronomer who had said it was scientific poppycock. Was it? Did it matter?

I took the manuscript home and read it apprehensively. But there really seemed to be little to worry about. *The Big Eye* is not one of the all-time masterpieces of the field. But it kept my interest all the way through, and I was satisfied that it would do the same for most readers. There was one short passage that I thought needed a fix, so I wrote in a couple of insert pages and sent it back. Brad expressed his gratitude with a bottle of Scotch, and later on, when the book proved out even more successful than he had hoped, with a fair-sized check. (He was under no obligation to do that, but I told you he was a gentleman.) And I began to sell him books.

My client Isaac Asimov, I happened to know, had a nearly book-length manuscript lying around, gathering dust because no magazine wanted to publish it. He had written it, on request, for *Thrilling Wonder Stories*, who hated it and sent it back. John Campbell had politely declined interest, and none of the other magazines of that particular time had much use for long stories. Let's try it on Doubleday, I proposed. They won't buy it, Isaac remonstrated; they want *book* writers, like this fellow Ehrlich, whoever he is, and I'm a magazine person. Don't argue with your agent, I explained. After some arm wrestling I got the manuscript away from him and shipped it off to Doubleday.

What did Brad know? He wasn't aware he only wanted book writers, or that *Grow Old with Me* (as it was called at the time) wasn't exactly what the readers expected of Isaac Asimov. All he knew was that he enjoyed reading it and, after some revisions, was perfectly willing to publish it. Which he did, after giving it a new title. As *Pebble in the Sky*, it has sold, and keeps on selling, a lot of copies.

That was Isaac's first book—not counting a part of a biochemistry text. He caught the fever at once. We followed that one up with another original, *The Stars Like Dust*, and then another, and another. Doubleday was not quite ready to pick up some of his famous older stories, heaven knows why, so they declined *I, Robot* and the *Foundation* series (and I sold them elsewhere), but they were willing to publish his new work almost as rapidly as he could write it.

My other clients were also getting into the act, and some of them with even fatter rewards. John Wyndham turned up with a new novel called *The Day of the Triffids*. Doubleday snapped it up, but I had to ask them to hold off publication because *Collier's* also loved it, and *Collier's* love expressed itself in the biggest check I had ever seen, five figures worth of fondness. My most cherished client (by then also my wife), Judith Merril, wrote a borderline science-fiction novel about New York City under nuclear attack, *Shadow on the Hearth* (later it became a TV special). Cyril Kornbluth was out in Chicago, playing hardboiled-newspaperman games with Trans-Radio Press and doing little of the science-fiction writing he was so good at. I sent him a note, explaining that it was raining soup and he looked silly standing there without a spoon, so he retooled and came on line. First he did a collaboration with Judy, flimsily based on a short story I had begun and abandoned years before; it appeared variously as *Marschild, Outpost Mars*, and a couple of other titles, in one edition or another, under their joint pen name of "Cyril Judd." Then he struck out on his own, with three or four chapters of something called *The Martians in the Attic*. It had to do with the first manned trip into space, and some kind of cockamamie Martians that complicated it. They also complicated the story line more than it would stand, and he bogged down.

Cyril and I worked together pretty closely, not just on the stories that bore our joint byline. When I was having trouble making a story work, over the years, it often helped to show it to Cyril for comments and suggestions, and he did the same with me. We replotted the novel all one late night in my kitchen, amputating the Martians. Cyril revised a few pages to accommodate the changes, and I showed the remaining fragment to Brad. Fine, said Brad, I'd love to publish it. But there's this one technicality. For the sake of the weekly editorial conference I need an outline of the rest of the book before I can put through a contract.

When I reported this to Cyril, he pursed his lips, borrowed one of my typewriters, and holed up in the small, old, once-theatrical Hotel Latham, a block or two from my office. They had a room just right for writers, on the top floor, next to the elevator motors; it was noisy enough on its own that a little typing disturbed no one, and I used the same room myself for the same purposes now and then. He emerged forty-eight hours later with the completed manuscript. I turned it in to Brad, explaining that most writers disliked writing outlines but Cyril really hated it, and Doubleday published it as *Takeoff*.

Other book publishers were falling in line, and the specialist science-fiction magazine market was beginning to swell toward its biggest boom. *Ellery Queen* decided to diversify with a one-shot called *The Magazine of Fantasy*. It seemed to work out, and under a slightly expanded title it is still being published today. An Italian publishing company had done so well with soap-opera comics that they proposed to try them out in America. For makeweight they added a couple of other titles; one was *Galaxy*, with Horace Gold as editor, and it too survives today. The agency was prospering, and not just in science fiction.

It seemed to be decision time, get all the way in or get out.

I was under no illusions about the money. It would be a long time at best before the agency would net me as much taking-home money as Popular Science was reliably handing over to me every week. But then I didn't really need that much money. With a little luck, at least I might not starve.

Moreover, it felt like time to move on. George Spoerer remained a marvelous man to work for, but the person I really enjoy having as a boss has not yet been born. I had talked about quitting once or twice before. Each time the company had come through with more money and assorted other kindnesses. This time I was serious. In November of 1948 I resigned from Popular Science and set out as a full-time literary agent.

It all came to nothing in the end. But my, it was fun for a while!

I had, all worked out in my mind, a clear description of what an ideal literary agent would be. The ideal agent would not concentrate on selling books or magazine pieces. He would represent writers. The ideal agent would not make deals and then find writers to carry them out. He would learn what each writer's strengths were, and find ways to help him develop them. The way to measure the success of an agent was not to tote up the dollars in his bank account, but to see whether his writers were producing regularly and well.

You see, each literary agent is free to do business in the way that suits him best, and some of the ways that are best for him are worst for his writers.

But no, you say, that's not possible! After all, he gets nothing but a ten percent commission on whatever his writers make. Obviously, whatever is good for his writers is exactly one-tenth as good for him, right?

Wrong. Let's do a mind experiment. You be an agent. You open your mail in the morning, and here is a story from a writer. Because you are a smart agent, you know that you can sell it to X, and he will pay you a thousand dollars for it. Or, alternatively, you can try to sell it to someone who will earn, maybe, two thousand dollars for you with it—Y, or Z, or Q, or W. The trouble is, none of those are a sure sale.

You'll have to try all four of them, maybe, before one will buy it.

So which is a better return on your time, as a literary agent? The fast, sure thousand-dollar sale, or the slower, more problematical sale for twice the money? If you are running a factory, you go for the fast grand.

But now be the writer, and see how different the view is from the other side of the desk. You have spent exactly the same amount of time in writing the story, no matter how long it takes to sell it; one way will bring you exactly twice as much return as the other, so which do you-the-writer prefer? Of course you do; but your agent's cost/effectiveness studies may lead him to the other course.

Things are rarely that simple, but the choices are real. Book contracts are pretty complicated. When the complications have to do with how much money the publisher is going to pay you, then the agent's interests are pretty close to those of the writer. But there are many other clauses in a contract. For example, when you sign a publishing contract, you usually sign your name to a clause that says that if anyone brings suit for libel or plagiarism or one or two other actionable possibilities, then it will be you, not the publisher, who will take the rap. That's reasonable. But sometimes the language of the clause is not; it requires you to pay costs that you may think out of line, or to accept responsibilities that are not properly yours. That doesn't affect your agent, particularly. His neck is not on the line. But yours is. He may be willing to horse-trade a bad indemnity clause for a better share of subsidiary rights with the publisher . . . but are you?

Some agents made a specialty of making package deals—supplying the entire contents of a magazine, or a line of specialized books. I don't know of any case when these captive markets were what any writer would want to aim at, but in the aggregate they could

amount to tens of thousands of dollars of sales for
the agent. Of course, the agent would have to throw
in something by his big-name clients now and then to
sweeten the pot. It seemed to me that that was a bad
deal for all the writers concerned: for the big names,
obviously, but also for the trained seals who turned
out the mass copy, because what they were being paid
to write seldom had anything to do with what they
were good at.

Now, none of this is meant to say that all agents, or
even any agents, are crooked or malevolent. Most of
them do a better job than their writers ever know. But
they are human beings, and they have diverse styles,
and after some observation of a lot of them, as editor
buying stories for them, as client and as competitor,
I had worked out just what I thought was right.

I didn't, for instance, want to get into supplying captive markets. I didn't want to divert writers from what
they did well to what would surely sell.

But many writers actually liked writing for those
markets because they meant sure sales. Writers, too,
like to eat.

I invented a solution for that. One of my most
promising, but least solvent, writers was a young Cali-
fornian who was averaging about one sale for every
ten stories, not enough to live on. He was not the only
writer in the world with that problem, but he was making a serious effort to support himself and his family
by writing; he had no resources, and unless he could
count on scratching together at least enough to pay for
groceries, he would have to give it up.

In similar circumstances, any number of writers have
either turned into hacks or gone out and got a job
and deferred, maybe permanently, their writing careers.
But it seemed to me there was an experiment worth
trying, and so I made an arrangement with him. I
undertook to pay him an advance on every story he

turned in, so much a word, immediately on receipt of manuscript. He could write whatever he liked. I would worry about where and how to sell it. But every time a page came out of the typewriter he could count on a few bucks—not maybe, not later, but then.

Actually, it worked pretty well. Without the constraint of desperately needing to please some editor, he was able to write what he was good at. His sales began to pick up. I mentioned this to Cyril, and he allowed as how he would like the same arrangement; I agreed, and it worked for him, too. Jim Blish and Damon Knight wanted to try the same arrangement, and it also worked for them. By and by I had twelve or fifteen writers doing their own things, liberated from the need to slant, and, by gosh, doing very well. If you look at the major sf magazines of the early 50s, you will find that around half of the stories in them came from my agency; and of those I think at least half, including many of the best ones, were written under that arrangement, and mostly *would not have been written without it.*

I am really rather pleased with myself about this. Most of the writers involved were producing at the top of their form. The stories themselves comprise a solid part of the literature of sf. They are still being reprinted, and even taught. While it isn't as good as having written them myself, it still isn't bad; they are my stepchildren, with whom I am well pleased. It wasn't all roses. What was most wrong with it was that it required substantial amounts of capital—which I didn't have. But what was right about it was that it made it possible for good writers to do their best work without worrying about pleasing some nut of an editor. And shielding writers against editorial insanity, it seems to me, is an agent's principal task.

I tried to do that in as many ways as I could, and sometimes it worked pretty well. For instance, Hal

Clement wrote a marvelous sf novel called *Mission of Gravity*. He had had a temporary aberration of his own and submitted it in some kind of fruitcake "best novel" contest run by one of the semipro publishers, which I was desperately afraid the book would win; untangling it from them was my first and hardest job. But then I sent it off to John Campbell, who sent it back with the sad news that although he, of course, loved it, it would be impossible for him to run it as a serial since it did not break naturally into three installments.

Now, this was clear lunacy. I have no idea what made John say a dumb thing like that. John was about the best editor sf ever had, but even the best can go out of his mind at certain phases of the moon. I was never any good at winning arguments with John Campbell, but in this case I was certain he was wrong, and it was my clear duty, to him as well as to my client, to save him from his folly. So I took the manuscript out of its box and thumbed through it. It ran about 270 pages. I turned to page 90 and found a paragraph that could be construed as a cliffhanger, and penciled under it "End of Part One." On page 180 I wrote in "End of Part Two." I turned the manuscript over to my secretary with instructions to retype three or four pages before and after each break. I put it in the file for three weeks and then sent it back to John with a note saying that I hoped he would find that the revisions made it suitable for serialization. Of course he did, and it wound up as one of the best-loved serials *Astounding* ever ran.

I tell this story, not to make fun of John Campbell, but to illustrate the point that all editors, even he, sometimes say crazy things. If they are taken seriously, they can mean lost sales and wasted work for writers. One of the hardest things an agent has to do is to know when to reject a rejection. "How" is even harder.

With Horace Gold at *Galaxy* I was on easy terms.

Half a dozen times I refused to accept his turndown of a story and kept sending it back until he weakened and bought it. (Half a dozen other times I didn't persuade him.) With most editors I was less forthright. The simplest ploy was to hold a manuscript for a month or two and then send it back as if it had been revised. I tried not to lie outright, but I was willing to send off a letter that said:

"You know, Charlie, I think you've put your finger on a good point in Sam's story. I'll see what he thinks."

And then, a few weeks later:

"Here's Sam's story back, as we discussed. I really think it's a winner now."

What made it easy for me to play tricks was that I had a lot of leverage in science fiction, and the science-fiction field was booming. I used the muscle when I could, not just for my own writers. The reason the prevailing rate went from two cents a word to three in the early 1950s was a complicated three-way squeeze play that I planned and flawlessly executed.

When I went into the Army in 1943, I had helped Damon Knight get my old job at Popular Publications; now he was getting tired of it and looking for something with more authority to do. He stopped by my office and asked for advice. I had heard some trade gossip about Alex Hillman, then proprietor of a magazine chain, and suggested Damon hit on him for a science-fiction magazine; Damon did, and Hillman was willing to give it a try. Then Damon came to my office and asked how he could get a look at some of the stories that were going to Horace Gold and John Campbell. "Pay more than they do," I said, and Damon thought it over, and took it back to Hillman, and got a budget that allowed him to squeeze out an extra penny a word. That was step one. Step two was for me to trot down to Horace Gold and tell him that he now had powerful competition for a first look, and what was he going to do about it? "Let me talk it over with the publisher," he said, and did, and then *Galaxy* went to three cents a word. Whereupon I called up John Campbell and told him that the two-cent line had been broken; and a few weeks later *Astounding* followed suit. Well, no doubt all of that would have happened sooner or later, anyway; but it happened when it did because I squeezed.

All these things pleased me a lot; forgive me if I dwell on them, because some of the other things weren't very pleasing at all. I was having a lot of fun, but one thing I was not doing was making a profit.

Although the gross kept growing, the cost of doing business kept growing just a little faster. Advances. Rent. Salaries. Taxes. Telephone. Entertainment—I didn't do nearly as much of this as many agents, but still it was an item. Stationery! We used a lot of it, and most of it was custom-made. I designed a really handsome die-cut manuscript folder. They did exactly what they were intended to do, protected the scripts and made ours stand out from everyone else's, but they also cost the earth. Every time we ordered a new batch it blew the commissions on half a dozen sales. I designed locater cards and rights cards, ten times as good as the stock varieties, and at ten times the price.

And then there were those special and inevitable costs, like Christmas.

Christmas! It's a quarter of a century since I had my agent's office in New York City, but I can still barely force myself to send out a Christmas card. The jolly Yule spirit does not survive being an entrepreneur. Early in November the vultures start to gather. Building-service personnel you hardly see all year round

make sure to wish you a happy holiday. The elevator
people give you a group card, with each name carefully spelled out. The cleaning women identify themselves. The gnomes that toil in the caverns underground, fixing the pipes and feeding the boilers, every
one makes himself known to you, and every one expects a little token of affection. And the Post Office!
God must love mailmen, he made so many of them.
The First-Class Delivery men present you with their
collective card. Then the Bulk Mail deliverers give you
theirs. Then the Special Delivery and Registereds come
along. Then the Pickup Men, who empty out the box
in your building. Then the for God's sake Sorting
Clerks send a deputy out to visit your office, Christmas
card in hand, cheery smile on face, and larceny in
heart.

Taken all in all, a lot of money was funneling
through the agency checking account, but it all
seemed to belong to someone else. Somehow or other
we managed to go on eating, but not out of those
ten-percent commissions. Popular Science had been
reluctant enough to see me go to ask me to continue
with odd jobs on a free-lance basis, and so from time
to time I packaged a new book for them, photography
manual or fishing guide. There was not much satisfaction in them, but they were easy work for the money
and kept body and soul together.

But I kept thinking I would like to do some real
writing.

The thing was, there was a moral question involved.
Selling my own writing meant competing with my
clients. Ninety-five percent of the time, that would
make no real difference to anyone, the work sold on
its merits, the editors were glad to have it, there was
never enough really good stuff to suit them, anyway.
But now and then there would be conflicts, inevitably.
A slick magazine would want to try *one* science-fiction

story as an experiment. Whose? Bob Lowndes would have a cover and need a story written around it. Whom should the assignment go to?

For a time I compromised by editing a few anthologies. Brad had asked Bob Heinlein to do one for Doubleday, and Heinlein had objected that he didn't know enough about what had been published or how to secure permissions. Brad asked me if I were willing to ghost it, and I was, provided I could share it with Judy; and so the two of us put together *Tomorrow, the Stars*. It turned out very well, in fact I still get royalties on it, twenty-odd years later, and so Brad asked me to do some more in propria persona.

But it wasn't quite the same as writing.

I should say that the desire to write is really independent of the need to make a living. Not just for me. Harlan Ellison and I were talking to some fledgling writers a year or so ago, and he said, "No one should consider writing if he can possibly imagine doing anything else." I was struck by the wisdom of the remark because it defined exactly my own unexamined attitudes. Writing is the way I make my daily bread; but it is also my hobby, my vice, and my ongoing and most valued psychotherapy. Most writers would be straight up the wall if they didn't have the typewriter to fantasize through. James Branch Cabell once wrote a tenderly critical little jape about a writer: gauche, self-obsessed, petulant, he cried out, "I am pregnant with words! And I must have lexicological parturition, or I die!"

And I was beginning to bulge.

In the beginning of the 50s Judy and I took a summer place up on a hill overlooking the Ashokan Reservoir, a strange, comfortable old house with the upstairs where the downstairs ought to be: the ground floor was all bedrooms, while the upper part was mostly

an immense open drawing room with a big fireplace.
One weekend I felt the need to do some kind of writing badly enough to exhume my wartime novel, *For
Some We Loved*. I sat in front of that fireplace all
night long, reading it page by page. And as I finished
each page I threw it in the fire. It was, boy, *bad*.
Scratch *For Some We Loved*. I had achieved my purpose in learning enough about the advertising business to write a novel about it, no doubt. But not that
novel. It was too immature and incompetent to salvage. I thought of starting over again from the beginning, same premise but better resources and maybe
even better skill at writing, since I had learned something in the years between. But by then Fredric
Wakeman had made an immense success with *The
Hucksters*. The idea's virginity was gone.

A year later Judy and I were weekending at Fletcher
and Inga Pratt's immense old place in Highlands, New
Jersey, tenderly called The Ipsy-Wipsy Institute. It was
a literary sort of place to be. Fletcher himself used to
set up his typewriter in the billiard room; he would
type a few lines, pause to chat, toss cards into a hat,
have a drink, feed the marmosets, then go back and
type a few more. I have never understood how the
man could string sentences together to make sense
under conditions like that, but his example was a
prod. The other guests were people like Willy Ley,
John Ciardi, Sprague de Camp, Bernard de Voto, all
of them with writing of their own to do, and I felt left
out.

So I took my lavender typewriter out on the lawn
and began typing something called *Fall Campaign*. It
seemed to be the beginning of a science-fiction novel
about advertising. I didn't know where I was going
with it. I especially didn't know what I would do with
it after I wrote it, but it seemed like an interesting
thing to do; and in any event, the problem of what to

do with it would not arise until I had it written, which seemed comfortably far in the future.

As time permitted, for the next few months, I added a page now and then. Time didn't permit a lot. Putting in seventy hours a week as a literary agent did not leave many hours for writing, but, even so, by the summer of 1951 I had some twenty thousand words of very rough draft on paper, and the novel seemed to have solidified itself.

Then along came Horace Gold.

I had been selling him at least half of what he printed, as an agent, and besides, we had become good friends. I fought temptation for a while and then bashfully admitted I had a novel of my own in the works. Show me, said Horace. I did. Finish it and I'll print it, said Horace.

Fine! But how? I was still putting in seventy-hour weeks. At the current rate of progress it was two or three years in the future, at best, and here Horace was talking about having a cover painted and scheduling it as soon as Alfie Bester's *The Demolished Man* was through.

By then Judy and I had bought the big old New Jersey house I still live in, just across the river from Red Bank, and we had house guests. Cyril Kornbluth and his pregnant wife, Mary, had come to stay with us while they sorted things out. Cyril had quit his job as a wire-service news editor in Chicago to come east to free-lance. Naturally he was one of my clients. He was also my tried and trusted old collaborator. And he was right there in the house.

I showed him my twenty-thousand-word fragment. We chatted for a while about where I thought I was going. Phil Klass, alias William Tenn, had made a suggestion about having the hero do the Haroun al Raschid bit, wandering around the planet as a plebeian instead of an upper-crust advertising executive, and I thought that was a profitable area to explore. Cyril agreed and took the manuscript away, and when I saw him again he had rewritten the first twenty thousand words and added a whole new middle section. The last third we wrote turn and turn about, and then I put the whole thing through the typewriter one more time, and what came out *Galaxy* serialized as *Gravy Planet*.

As *The Space Merchants*, the book has had quite a career. I have a shelf made up of nothing but editions of it, in some twenty-five languages: French, Italian, Spanish, Portuguese, German, Russian, Latvian, Japanese, Serbo-Croatian, Dutch, Swedish, Hungarian, Romanian, and a dozen others. There are seven different English-language editions, from seven different publishers. We sold the film rights for a pretty penny: * it was broadcast on CBS's Columbia Workshop, and you can still buy pirated tape cassettes of the dramatization. For that matter, you can still buy the book. I don't know how many copies of it have been printed worldwide. There's no good way to tell, since there are several pirated editions I know of only from hearsay, not to mention the Eastern European editions on which no royalty statements have ever been furnished (or, of course, royalties paid). But it may be somewhere around ten million.

Not bad, right? And obviously, any book with that kind of potential had to be snapped up by the first book publisher to see it, right?

Well, it didn't happen that way. The book market for science fiction was booming when *Gravy Planet* came out, and I had little doubt that we would find a home for it. Unfortunately, the book editors didn't see it that way. I submitted it to every trade publisher,

---

* Actually five million pretty pennies. But they've never made the film. Movie people are crazy.

one by one, in the United States with a science-fiction line—toward the end, with even a hope that they might *consider* having a science-fiction line. And, one by one, they turned it down.

You must remember that I was not some rank outsider trying to get my first lucky break. As an agent, I was selling big chunks of material to all of them. Most of the editors were personal friends. But they didn't allow that to influence them, and in fact one or two were not even very kind about it. One very good friend handed the manuscript back to me and said, in tones of great sorrow, "Fred, look. I don't know how to tell you this, but it's no good. There are a couple of good ideas, sure. But you don't know how to handle them. What you need is some good professional writer to pull the whole thing together."

I never did find that good professional writer. What I found was an unprofessional publisher. His name was Ian Ballantine.

Judy had worked for him for a year or two, when he was president of Bantam Books and she was their science-fiction and mystery editor. Bantam mostly limited itself to reprinting hard-cover books, and so I had little to do with them as an agent. But I came to know some of the Bantam people pretty well— Arnold Hano, the managing editor (who greeted me with the tepid enthusiasm reserved for the husbands of colleagues until he found out I had written the copy for the "huge white bride's bed" ad he had tacked over his desk), and Ian Ballantine himself.

Ian had started Bantam and made it thrive. But in 1951 he and they had come to a tight place. He wanted to try some new ideas; Bantam's owners were happy with the good old procedures that were working very well, thank you. And so Ian took his courage in his hands and set up his own publishing house of Ballantine Books.

Ian Ballantine is not a physically dominating figure. He is short, and shaped mostly like a penguin. He has flaring John L. Lewis eyebrows and a habit of replying at right angles to any question. His wife, partner, and chief executive officer, Betty, makes up the difference. She is not only beautiful and sexy but a good fifty percent smarter than most publishing people; but I don't believe even Betty always follows Ian's logic.

No matter. A genius doesn't need logic. Ian Ballantine is a publishing genius. Half the major categories of paperback books on the stands today are there because Ian Ballantine had the wit and courage to try them out when no one else dared. He was the first paperback publisher to do serious amounts of science fiction, the first with books on the ecology, with mass-market art books, with war books; with books in unusual formats, sold through unusual channels. Without Ian Ballantine the paperback book business would be far tinier and more dull than it is.

All of this is true, and is one of the reasons why Ian Ballantine was my favorite publisher for a quarter of a century, but not all of it was evident in 1951 and 1952. The firm of Ballantine Books, Inc., was operating out of Ian and Betty's Chelsea penthouse. It was a big, handsome apartment. It probably would have been gracious and luxurious if it had not been crammed full of card-table desks and cardboard-carton filing cabinets. Their editorial staff was there, notably Bernard W. Shir-Cliff and Stanley Kauffmann.* So were

---

* Bernie Shir-Cliff has stayed in the paperback business and is now boss editor for Warner Paperback Library. Stanley Kauffmann had a marvelously interesting career after deciding against continuing as a book editor. For a while he was the first-string drama critic for *The New York Times*. That lasted, if I remember correctly, about three weeks; almost the first thing he pub-

most of the business department, and the art department, and the publicity department, and Ian and
Betty's ten-year-old son, Richard, whose bedroom was
the only corner of the house not ceiling-high with
manuscripts and galley proofs. Fortunately for the
sanity of all of us, after a couple of months Ballantine
Books found office space on Fifth Avenue. From then
on, having dinner with Ian and Betty was just as
stimulating, but a lot less athletic.

Ian's principal innovation was a decision to publish
both hard- and soft-cover editions of all of his books
simultaneously. The skeptics said it would never work.
Who would pay hard-cover prices when they could
pick up a paperback of the same book for a tenth of
the money?

In the long run, it turned out that the skeptics were
right, or almost so. But they were right for the wrong
reasons. The customers seemed perfectly happy to
accept both editions; I saw with my own eyes a good
many people carrying around three-dollar hard-cover
editions of Ian's first big bestseller, Cameron Hawley's
Executive Suite, right past newsstands where the paperback was on sale for thirty-five cents. But the wise
old hands of the publishing business *knew* it wouldn't
work. The terrible thing about these wise old hands is
that even when they are wrong, their convictions make
them right. When dealers, jobbers, wholesalers, and
salesmen think something won't work, they pull back,
and the prophecy becomes self-fulfilling.

Simultaneous hard- and soft-cover sounded pretty
jazzy to me, so I showed the tear sheets of *Gravy
Planet* to Ian. Poor fellow, he was just too inexperi-

---

lished was a reasoned analysis of the influence of homosexual
playwrights on the New York theater scene, and they had his
heart for breakfast. He is now a specialist in the art and history
of film.

enced a publisher to know it was no good. So he published it. And kept on publishing it, for twenty-some years.

Not only that, now that he had caught the sf fever he wanted more. I trotted out half a dozen candidates from the limitless resources of my agency, and he bought them all. We will do one science-fiction title a month, Ian decided, but in order to assure a supply, we will have to figure out some way of keeping our image bright in the memories of all science-fiction writers. How do we go about that?

Well, I said, you could publish an anthology. There is nothing like getting checks, even smallish anthology-sized checks, to make a writer aware of your existence. Come to that, I'd be glad to edit one for you.

Ian pondered that for a moment, and then his face lit up. No, he said, I don't want to do what all the other publishers have done. I want to do something original—in fact, what I want to do is an anthology of all original stories. You edit it. We'll outpay the magazines, to get the very best. We'll call it—we'll call it— well, never mind, we'll think of something to call it. You get the stories.

That's how *Star Science Fiction* was born. There have been a good many imitations of it since, but *Star* was the first regular series of anthologies of originals.

And, you know, not bad, either. It should have been pretty good; I had everything going for me. So many of the best writers in the field were my clients that I could easily get first look at the cream of the crop. I couldn't shortstop it all. I had, after all, some obligations to the editors I had been dealing with. But I also had some obligations to my writers, and Ian had opened the treasure chest wide enough so that we were paying twice as much as the magazines.

So I began assembling stories, first by checking out

what my own clients had to offer. About that time I realized that it wasn't entirely fair for me to take a commission on sales I made to myself, so I waived the ten percent (which meant that a sizable fraction of my earnings as editor was lost back in forgiven commissions). Even so, I was pleased to be able to print Cliff Simak's "Contraption," John Wyndham's "The Chronoclasm," Isaac Asimov's "Nobody Here But—," Judy Merril's "So Proudly We Hail," H. L. Gold's "The Man with English"; Fritz Leiber did a wildly funny burlesque of Mickey Spillane, "The Night He Cried"; William Tenn and Robert Sheckley had bright, satirical stories called "The Deserter" and "The Last Weapon" . . . and then there was the case of Joe Samachson. Under his pen name, William Morrison, Joe was one of the great unrecognized all-time pros of science fiction. He was always competent, and once in a while great—as in "The Sack." This time he had a peak again, with my favorite story in the whole book, "Country Doctor."

That was more than half the lineup. I didn't want to publish only the work of my clients, and fortunately by then the word had got around that this new volume would be worth appearing in. I was able to get first-rate stories from Lester del Rey, Ray Bradbury, Murray Leinster, Arthur C. Clarke and Henry Kuttner and C. L. Moore. It all worked well, and over the years we did half a dozen more just like it.

It also gave me perhaps the sweetest moment of revenge I have ever tasted, on the hapless body of Horace Gold.

The thing about Horace was that he was a dynamite editor, energetic, talented, skilled, but he had this one little fault. He could not keep his fingers off his writers' prose. He got his training under Leo Margulies, in the old pulp-chain days when an editor's productivity was measured by the proportion of pencil markings on the pages he sent to the printer. Horace never forgot the lessons learned at Leo's knee.

He drove some writers wild. Even Cyril Kornbluth, compleat pro, casehardened against all editorial madness. Even me. We all muttered in our beer about the way Horace tinkered with our words. Most of us tried to tolerate it—he was, after all, putting out just about the best magazine in science fiction. But we hated it. It was the kind of curse that seems put upon the world to strengthen our spirit, like hemorrhoids or the torment of psoriasis.

And then Ian gave me *Star* to edit, and Horace gave me the manuscript of his story, "The Man with English."

Cyril dropped into the office just as I was finishing reading it, and I told him what it was. Are you going to buy it? he asked. I told him I was, and he looked pensive. You know, he said, I'd like to buy a story from Horace. I'd like to buy it, and then edit it. I'd like to go over it from beginning to end, with twelve sharp pencils, and then—

He stopped, and we looked at each other. Inspiration was born.

So I sent Cyril out for a bottle while I had my secretary type up another copy of the script. (There were not yet Xeroxes in every office!) I prepared the new copy for the printer and sent it off, and then Cyril and I settled down to enjoy ourselves.

Ah, the creativity of that evening! No manuscript has ever been as edited as that one. We changed the names of the characters. We changed their descriptions. If they were tall, we made them short. We gave them Irish brogues and made them stutter. We switched all the punctuation at random and killed the point of all the jokes. We mangled his sentence structure and despoiled the rolling cadence of his prose, and then we came to the point of the story. The hero

of "The Man with English" has somehow had his
senses switched around, so that he hears light and sees
sound. At the end of the story he thinks he has had
them straightened out, but then he wrinkles his nose
and asks, "What smells purple?" We argued over that
for half an hour, and then crossed it out and wrote
in, "He said, 'Gee, there's a kind of a funny, you know,
sort of smell around here, don't you think?'"

And then, with great cunning, I let the manuscript
be mixed in with some others intended for Horace,
as if by accident, and dropped them all off at his apartment on my way home from work. And by the time I
walked into my house the phone was ringing.

If you ask Horace about it now, he will tell you,
sure, he knew it was a gag all the time. Don't you believe him. "Fred," he said, "uh, listen. I mean—well,
look, Fred. You know I'm a pro. I don't object to
editing. But . . ." Long pause. Then, "*Jesus*, Fred!" he
finished.

Well, in the long run it made no difference; Horace
kept on doing what he always did, making authors
weep and putting out a fine magazine. But one thing
it did do. For a while one evening it made Cyril and
me feel a lot better.

First to last, I was an agent for seven years.

Being an agent is almost like being an editor. It
satisfies the god complex. John Campbell once told
me that if he hadn't been an editor he would have
been either teacher or preacher, and I guess so would
I. Problem-solving is always a great high. Other people's problems are always the easiest to solve, and I
enjoyed doing it. I liked taking brand-new writers like
Robert Sheckley and A. J. Budrys and breaking them
into top markets. I liked opening new areas for established writers—a nonfiction book condensation and
then a movie sale for H. Beam Piper, their first TV
assignments for James Blish and Joe Samachson. Be-

cause I got him into book writing in the first place, I am almost as pleased about Isaac Asimov's scores of books as he is,* and all that was fun.

But among the great pluses I could count from my career as a literary agent, making myself rich was not one. In fact, I was running out of money. I was certain that I was on the right track. In the long run it would all pay off. But the trouble with the long run, as John Maynard Keynes is supposed to have said to Franklin D. Roosevelt, is that in the long run we are all dead. Even after I had managed to get the enterprise feebly into the black, even when I had begun doing outside editorial work and even some writing, I still was netting a lot less than I had taken home every week, headache-free, from Popular Science, and the strain was beginning to be hard to take. Among other things, it was messing up my personal life.

After Judy and I married, we had a couple of pretty interesting years. It probably was not highly intelligent of us both to quit our well-paid jobs at the same time, but I wanted to spend more time at agenting and Judy wanted to write *Shadow on the Hearth*, and we took the plunge. We didn't have much money. On the other hand, we didn't need a lot. Our first apartment (which had been Judy's apartment, until I moved self and typewriter in) was a basement in the East Village, about as cheap as an apartment got. It was large and rather nice—assuming you didn't mind squeezing past the steam pipes and the laundry room to get to the door—and we had a lot of good parties there. It didn't matter much if we were noisy, and that was good. Sometimes Jay Stanton would bring his guitar, or Ted Sturgeon would bring his. There was a piano, and usually someone to play it. Most often it was a young girl named Gerry Schuster, who was rehearsal pianist

* Well, no, not *that* pleased.

for the Ballet Theatre and once or twice brought actual dancers and choreographers around.*

Considering how little money we had, Judy and I got around quite a lot. We made it to Toronto for the 1948 World Science Fiction Convention (the first one to take the word "world" seriously, or a little bit seriously, by having the site actually outside the United States). George O. Smith and Chan Davis drove up to Toronto and back with us. That's where I first met people like Poul Anderson and Gordon Dickson, young fans just beginning to break into print, and on the way back George O. achieved his life's ambition by bellying up to the rail at Niagara and urinating into the Falls. We had a summer place at Ashokan one year. We were on Cape Cod, visiting Chan Davis's family, when the Korean War broke out. We got to the Cincinnati convention in 1949, sharing our twin beds with Chan and his new bride when they arrived too late to get a room.† The 1950 convention was off in some unexplored area like California, and we didn't see how we could make that, but we beat the system by holding our own convention in New York City.

New York-1950 was the first convention I had actually participated in organizing, and if God spares my reasoning powers, it will be the last. It was a harrowing experience.

By now there have been hundreds of conventions. There is a great body of accumulated wisdom, passed on from committee to committee. Hotels have become aware of sf conventions and usually welcome them, sometimes compete furiously to attract them. But in 1950 there was much ground still unbroken. Hotel

* Once she borrowed the apartment to give a party for the whole troupe—Nora Kaye, Danilova, everybody! In my own home! But I was out of town and missed it. I could have killed her.

† One couple to each bed, of course, what did you think?

managers were not at all sure of what they were getting into; they wanted guarantees. Registration fees were modest. No one had yet thought of converting sf conventions into Farmer's Markets for hucksters of books, magazines, and trinkets, so there was no income from renting out sales space. There wasn't very much money at all to work with, and certainly none to pay speakers. Nevertheless, we got several hundred people out, and all in all, it was one of the best conventions of the decade.

It even attracted media coverage. *Life* sent a crew around, and published a group photograph of the banquet. The saddening thing about the photo, looking at it now, is that so many of the people are dead: Willy Ley, Will Jenkins (a.k.a. Murray Leinster), my old boss George Spoerer, Rita Pringle (Dirk Wylie's sister-in-law; Dirk himself had died a year or two earlier), Jim Williams of Prime Press. The other saddening thing, or at least the sort of rueful thing, is to observe how many of the couples there are couples no longer, or are coupled with different partners. My wife, Carol, is in the picture, but not only were we not yet married, we had barely met.

The convention committee, besides Judy and myself, were Jay Stanton, Lester del Rey, and Harry and Evelyn Harrison, a small and incestuous world. A few months later Jay married Carol; that lasted not quite a year. Harry and Evelyn Harrison split up, and Evelyn marred Lester del Rey. A sociology student named Jean Haynes came into the Hydra Club around that time and decided to do her master's thesis on kinship ties in our social microcosm. She spent three months trying to sort out who was married to whom and which had been married to what, not to mention less formal alliances, and gave up in despair. The game was Musical Beds. At its peak it was hard to get a quorum of the Hydra Club to transact business, since so many of its officers were divorcing and remarrying so many others.

At the time of the New York convention, however, Judy and I were pretty solidly married. We had even decided to risk parenthood, and two or three months later, on the twenty-fifth of September, 1950, our daughter Ann was born.

Judy already had a daughter from a previous marriage, Merril Zissman, so I was not unused to being in loco parentis. What I was not used to was newborns. She was so *tiny*. On one side of her face she was one of the prettiest babies ever seen, but the other side was somewhat squeezed from the business of being born, and so I worried intensely (and privately) that she would grow up hideously deformed in the right profile. No matter! I would protect her! If the other kids tried to make fun of her, well, I would know how to deal with those lousy other kids. . . . As a matter of fact, within a week or two the right side of her face filled out to match the left, and she turned into a beautiful child.* And that winter, with Annie beginning to crawl and Merril well into her school career, Judy and I began to discuss where we wanted to make a permanent home for the kids.

C. Northcote Parkinson says that when institutions finally get themselves into permanent headquarters, that is the sign that the peak has passed and they are on their way to oblivion. So it was with us. In the spring of 1951 Judy and I bought the house in Red Bank, and three months later we had decided to get a divorce.

To my surprise, shock, and anger, the divorce was not in the least amicable. I wasn't ready for that. After all, it was my third. I was beginning to think of my-

---

* She is now a beautiful adult, with two spectacular tiny children of her own, in Canada.

self as an acknowledged expert in the field. The procedure was all pretty routine: one party decides to call it off, the other party agrees, you sign some papers, and pretty soon both of you are married to somebody else and no harm done.

But it wasn't that way at all.

What made this divorce unlike any other was Annie. We both loved her. We both felt we could do more for her than that rotten other person. The first steps toward divorce were painless enough, but when we got to the question of custody, we wrangled bitterly and interminably, through the courts and outside them, for years. I wish we could have avoided all that.

But I am not sure it could have happened in any other way. I think I can explain it all in terms of nuclear physics. It is a question of pair formation, and the conservation of net charge. When a positively charged + male and a negatively charged − female annihilate each other in divorce, they instantly become free-flying photons with a 0 neutral charge, and the law of conservation is maintained. Time passes. Each photon ultimately interacts with another, and so another electron-positron pair is formed. But. When the pair has formed some smaller particle, they no longer have the capacity to act as leptons. They cannot separate to lead the carefree lives of photons. There is a piece left over. Charge-conservation is violated, and the result is acrimony and pain. So Doë and I, and Tina and I, could end our marriages and still be friends. Judy and I could not, for years.

Of course, that was years ago, and I think we have now settled into a position as old and good friends. Which leads me to something I want to say. I don't quite know how to say it. I am hesitant to speak of "my ex-wives" as if the term defined them as a class. The principal thing that the ladies I have been married to (and some ladies I have not been married to) have in common is that each is very much an individual, with talents and graces far beyond the usual allotment. I keep running into people who speak of lives damaged by mates so malevolent and self-centered that the marriage is a constant pain. It has never happened to me. It is hard for me to believe that these closet beasts and termagants exist. Barring the odd dissonance in the relationship—well, maybe barring a *lot* of dissonances—the women who have shared any part of my life have each been a treasure, and a joy.

But the dissonances with Judy were immediate and painful in 1951 and after, and they were made a lot worse by the dissonances in my work. I ran out of money.

Part of the reason was my wonderful invention of advancing money to my clients so that they could write what they chose. It mostly all did pay off in time,* but I was undercapitalized. I began operating on float, drawing against funds between the time I wrote the checks and the time they would be presented for collection. Now and then, and then more and more often, my checks began to bounce.

I decided to trim expenses to the bone, got out of the Fifth Avenue offices, and moved to a tiny single room on West 10th Street, in the same building as Marty Greenberg's Gnome Press. Marty was also suffering undercapitalization woes, and when things got too grim in my office I would wander down the hall to his to compare notes on disaster. I cut down to one secretary, no messenger, no assistant. It turned out that the extra people were not necessary to the work of the agency. The monthly sales figures con-

---

* Ultimately all the advances were repaid except for one or two writers amounting to a few thousand dollars, but I have spent more for things I valued less.

tinued the trend upward. But their absence was very expensive in terms of my own time. I was working eighty hours a week and more, and it was beginning to be more pain than it was worth. My writers were generally sympathetic, but they were also getting worried.

Gossip carried the word around the publishing business that I was having money troubles, and other agents began to send out feelers. Would I care to sell my contracts for a capital-gains payment? Sell the agency entire to another agent? A new agent, Rogers Terrill, once my boss at Popular Publications, urged me to come into partnership with him, and that was tempting; Rog was a prince of good fellows, as well as a capable and industrious person.

But the Fool-Killer was loud behind me, and it no longer seemed worth struggling to survive as an agent.

In 1953 the agency at last threw off enough net profit to equal the salary I had had from Popular Publications. That in some way satisfied a need, and so I packed it in. I made cash settlements where I could, turned the authors loose, and toted up my losses.

Counting everything, I was in hock for around thirty thousand dollars.

Years later, my lawyer asked me why I hadn't considered bankruptcy. I didn't know what to tell him. I don't know now; I just never gave it a thought. I intended to pay off the whole thirty thousand, and I did; but it took me nearly ten years.

٩

Four Pages a Day

For the next seven or eight years I was a pretty nearly simon-pure free-lance writer.

In the minds of most civilians, the life of a writer has got to be glamorous and exciting. Well, it is, some of the time. A writer often gets to meet special people, visit fascinating places, do exciting things. But none of these occur when he is actively engaged at his employment. When he is writing, he is the nearest thing to a vegetable that you will find registered to vote. He sits.

He doesn't even have the apparent function of pushing typewriter keys most of the time, because during most of that sitting time the activity is all internal and thus invisible.

Let me show you the numbers: Any jackleg typist can manage seventy-five words a minute. If you type at that rate from nine to five every day, with time out for lunch and a ten-minute break at the end of each hour for flexing the fingers, you will produce the equivalent of two 75,000-word novels in every five-day week.

It is an observed fact that writers do not ordinarily produce two novels a week. Most don't even manage two a year. Therefore it is demonstrated that writing is not merely a matter of putting words down on the page. Some other activity is taking place.

The name of that process is "thinking."

The trouble with a career in which ninety-five percent of your working time is spent thinking is that, therefore, ninety-five percent of the time you don't *look* as if you're working. Or even thinking. What a writer looks like he is doing, generally speaking, is watching TV, playing solitaire, cleaning his typewriter keys, or taking a nap. Writing is not much of a spectator sport. I have had one or two nonwriting friends whose curiosity was so piqued that they coaxed to be allowed to watch me write. After ten or fifteen minutes they always fled to some other room. The boredom reaches criticality very soon. It does for the writer, too, unfortunately, so that actually getting words on paper becomes a test of strength, will power against terminal tedium. Which is why it is said that writing is the art of applying the seat of the pants to the seat of the chair.

Writing is the only job I know that your wife will nag you *out* of. Why wouldn't she? There you are, sprawled out on the living-room sofa, rereading the real-estate section from last Sunday's *Times*—although it is known that you have no extensive real-estate holdings, and little prospect of acquiring any. Meanwhile, the dishwasher needs fixing. Poor soul! How can she know that if she interrupts you now, you will lose a precarious train of thought that has taken you four hours to construct?

The other side of the coin is that sometimes your wife is right, and you're just loafing. There simply is no external way to tell when a writer is working, and maybe even the writer himself doesn't know.

Nevertheless, the end product is easily recognizable. If the writer *is* a writer, at some point words will come

out, and finished works, and if he is any good they will
sooner or later be published. This is conclusive diagnostic evidence. Pity it doesn't come along in time
to be useful when you need to know whether the dishwasher should be fixed.

I don't write all the time—I don't know many writers
who do. There are periods when, for reasons not easy
to identify, I write regularly and well for months on
end. There are other times when I don't.

The times when a writer isn't writing are called
"writer's slump." Everybody has it, at least now and
then. Nobody, or nobody I know, is wholly successful
in dealing with it. I don't know how to deal with it
any more than anyone else, but what I do know is a
way to postpone its happening, pretty well, most of the
time, in a fashion that works, more or less, for me.
What I do is to set myself a daily quota of four pages.
No more, no less; and I write those pages every day,
no matter where I am, no matter how long it takes,
if I die for it.* Sometimes it takes forty-five minutes.
Sometimes it takes eighteen hours. Sometimes I am
reasonably satisfied with the words that go onto the
paper, and quite a lot of the time I loathe them.

But I *do* them. If I miss, if I skip *one day*, the
rhythm of the stride is broken and the shattered edifice
of my life tumbles down on my head. So I do it every
day, which means every day there is, including Satur-

* These particular pages, for instance, were written early on
a Saturday morning in a hotel room in Cleveland, Ohio. Chip
Delany was right across the hall. Joe and Gay Haldeman, Annie
McCaffrey, Judy-Lynn and Lester del Rey, and other boon companions were only a few doors away, and I was certain, absolutely, despondently certain, that they were all getting ready to
have a fun brunch, laughing and chortling and having a hell of
a great old time, while I was slaving away on my decrepit French
portable. But I stuck it out and postponed collapse for one
more day.

days, Sundays, Christmas, my birthday, the day I'm
going to the dentist to find out if I'm going to need
a root-canal job, the day I fly to London, the day I
am so badly hung over that my eyelashes bleed. I do
my quota in airports, on boardwalk benches, and in
commuter trains. I have been known to take my typewriter along on a weekend date. "Every day" means
"every day," and this is the first rule of writing for me.

Of course, with all this terrible strength of character,
the times do come when I fall. I've missed a day, never
mind why. Then everything is at risk. If I can climb
right back on the wagon, maybe it will all be all right
again, but maybe it won't—and sometimes that single
day has extended itself to months.

But that is what it is like to be a writer (for me,
anyway), and that is why there is not a great deal
to say about what occupied the greatest part of my
attention for the remaining years of the 1950s. I wrote.
And was a damn dull spectacle doing it.

So will you imagine, please, that all through this
chapter I am—whatever else I am doing—writing about
forty short sf stories (and a couple of dozen other short
pieces) and about a dozen science-fiction novels (and
eight or ten other books).

I did manage to get away from the typewriter long
enough to do a few other things, and one of them was
to get married again.

The girl was (and is!) a tall, leggy, strikingly beautiful blonde, neé Carol Metcalf Ulf. A brief marriage to
Jay Stanton left her with a brand-new daughter, Karen,
who in the twenty-odd years since has changed from
a tiny scarlet bundle of flesh, with an eye that wandered northeast and a foot that pointed southwest,
to the kind of beauty who stops conversation when
she comes into a room . . . and with intelligence,

creativity, and personality to match.* So Carol and
Carol's Karen, and me and my Annie, at least when
the varying vicissitudes of my struggles with Judy gave
me custody of Annie, set up housekeeping. First it was
a tiny apartment on the far East Side of New York.
The 10th Street bus paused to gather its strength for
the westward run right under our window, so that the
noise of idling Diesels kept things lively all night long,
and there were mice. But it was a pretty nice little
apartment. It was only a few blocks from Horace
Gold's place in Stuyvesant Town, and our Friday
nights were given to Horace's poker games. It was
very good that this was so. We didn't have money for
baby sitters and shows, since I was trying to make a
dent in paying off thirty thousand dollars.

Those Friday-night games were fun. Horace edited
Galaxy from his apartment, and a lot of the regulars
were *Galaxy* writers: Bob Sheckley, William Tenn,
A. J. Budrys, sometimes Lester and Evelyn del Rey,
Tony Boucher when he was in town. Not everyone
was a writer. John Cage showed up occasionally, a
gentle, humorous man who clutched his cards diffi-
dently, bet insecurely, and seemed to win a lot. Years
later, when Karen-grown-up was taking a course in
Cage's music, she was startled to learn that she had
met him as an infant, between Spit in the Ocean and
High-Low Seven, when we took her out of the carriage
for her ten o'clock feeding.

Before long we were back in the house in Red
Bank, trying to fill up fourteen rooms with what
furniture we could acquire on a budget of hardly anything at all. Carol was superb. Former art student and
fashion model, she made most of her own clothes—
as well as drapes, spreads, and slipcovers for the tatty

---

* You probably have noticed by now that I am fond of my
kids, but all this is objectively true, I swear.

furniture—naturally clothing the babies on the same sewing machine. Moreover, she was handy with pliers and paintbrush. Before long she had made the house eminently livable. Even partyable. We began inviting friends out, at first a few at a time, then overnight parties of dozens of people which climaxed, when the weather was warm enough, with a little daybreak swimming in the lake down the street.

We had a great natural resource to draw on, because the fabulous Ipsy-Wipsy Institute was not very far away. The Ipsy was the immense house in Highlands owned by Fletcher and Inga Pratt, twenty-three rooms, on acres of land rolling down to the Shrewsbury River. (I suppose that the reason I wasn't afraid to acquire a fourteen-room house of my own was that, seeing it for the first time after a weekend at the Ipsy, it seemed charmingly compact.)

The Ipsy-Wipsy was some two hundred years old, with sculptured plaster ceilings in the billiard room and immense fireplaces in the drawing room and the dining hall, and a strange, huge painting that went with the house (because there was no way to remove it) on the landing of the stairs. The Pratts had bought it cheaply enough, but I cannot imagine how many tens of thousands must have gone into jacking up the fireplaces, stopping the leaks in the roof, replacing wood that had rotted and plaster that had peeled away. Owning a big old house is a career. They are like beaver dams, a dynamic interplay between creation and decay. If you take your eyes off them for a moment, they are down around your ears: the heating system goes, the roof tiles separate and blow away, water stains the walls you have just repainted, the floors begin to pop. But it's worth it. *Maybe* it's worth it. It's worth it if you enjoy the house, and if you keep it filled with life.

The Pratts surely filled theirs, with people, books,

and marmosets. Fletcher raised the little wooly monkeys; they lived in bird cages in the billiard room, huddling under scraps of blanket and peering out with their old-man faces cocked to one side, wistful for a mealworm or a grape. Fletcher, who was the dearest man alive, looked like a marmoset himself, with his own head held in exactly the same position, and with his marmoset beard and bright marmoset eyes. Sometimes we borrowed the Ipsy's company. Sometimes they borrowed ours. Basil Davenport was an Ipsy-Wipsy regular, a Book-of-the-Month-Club editor who came out one weekend in great exultation because he had persuaded the Club to take an Arthur Clarke book as an alternate selection, and thus struck a great blow for science fiction. St. Leger Lawrence was another. So was John Ciardi, paying his bills by teaching in a New England college and doubling as a science-fiction editor for Twayne while waiting for poetry to pay off. So were any number of literary skin divers, former dictators of obscure countries, rocket millionaires, space chemists, and, naturally, science-fiction writers: Ted Sturgeon, Fritz Leiber, Katherine Mac-Lean and her husband, Charley Dye, the Kornbluths, the de Camps, the del Reys. William Lindsay Gresham was there a lot just at the end of his life, an irascible, mean-mouthed man who was having troubles he could not handle, and one night a little later, checked into a Times Square hotel and killed himself. Willy Ley and his wife, Olga, came out frequently with their two small girls (enough bigger than ours so that we had inherited Xenia's crib for, successively, Annie and Karen). When Doña and John Campbell were divorced, Doña married George O. Smith, and by and by they came to the Ipsy not as house guests but to live. (The old original house, four or five rooms of it, was still part of the structure, with its own independent facilities and entrances, and it became theirs.) Laurence and Edie Manning came for a few weekends. Larry had written *The Man Who Awoke* and many other science-fiction stories in the old days and now was the proprietor of his own mail-order nursery; they made up their minds quickly, bought a piece of Fletcher's property, and built a house of their own next door. Meanwhile, the del Reys had come out to spend a weekend with Carol and me, stayed several months, and then moved into their own place down the street. The science-fiction population of Monmouth County was growing by leaps and bounds.

Saturday was the special day at the Ipsy-Wipsy Institute. At five the cocktail flag was hoisted while Fletcher tootled the trumpet, and the guests began to assemble. We drank for hours around the huge oak cocktail table in the billiard room, before dining on the quail or eel or roast hump of bison. Fletcher, God save him, was a lousy cook. He did not believe in overexposing food to fire, and so it was always all bloody. (He actually served the only rare bouillabaisse I have ever encountered.) What saved us all from terminal trichinosis was Grace, the all-purpose maid, who lied to him about cooking times.

Ceremonial was a joy to Fletcher. He had been born a Buffalo farm boy, achieved prosperity and fame,* and set out to re-create himself in the image of a landed gentleman. The Ipsy-Wipsy made it all come true. The port. was always passed to the left. The after-dinner liqueurs were drunk to courteous toasts and responses. It was easy to tease Fletcher for his pretensions, but he knew what game he was playing. He saw as much humor in it as anyone else, and there was nothing mean or pretentious in it, or in Fletcher. He made the world a nicer place.

* Not just in science fiction. His *Ordeal by Fire* is the best one-volume history of the Civil War ever written, and taught me most of what I know about the writing of nonfiction.

In 1957 he began to feel ill. Staunch Christian Scientist, he would have nothing to do with the doctors of the flesh. By the time Inga bullied him into seeing one, it was too late. He died of cancer of the stomach.

A year or two later Inga remarried and moved away, and the Ipsy-Wipsy Institute was sold to a dentist from Jersey City. One night it burned to the ground. The dentist cleared away the rubble and built himself a split-level ranch house on the spot. It may be a nice enough place, but it has nothing of the majesty of the Ipsy, or of the memories.

Early in the 1950s something else happened that changed my life in ways I had never anticipated, and it began when I subscribed to *Scientific American.*

I had a fair grounding in science and mathematics from Brooklyn Tech and Chanute Field, but I was not terribly interested in the subjects. *SciAm* began to turn me on.

The precipitating incident was a brief, popularized article on the theory of numbers. At that time it was a terribly arcane subject. Now it is less so, particularly for ten-year-olds, because the "new math" of the public schools leans heavily on number theory: which is to say, the properties of numbers.

Now, I don't really expect you to sit still while I explain number theory to you. I am not sure if I could even answer the question if you were to ask me if it mattered at all. One answer would be, "My God, yes!" Another would be, "Of course not." The best answer would be that it has the same importance as God has. Either it is of transcendental concern or it doesn't matter at all, and which it is to you depends on you.

The article was only a teaser, but it included a bibliography. I had my secretary order all the books in the bibliography and I read them—not, dear God, without pain! They stretched my head to its limits. I found that they were teasers, too. I found that number theory was one of the very few domains of science and mathematics in which an amateur might well achieve something all the professionals had always missed, and, in fact, in which quite a few amateurs had done so.

Well, that seemed like pretty jazzy fun, and so I plunged into a couple of the classic problems. The seductive thing about them is that they are almost all quite easy to understand. Solving them, not so easy.

For instance, there is the case of Fermat's last theorem.

This fellow, Pierre de Fermat, who died some three hundred and more years ago, had some flaky habits. There is no question that he was a genius of a mathematician, everyone knew that. The trouble was that he knew it, too, and knew it so well that he never felt any obligation to prove it to anyone. Most of what he said he mentioned offhandedly in casual letters to friends, or even in little scribbles to posterity in the margins of his books, and one of those scribbles has caused immense pain to all the world's greatest mathematicians—and also to me!—ever since.

It goes like this:

When you were in high school, you learned that the sum of the squares of the sides of a right triangle equals the square of the hypotenuse. You learned to write it as $a^2 + b^2 = c^2$. That was a powerful discovery in itself, but it wasn't made by Fermat; a fellow named Pythagoras laid that one on us two thousand years ago.

A different ancient fellow named Diophantos looked at the equation in a different way and proposed a general solution for the formula; and there matters languished till flaky old Fermat came along. And in his copy of Diophantos's book he wrote:

It is impossible to write a cube as the sum of two cubes, a fourth power as the sum of two fourth powers, and in general any power beyond the second as the sum of two similar powers.

That's not news in itself. It means that equations like $a^3 + b^3 = c^3$ or even $a^{115} + b^{115} = c^{115}$ might as well never be written, because they don't mean anything—there aren't any numbers you can put into them that will make them come out with exact answers. But everyone rather suspected that, anyway.

But Fermat didn't stop there. He added one more sentence, which was the kicker:

For this I have discovered a truly wonderful proof, but the margin is too small to contain it.

Now, what a spot to leave generations of mathematicians in! It cannot be ignored. You or I could write that in the margins of anything we liked, and no one would lose a moment's sleep. But Fermat did not make claims he could not support, ever.

Well, I never found that "truly wonderful proof." No one else has, either. But in looking for it I came across half a dozen other brain teasers: verifying Goldbach's conjecture,* looking for a formula for primes.† Finding a general rule to explain the recurring rhythms in sums of powers—well, never mind about that one; I may get back to it someday.

From first to last, I must have spent a year on num-

* "Any prime number can be written as the sum of two primes." It's true, as far as anyone knows. But prove it?
† That is, some mathematical formula into which you can substitute arbitrary numbers on the left-hand side of the equation, and for which the solution on the right-hand side will always be a prime number. I *still* think that one can be solved, but I no longer think it will be by me.

ber theory, reading papers in things like *Scripta Mathematica*, doodling endless series of numbers. About half of what I did that year could have been done in minutes on a computer, or in a few days, anyway, on a pocket calculator of the kind my son carries in his shirt pocket to classes, but I didn't have them. Then finally the fever spent itself.

But there were sequelae. I'm not fully recovered yet.

I discovered that I could learn quite a lot about a particular subject; having demonstrated this on one subject, I tried it on some others. I became interested in recent American history and began to look into the causes and consequences of the Great Depression. After a time I realized I knew enough to write a book and began systematically to prepare it. That one never made it to print—not yet, anyway *—but first-century Rome also interested me, and that one did turn into a book, *Tiberius*. One on the Ku Klux Klan made it all the way to final draft and a publishing contract, but then I found I was dissatisfied with it and withdrew it, meaning to go over it one more time when I found an opportunity. (It hasn't come yet.) I learned the uses of reference collections and the microfilmed periodicals in the big Fifth Avenue library. I developed an appetite. School had never sated it, or even let me know I had it.

I don't think of myself as a scholar. I think I have the same relation to knowledge that your brother-in-law has to the Los Angeles Rams. Learning—all kinds of learning, but especially history, politics, and above all, science—to me is the greatest of spectator sports. It gives me pleasure.

* I wound up with three quarters of a million words of notes and about fifty thousand words of the text of what was called *Say, Don't You Remember?* But while I was doing that, several other people noticed the need for such a book and beat me into print.

Real-fun, kicky pleasure? Well—yes, maybe. Pleasure in the sense that sex is pleasure, but also painful in the sense that unfulfilled sex can be a yearning and obsessive pain. It *hurts* me to be ignorant. It is unpleasant, in an interior, unfulfilled way, for me to discover that there is a whole space of knowledge I don't share.

God knows, I am no scientist. There is no prospect at all that I will ever make any fundamental discoveries in physics, chemistry, or biology. I don't have the equipment. I don't just mean the skills, although they are daunting. I mean the hardware that is pretty fancily outside my amateur reach: mile-long particle accelerators, radio-telescope dishes with hearts of liquid helium and skins that spread across a valley, whole populations of nude mice and genetically pure tree frogs. I can accept that. Scientific discovery is not the sort of challenge that I feel compelled to take up personally. I really want to know very much what the world of Venus is like under its opaque, searing clouds. But it's all right to leave the problem to the Soviet and American space establishments. Little by little, they are fitting the pieces together, and when they learn something new, the JPL or Carl Sagan or Walter Sullivan will be sure to tell me, one way or another. I am content with that. I think that somewhere I have a basic religion, and its dogma is that the purpose of life is to understand the world and all it contains. I don't need to make the discoveries. But I do need to know about them.

And so I read *Scientific American* and *New Scientist* and *Science* and *The Bulletin of the Atomic Scientists* and *Spaceflight* and the *Journal of the B.I.S.* and, oh, hell, I don't know, maybe a dozen other publications. And when in one of them somebody says something new and elegant, it is almost like it used to be when Roy Campanella drove Jackie Robinson across the plate in the old days.

Sometimes people ask me what my scientific background is, and I have worked out an answer. I point to my friend Isaac Asimov, who is about the same age as I am. We met when we were both still in high school. I dropped out without graduating, and most of what I have learned I have picked up catch-as-catch-can. While Isaac did graduate from high school, and went on to college, and got a bachelor's degree, and then a master's degree, and then a doctorate, and finally became a professor. And that proves that, when the will to learn is present, obstacles can be overcome; because when you come right down to it, Isaac knows as much science as I do.

The 1950s were boom years for science-fiction magazines. At the peak there were some thirty-eight of them, and anybody who could write science fiction at all could get published in one or another of them. (So did a lot of people who couldn't.)

Making a living was something else. A lot of the word rates were low—well, they were all low, compared with the kind of money sf writers expect now. Three cents a word was a good price. Horace paid me four, and that was super. In that decade I was *Galaxy*'s most prolific contributor, with some seven serials and about thirty shorter pieces; I counted on some three or four thousand dollars a year from *Galaxy*, and somewhat more than that amount from all the other markets combined. In the 1950s eight or ten thousand dollars a year was well above the poverty level, and if I hadn't had that thirty-thousand-dollar millstone hanging around my neck, I would have felt pretty prosperous.

Unfortunately the debts did exist. I paid them off as best as I could. In the process new debts developed. I discovered that my local grocer would let me charge. So, a while later, did my friend and down-the-street neighbor, Lester del Rey. Within a year or two we each had four-figure tabs with the poor grocer.* He was *incredibly* good about it. As prosperity seeped back, Lester paid him off and he built a new entrance to his store. A little later I did, too, and he built a new store.

After *The Space Merchants* Cyril and I began a new novel,† and when it got far enough along to show, I turned it over to Horace Gold. Fine, he said, I'll publish it. I'll do more than that. I'll consider it as an entry in the *Galaxy* $7,000 Prize Novel Contest, and I can tell you right now, from looking at the other entries, it's practically a sure thing to win. Only thing is, you have to use a pen name. Why is that? I asked. Because I say so, he explained. But the rules don't say anything about it having to be by a new name, I protested. No, but the purpose of the contest is to discover new talent, and I by-gosh will discover new talent even if I have to find it in *you*, he clarified.

So I went home and talked it over with Cyril, and Cyril shared my view: seven thousand dollars was mighty attractive numbers, but not, when you come right down to it, any more than we would get anyway from serial and book sales, and we liked the book, which meant we wanted to have it under our own names. I told this to Horace, and he accepted defeat gracefully enough; he did serialize it, just as planned, without involving the contest at all.

I do not think I was a good enough person to refrain from telling Horace I had told him so. I had. Prize contests are a *terrible* way to find talent. I do not believe they have ever worked well, and mostly they don't work at all. So it happened with Horace's. As the deadline approached and he read through the hun-

* I would like to pay him honor by mentioning his name. But I did that once, on the air, and he was far from pleased. He said that within forty-eight hours a dozen regular customers began asking for credit, and would I please not *ever* do that again?
† *Gladiator-at-Law*, Bantam Books.

dreds of entries that blocked every doorway in his apartment, it became clear that there was nothing there that was really outstanding, and an awful lot that was preposterously bad.

By then Lester and I had gotten together on a novel about the future of the insurance business, *Preferred Risk*. *Gladiator-at-Law* was already in type, and I offered the new one to Horace. He read it and called me up: Uh, Fred? How about if we make *this* one the winner?

The stipulation was the same: we had to use a brand-new pen name, and everyone concerned was to pretend it was a real person. I talked it over with Lester, who is philosophical about the vagaries of editors. Why not? he said, and we proceeded to cook up a pen name. We divided the labor equally. I chose the first name—"Edson"—and he provided the other—"McCann." And then a few days later he came to me with the look of wild pleasure that serendipitous flakiness always gives Lester and pointed out that the initials E. McC. could equally well be written $e = m c^2$.

All of this was a terribly deep secret. We made up a whole life for this Edson McCann person, celebrated nuclear physicist, so heavily into classified research that he did not dare show his face in public. But the secret was really no secret. Five or six years later, when I went to work for Bob Guinn, *Galaxy*'s publisher, he let me know as gently as he could that he had found out about it long since.

Collaborating is a familiar life-style to me, I've done it with at least a score of writers, some of whom I've never met. But this time was especially tricky. Lester and I do not collaborate well. He has his own very idiosyncratic way of working. While I have, of course, a well-thought-out and admirable set of work habits of my own. The two do not meet at any point, and the whole exercise took twice as long as it should have, with ten times the trouble. Lester and I have been close friends for a very long time. One reason we have stayed so is that, after *Preferred Risk*, we never collaborated again.

Especially not for Horace Gold, who added a whole other dimension of complication to the effort. With *Preferred Risk* the complication was almost entirely in the Byzantine conspiracy of silence. In the work with Cyril Kornbluth it was at every step. Working with two individuals as quirkily brilliant as Horace and Cyril kept me on my toes twenty-four hours a day. Horace *would* edit. He would also come up with suggestions as the work was going along, great gobs of them, some bright and some lunatic. To the maximum extent possible I believe in humoring editors, and so, at Horace's special request, we, for instance, added a couple of chapters to the serial version of *Gravy Planet*, carrying the action of the story onto the surface of the planet Venus. (It was easy enough to drop them out again when we came to publish the story in its book form as *The Space Merchants*.) But when Horace asked for something of the same sort on *Gladiator-at-Law*, I flatly refused. As far as I was concerned, that closed the matter. Cyril and I had a working treaty. After the rough draft of the book was done, he was out of it. I always did the final revisions (except on the last novel we did together, *Wolfbane*), and I always did all the dealing with editors and publishers. But with *Gladiator-at-Law* Horace outwitted me; he got on the phone with Cyril when I wasn't looking, and persuaded him to borrow the setting copy of the manuscript and write in some additional scenes.*

---

* Also dropped from the book version. Working with Cyril, by the way, was one of the most rewarding experiences of my life. If I say comparatively little about it here, it is because I have already said a great deal about it in three other books,

Working with Horace was always a challenge, sometimes delightful and stimulating, sometimes with a lot
of screaming at each other. He personalized the editorial function more than any other person I have
ever known, even John Campbell, who sometimes
seemed ordained by God to sit at a desk and tell people
how to write their stories. With Horace, editing involved every aspect of his personality. Editing was not
only what he did, it was what he was.

Horace was a medium-tallish, mostly baldish, and
slightly plumpish sort of person. He never left his
apartment. He made the world come to him. When
it was unwilling to do so, he pursued it on the phone.
Most of his dealings with writers were telephonic, so
that wherever you were, at whatever time, the phone
might ring. There would be Horace on the other end,
lying on his back on his bed with cigarettes and ashtray at one hand and your manuscript in the other,
ready for as long and complicated a talk as was needful
to get you to do what he wanted.

Horace's phone bills must have been immense, and
so was his determination. He knew what he wanted.

Horace's battle to substitute his own conception of a
story for the writer's caused fury and frustration. But, my
God, the stories he got! Sheckley, Knight, Kornbluth,
Leiber, Bester, Sturgeon, Tenn, and fifty others never
wrote better than when they were writing for Horace
Gold's *Galaxy*. He took mediocre writers and made
them at least momentarily pretty good. He took good
writers and stretched them as far as they would go. He
wasn't always right in what he asked for. Sometimes
he was terribly wrong. That didn't really matter. The
creative synthesis of the dialectic was at work; in the
struggle between Horace-yin and writer-yang something

The Best of C. M. Kornbluth (Ballantine), *Critical Mass* (Bantam), and *Before the Universe* (Bantam).

came out that was better than either could have
achieved alone.

If Horace had a failing as an editor, it was that
when a perfectly good story came along his responses
faltered. He had no way to improve it, and sometimes
he rejected it. He turned down a couple of my best,
I think. He also turned down Jim Blish's A Case of
Conscience and Danny Keyes's Flowers for Algernon
and—well, quite a few good ones. That didn't really
matter, either. While Horace was in swing, Galaxy was
where the action was.

Apart from editorial dealings, of course, we were
friends, Horace and Evelyn and Carol and I. When we
lived nearby we saw each other frequently. When
Carol and I moved to New Jersey, not as often, but
we still kept in touch.

As our lives began to settle down, Carol and I decided that having a child of hers and one of mine
wasn't quite enough, and so we opted for one of ours.
Horace was delighted, called anxiously all through
the pregnancy, and was the first person I phoned when
our son, Frederik Pohl III, was born in the cold
November of 1954.

He was a big, strong, beautiful baby. He came home
from the hospital with a slight cold, or something of
the sort. The pediatrician thought it would clear up
quickly. It didn't. He became seriously ill, and then,
very quickly, he died.

If I could go back and rewrite my life with the
privilege of editing out one experience, that is the one
I would pick to obliterate. Even now I cannot think of
it without rage and pain. Friends tried to console us
with the promise that as time went by we would forget.
They lied. The only thing that happened was that
the pain receded and became bearable. Even that took
a long, long time.

What made the world begin to look promising

again, fifteen months later, was the birth of another son, to whom we gave the name Frederik Pohl IV. Since he is now a man grown, I dare not say what I would like to say about his infancy, because he would have my heart out. But when he came into the house the world brightened. Rick was born in January, 1956. Cyril and I were just finishing a novel called *Presidential Year*. We were into the last chapter when Carol announced that it was time; I took her to the hospital, came back, wrote the final pages of the novel just as the phone rang to announce the birth. I am not so enslaved to writing discipline that I would do that sort of thing as a matter of course. With *Presidential Year* we didn't really have a choice. It was about—well, it was about a Presidential Year, which 1956 was; if we wanted it out in time to do anything, we had to get it to the printer.

In the event, the novel was only a marginal success. It sold a reasonable number of copies, got some friendly reviews, and earned a little movie money. That was it. It is more or less irrelevant to these radically different post-Watergate political days, and so I have to call it at best a passable accomplishment; but the son was a triumph.

Presidential Year was written for Ian's Ballantine Books, as were more than half the books I have written for anyone in my life so far.*

By 1956 Ian had gone through a burst of opening splendor, a fairly catastrophic fallback, and a return to reasonable prosperity. The thing about Ian as a publisher was that he couldn't help seeing the authors'

* I don't really know how many books there are. I used to. I used to write the title and date of every new book on the wall of my office as they came out. Then Carol painted the wall. The total is somewhere around a hundred, give or take half a dozen or so.

side of it. When he started, every paperback company in the United States was paying 4 percent royalty to its authors. Ian decided to pay eight. Every other paperback publisher was sticking pretty close to Westerns, mysteries, and best-seller fiction. Ian chose to let his writers try new things. He was not only a publisher but a friend, and he was something else, too. Ian was my bank. When the well ran dry I would go to Ian and say, "More money, please, sir." And he would give me an advance on some future book, not only not written but not even thought out yet in my head.

For all those reasons Ian Ballantine became my principal publisher and stayed so as long as he was head of the company that bears his name. I am not sure whether this was wise or not. There is a limit to how many books by one writer any publisher can keep in print. If the writer is Joseph Heller, publishing a book every eighteen years or so, that is one thing. If the writer is Isaac Asimov, or Robert Silverberg at his most fertile, emitting books every twenty-eight days as the moon grows full—a little blood and a few days' discomfort, and there's the book—obviously no publisher in the world is going to keep up with him. If the writer is somewhere in between, like me, then the problem is hard to solve. My trouble is that I have monogamous instincts. Flitting from publisher to publisher has always seemed sort of vaguely promiscuous. So I had an adolescent fling with Gnome Press, and an occasional dalliance with Doubleday, and a few one-night stands here and there, but then it was back to hearth, home, and Ballantine Books.

As Ballantine with books, so *Galaxy* with serial rights was my main outlet, but there I was even more often led astray. There were so *many* magazines!

Some were edited by old and good friends, for whom I really wanted to write. When Bob Lowndes's science-fiction magazines at Columbia Publications were shot down by the war, he stayed on as general editor of the pulp group. As science fiction began looking good again, he revived them. Bob is a skilled editor, particularly in dealing with some kinds of writers, and although his rates were seldom competitive with the top of the field, he put together attractive magazines. Larry Shaw, who had briefly been one of my employees during my agency days, became editor of Jim Quinn's magazine *If*, in Kingston, New York. Leo Margulies, once head honcho for *Thrilling Wonder* et al., started a new magazine called *Fantastic Universe*. Out in Chicago, Ray Palmer left *Amazing Stories* to start his own science-fiction magazine. The magazines swelled tall in fairy circles after every rain, thirty-odd separate titles on the stands at one time. Although I was writing a hundred thousand words a year, I couldn't appear in all of them. But I gave it a royal try.

Then, suddenly, it was harvest time. The magazines fell like threshed wheat.

A lot of them, of course, were well ripe for obliteration, put together in a hurry by people who knew nothing of science fiction, printing derivative yard goods and living off the reputations of their better brethren. But some of the good ones fell, too. Bad science fiction hurts good. The in-and-out readers who have not yet developed a major habit don't always distinguish between magazines—or between authors, either—and if the last two or three sf books or magazines they've read have displeased them, it may be a while before they buy any more science fiction at all.

But that was not the major reason for the collapse. What did them all in so massively and fast was the sale of the American News Company.

I think I have to explain what the American News Company was. It was a nationwide distributor. When a publisher brings out a magazine or a line of paperbacks, he does not walk down to your corner news-

stand to put them in the racks. He employs inter-
mediaries for that purpose: a national distributor,
who in turn supplies a large number of local wholesalers, six or eight hundred sizable ones in the United
States.

American News had its own local wholesalers in
every community. They were not a monopoly. There
were a dozen or more other national distributors, collectively called "the Independents." They jointly supplied another complete network of local wholesalers,
so that in every community there were two sources
from which newsdealers got their publications: the
ANC wholesaler, and the wholesaler for the Independents. ANC was big, mighty, and old. It had been
around so long that over the years it had acquired
all sorts of valuable real property. Land. Buildings.
Restaurants. Franchises. Items of considerable cash
value, acquired when time was young and everything
was cheap, and still carried on their books at the pitiful
acquisition costs of 1890 or 1910. A stock operator took
note of all this and observed that if you bought up
all the outstanding stock in ANC (a publicly held
corporation) at prevailing prices, you would have acquired an awful lot of valuable real estate at, really,
only a few cents on the dollar. It was as profitable as
buying dollar bills for fifty cents each. And it was
legal.

So he did. He bought a controlling interest and
liquidated the company.

Now, all this is perfectly legal. It is even common.
It may seem strange that you can buy dollar bills for
fifty cents each in this way, but that's because most
of us still believe in the legends we were taught at
our mothers' knees: Santa Claus, the Tooth Fairy, and
the validity of the pricing mechanisms of the Free
Market. Let's have a short multiple-choice quiz:

Q. What does the price of a share of stock reflect?
I. Its proportionate value of the assets of the corporation?
II. The expectation of future earnings?
III. The growth expectations of the corporation?
IV. The security of the investment?
A. None of the above.

What the price of a share reflects is nothing more or less than the state of mind of the people who buy it.

The New York Stock Exchange is basically a big parimutuel machine which balances off optimism and gloom.* When optimism is high, the price goes up. When optimism goes down, the price does, too. Investors do not *really* know what they are doing, you know. During the excitement of the early days of commercial air transport, thousands of them spent millions of dollars to get in on the ground floor by buying a stock called Seaboard Airways. (It turned out to be a railroad.) And more recently, remember the misery of all the wise old institutional investors who bought gold.

So there was old American News, ripe for the scavenging, and it was scavenged. The operator bought up a controlling interest, sold off everything that could be sold, and liquidated the concern. He made quite a nice couple of capital-gains bucks out of it all, and in the process American News Company ceased to exist.

Oh, the panic, the terror! All the magazines that had been distributed by ANC now had no way to get their next issues on the newsstands!

The publishers came running to the offices of the various Independents, hats in hands, tears in their eyes. Most of them were turned down flat. There was

* See *Gladiator-at-Law*, by Frederik Pohl and C. M. Kornbluth, Bantam Books.

just so much volume that each Independent was capable of handling, and they picked and chose. *Life* and *Time* they were glad to take. But who wanted to bother with some bimonthly pulp about spaceships and monsters? Especially if the publisher was rather inadequately financed and in the habit of hitting up his distributors for advances to pay the printers?

This period in history is referred to by scholars as "the final solution to the sf magazine boom," and, one by one, they went to the gas ovens. Some were spared, of course. The luckiest of the lot was *Galaxy*. Horace Gold had heard rumblings and warned Bob Guinn only a matter of months before that it was time to move. So he had taken his business from ANC to one of the Independents just before the stock shuffle began, and in the panic that followed, Bob could look on with compassion and complacency because he already had his contracts for distribution signed.

But for the others—a score of them, at least—R.I.P. Their like shall not come this way again.

All was not smooth sailing for *Galaxy*, however. It did have a problem. The problem was the health of its editor, H. L. Gold.

Like Cyril Kornbluth and Dirk Wylie, Horace had come out of World War II as a disabled veteran.

For a man officially described as "disabled," Horace was fantastically able. In his dealings with writers, agents, artists, printers, and all the other fauna of the publishing environment, his problems did not slow him down for a second. What he could not accomplish by phone he managed by mail. When letters failed, he persuaded the people he needed to see to come to his apartment in Stuyvesant Town.

It did cost him. There were times when he would have five or six people visiting him at once, and abruptly they would be too many. Horace would retreat to the hall, looking into the room where everyone else was gathered; a part of the conversation, saying everything that needed to be said, but shielded by the doorframe. There were times when anxiety made decision-making unpleasant, then difficult, now and then impossible.

Editing a magazine is no easy spot for a person who second-guesses his decisions. There is a go or no-go decision to be made on every manuscript, a hundred times a week, not to mention all the serial decisions that go into the big ones.

When he could, he would ask writers and other friends for help. Groff Conklin did a great deal to assist; so did Evelyn Gold, Horace's wife. More and more he came to me. He would save up the slush-pile manuscripts until they filled every drawer of a bureau in his bedroom. Then he would ask me to deal with them, and I would take them away, a suitcase-full at a time. What I liked I would return to him with appropriate comments—"Buy this one," "Tell him it needs cutting," "The scene beginning on page nineteen kills the point of the story"—whatever. What I didn't like I stuck a rejection slip on and dropped in the mail.

It is not uncommon for an editor to have someone to do his preliminary reading for him. I've never done it myself, but then I was lucky enough to be able to read fast. In the late 1950s Horace began to go beyond that. At times he asked me to "ghost" the magazine for him: do all the reading, all the buying and bouncing, all the preparation of the magazine for the printer, all the writing of blurbs and house ads and editorials.

None of this was any sweat for me, really. If anything, I looked on the chance to edit a magazine again as a pleasant vacation from the reality of pounding the typewriter for a living.

Between times Horace functioned as always, acerbic, quick, opinionated. He had lost faith with all the

orthodox procedures for dealing with his problems,
and began about then to devise his own therapy. At
least twenty times he offered to share it with me, but
I wanted no part of it. I did not see that I had any
problems that needed psychotherapy at all. (Vanity,
vanity!)

It is my personal opinion that *any* therapy sometimes produces benefits, probably on the analogy of
kicking the Model T to see if it will start itself running. Horace's did—at least temporarily, at least now
and then, at least for some people. One of them was
Horace himself. He made it out of his apartment now,
at first experimentally, late at night; often I would
come by in my car and pick him up, and we would
drive around New York, stopping now and then to
let him get out and walk and stretch his limits. Then
he began to go off on his own, or with others, sometimes for a weekend.

Then, on one of his excursions, he was injured in a
taxi smash.

Together with the other threats to his health, his in-
juries were more than he could stand. He began to
lose weight. Horace is medium height, normally rather
solidly built. A hundred and seventy pounds would be
a good weight for him. He dropped down close to a
hundred. He could not eat. He was in constant pain.
And toward the end of 1960 it became clear that his
life was in danger, and that he was simply too ill to
continue with the magazine, or indeed with any activity not directly aimed at getting him better.

With Horace's approval I went downtown to see
Bob Guinn, the publisher of *Galaxy*, offering to fill in
for Horace on a temporary basis until things clarified
themselves.

Bob hemmed and hawed a little bit. He had had
ten years of an editor who never came into the office,
and if there was going to be any change, he would

have liked it to be in the direction of someone who would be where he could be watched forty hours a week. Well, this is against my religion. I said, as a concession, that I would be willing to come in maybe once a week, at least for part of a day, but that was as far as I could go; Bob mulled it over for a day or two and then called me up to say he agreed.

I stayed with *Galaxy* for just about a decade. The pay was miserable. The work was never-ending. It was the best job I ever had in my life.

10

The Finest Job in the World

In the middle of the 1960s, while I was editor of *Galaxy* and its satellites, I visited one of my writers at his regular place of employment. His name was L. J. Stecher, and what he did for a living was command the United States Navy guided-missile cruiser *Columbus*. The ship was tied up in the North River, a mean-looking low gray shape with threatening projections sticking out all over the deck, and when I came to keep our appointment, the Marine guard advised me to get lost. There were no visitors, and no exceptions. I mentioned tentatively that I had been invited by the captain. The Marine came to a Parris Island brace and said no more as he sped me on my way.

Lew took me around his ship with obvious love and pride. I am no fan of armaments. I would see every navy vessel in the world at the bottom of the Pacific if I had my druthers, except for a few light gunboats to keep the dolphin murderers and whale killers in line. But the *Columbus* was a mighty impressive machine. Those sticky-out things on the decks launched nuclear missiles. Those hooded electric-fan shapes radared the world. The fire-control room was fancier

238

and science-fictiony-er than the bridge of the starship *Enterprise*. From it, in time of battle, Lew could dispose enough muscle for his one ship, all alone, to have reversed the outcome of any sea battle in the history of the world.

We went back to his quarters, past the Marine guard. We were served a modest dinner by his mess orderly and chatted for a while, partly about the stories Lew had been writing for me, mostly about his ship. There were stars in his eyes when he talked about it. He said at last, "You know, I wouldn't change my job for any other job in the world."

I thought for a minute and said, "You know, neither would I."

From 1960 to 1969 I was the editor of *Galaxy* and its companion publications. Being an editor is not everyone's cup of tea. In the plate tectonics of the literary world, the place where the editor sits is right at the crunch. The Creative Integrity plate of the writer subducts under the Money-Market Morality plate of the publisher—or the other way around—and mountain ranges are thrown up, laws carven in granite are squeezed into fiery soup, and the flesh-and-blood creature who lives in the interface needs a lot of agility to keep from being maimed. An editor is a clearing-house for pressures. The printers want their deadlines met. The publisher wants a profit. The writers want— oh, God, what do they not want? An audience. The perfect freedom to say whatever it is they want to say. Cosseting. Coddling. Respect. And money. The agents want money. (And their writers kept off their backs.) The distributors want a product that sells itself. The advertisers want customers. The readers want—well, everything; and no two of them want quite the same everything. The artists, the assistants, the space sales-men, the columnists, the local distributors, the convention committees, the pressure groupies—all of them want something, and there isn't enough of everything to go around, and it is usually the editor who has to grant this and withhold that, steal a day on a printing deadline so an author can finish his third installment, spend a dollar more on a story and take it away from a cover artist, placate a reader who thinks there's too much smut in a story and calm down the writer who thinks too much of the smut has been edited out. I have said that all editors are crazy. Now you know why. The pressures precipitate psychosis, and anyway, nobody but a crazy person would take a job like that in the first place, especially at pitiful money. Which is what most editors of science-fiction magazines get.

But I loved it. I love it still. I have grown accustomed to a lot more solvency as a writer than I ever had from editing *Galaxy*, but if some sweet-talking devil came by tomorrow with an interesting proposition for a new science-fiction magazine, I would find it very hard to say no.

The great thing about being a science-fiction magazine editor, at least for me, is that it does so feed the vanity. I am sorry to have to admit to this character flaw in myself, but there it is. Those who are repelled by the sight of a naked ego will do us all a great favor by skipping the next paragraph, because in it I propose to brag:

In the decade of the 1960s I published a lot of science-fiction stories, by a lot of writers. Among them was nearly every writer of any importance in the field. For many of the best, I published all or most of the work written in that decade: Robert A. Heinlein, Cordwainer Smith, Harlan Ellison, Larry Niven, R. A. Lafferty, Fritz Leiber, Jack Vance, and a lot of others. Many of the stories, including many of the best, would never have been written if I hadn't encouraged,

coaxed, and sometimes browbeaten the authors. And
they were mostly pretty good stories. This is, of course,
my subjective opinion. But I think it's right.*

The man I worked for was Robert Guinn. He was
not really a publisher. He was a printing broker. Publishing was a sideline, operated out of one corner of
his office on Hudson Street, down where the trucks
line up to head for the Holland Tunnel and New
Jersey.

Bob Guinn was an easy person to like. He had a
salesman's professional affability, but he also had innate
intelligence. He did not always use his smarts in ways
that I liked, or his affability, either. What Bob was
really great at was reading a balance sheet, and he
kept perceiving ways in which we could pay a little
less and acquire a little more, all of which it was my
duty to resist. And when I came to him with proposals
for paying a little more and demanding a little less,
his affability took over and he would remember eight
new dirty jokes to tell me. So we tangled from time to
time, now and then with a certain amount of yelling.
But as far as what went into the magazines was concerned, he left me alone to do what I wanted. And
that *was* what I wanted.

All science-fiction magazines had been going through
hard times, partly as the result of the post-American
News comb-out. *Galaxy* was at a low point. It had
been cut back to bimonthly publication a year or two
earlier, and the word rate had been slashed. Once it

---

* There is, of course, no such thing as an objective opinion.
But if you take the Hugo awards as being as close to such a
measure as we've got, then look at Volume Two of Isaac
Asimov's *The Hugo Winners* and count up the numbers which
first appeared in my magazines as compared with those which
first appeared in all other science-fiction magazines combined.
(You can find the provenance in the copyright-acknowledg-
ments page.) The score is *Galaxy et al.* 9, all others 2.

had paid a three-cent minimum, averaging maybe three and a quarter. Now the average was down around a cent and a half. *If*, which Bob Guinn had picked up for small money when its Kingston publisher, James Quinn, got tired of it, had been bimonthly for a long time and was paying even less: flat penny a word, take it or leave it. Even at that, both were barely squeaking by.

I didn't like either word rates or the frequency. The proper publication schedule for a science-fiction magazine is every month, and don't argue with me, because I don't know why I am so sure of it. But I am. As to the word rates, John Campbell was paying *Galaxy's* old prices, three cents per and now and then a little more. I didn't feel I needed to be able to outbid John to get what I wanted, but I did need to be within striking distance. So my first two objectives were to get the rates and frequencies back where they belonged. When I explained this to Bob Guinn, he listened attentively, smiled comprehendingly, told me three quick dirty jokes, and gave me his considered opinion. "Forget it," he said.

If there is one thing I am sure of, it is that there is always a way to do whatever needs doing. All you have to do is find it. So I considered the options. Possibly I could cut the number of pages, and use the savings to pay more to the writers. But there was always the chance that Bob would say, sure, let's cut the pages and *keep* the savings. Besides, I liked having a lot of pages to play with. Or I might cut back on the art budget, or run a long (and free) letter column. Or— inspiration struck. I went over the inventories to see how much we already owned and how much we had paid for it. Horace and I between us, it turned out, had accumulated quite a few low-rate stories. I decided to accumulate some more. I went through all the submitted manuscripts on hand (there was a fair-ish backlog) and found a hundred thousand words or so that I liked reasonably well, without being in love with: the sort of story one is not ashamed to publish, but can face losing without distress. I made the authors low-rate offers on all of these, and most of the offers were accepted. Then I formally announced *Galaxy*'s return to the three-cent minimum, effective at once. By diluting the three-cent material with that handsome reserve of cheaper stuff, I could maintain an average per-issue cost well within the budget and still pay competitive rates for everything new I bought. That would last six issues, I calculated, and by then I would be prepared to fight it out with Bob for a budget increase.

What I wanted was to get first look at most of the uncommitted new material by the pros. In the long run I wanted more than that. I wanted first look at most of the amateur stuff, too, and I also wanted to loosen some of the pros' commitments to *Analog*, *F&SF*, and all, but I had other, slower-acting strategies in mind for those efforts.

The money was only Step One in the campaign. Speed of reporting was almost as important, and so I made my first order of business every week to read and respond to the incoming manuscripts, not only the professional submissions but the slush pile as well. It was easy to beat out the competition in that arena. John Campbell ordinarily took a month or more to report. Horace had sometimes been far slower than that. Most of the other magazines had a two-tier system, preliminary reader and then editor; I did all my own reading, and I did it fast, and for at least ninety-five percent of the manuscripts either a buy or a bounce was on its way within forty-eight hours of the time I first saw the script. Of course, most were bounces. I trained my secretaries and assistants, when I had any, to open all incoming manuscripts, put a rejection slip

on each one, and put it in an envelope stamped and
addressed to go back to the writer. In the event I
bought the story, that effort was wasted. But that only
happened to one manuscript in twenty or fewer; and
for all the others I could read them in the train on my
way home to Red Bank and drop them off in the mail-
box at the station when I arrived.

Of course, there was more to it than that, but just
that much gave me a crack at more than half the
stories I wanted. Nothing works perfectly. Some good
stories slipped through my net. When they were good
enough to make me covetous, I tried to let the author,
or his agent, know how I felt, hoping that the next
one would come my way.

Once or twice I lost out on a story I really had every
right to expect, and that was painful. Cordwainer
Smith was one of my favorite writers. He was also a
recluse, who didn't want too much contact with the
science-fiction world, but we had become friends and
he had voluntarily promised to give me first look at
everything he wrote. Unfortunately, he had taken on
an agent. The agent was willing to live by Paul's *
commitments, but he also had certain standard rules
of procedure. One was that he never under any circumstances submitted two stories by the same writer
to an editor at one time. When Paul happened to
finish two scripts on the same day and sent them off
to the agent in the same envelope, the agent sent me
the one he liked best and mailed the other off to
Fantasy and Science Fiction. By the time I found out
about it, they had already accepted it, which is why I

---

* "Paul" because his real name, of course, was Paul M. A.
Linebarger. Until his death he was a professor of political science at Johns Hopkins University and a frequent consultant on
sensitive Far East matters for the State Department—one reason
for his keeping his real identity secret.

didn't get to publish "On Alpha-Ralpha Boulevard"; but I then persuaded that agent to change that rule.

It was *Galaxy* that I was trying to make the leader in the field again. *If* was only a stepsister, but I had a good use for it. Most writers are in-and-outers, something good and then a few that are not so good. The best ones I wanted for *Galaxy*. The others I didn't. It's hard to deal with that sort of writer when you have only one magazine. You can't publish everything without sacrificing overall quality. But you know perfectly well (assuming the author is as good as you think he is) that someone else will publish the ones you turn down. There is always the risk that the suitor who soothes his feelings by buying the one you bounced will win him away with the next good one, too. *If*, with its lower rate, gave me a perfect dumping ground for the stories I didn't want to print in *Galaxy* but didn't want anyone else to have, either. *If* was also a good place to try out new talent.

There were, at least in my head, significant policy differences between the two magazines. Good gray *Galaxy* was the class leader. It paid a lot more for what it published, and took a lot more planning and care. *Galaxy* was edited for the mature, sophisticated science-fiction reader. If you could read only one magazine in the field but wanted to be *au courant parfaitement*, *Galaxy* was the magazine to read.

If was for the younger reader, and the newer, and the less involved. Editing *If* was almost recreational. If I had a whim not solid enough to call an inspiration, I tried it in *If*. In terms of literary quality and significance, I have no doubt that *Galaxy* was a better magazine than *If*, but *If* was a lot easier to turn around. It was cheaper to produce. Its budget was lower. It had less of a distinguished history for the readers to compare the current product against. I was able to make *If* show a profit long before *Galaxy* did.

And it was *If* that caught the fancy of the readers. What was fun for me seemed to be fun for them. Or maybe it was for another reason.

Early on I was sitting with another editor at a world convention banquet when Hugo time came around. He picked up the best-editor trophy. I was as generously congratulatory as my mean little envious spirit would allow. He mumbled something, glowered at his coffee cup for a while, and then leaned over and whispered in my ear: "You know, considering how little I've done on the magazine the past couple of years, it begins to look like the less I do the better the readers like it." It was almost the same with me. I never won a Hugo for *Galaxy*, but I won three in a row for its little stepsister, *If*.

By the time my stores of cheap stories were running low, the magazines were showing signs of returning financial health. I hit Bob up for a budget increase. He smiled and tousled my hair and told me six dirty jokes. I came back to it the next week, and the week after, and when he had used up all the dirty jokes he knew, he gave in. Sweet Old Bob! I always called him that. Or sometimes just the initials.

The next step was to make the magazines monthly, and that was a whole nother story. Alarmed by the fact that he had lost the battle of the budget, Bob summoned up reinforcements.

The thing about Bob Guinn was that he knew he wasn't a publisher, and so he decided to hire a publisher to do the job for him. Now, this will seem strange to many writers and editors. *What* job? they will ask. What is it that a publisher *does* do?

I can understand this confusion, because I have worked for and with a lot of publishers in my day, and I am still not sure exactly what it is that some of them were doing. One used to lock himself in his 16′ × 28′

office every morning and read comics. Another spent
his first year of incumbency in taking every single em-
ployee off the job he was doing and putting him on
some other job, so that no one in the office but he
would know exactly what was going on. Another spent
his time padding down the office corridors and peering
in at each desk to make sure the person was sitting
there. Another was hired, I think, mostly to yell. There
are some great creative publishers in the world—Oscar
Dystel and Ian Ballantine are the two I see the most
of—but there are also hell's own herd of turkeys.

Nevertheless, there are certain publishing functions
which have to be done. They aren't fun or glamor
things, but they make an immense difference to the
success of a publication. In large corporations they are
divided among a multitude of departments, and the
publisher's main function is as a sort of KP-pusher,
making sure that everybody does his job and knocking
heads together when needed. Galaxy Publishing Corporation was nothing like that. The editorial, promotion, publicity, and advertising departments were combined into one person, me. That left out a lot of
nitty-gritty, mostly production and distribution. Production is a matter of seeing that type is set and paper
is on hand and copies are printed and bound. That
was Bob's area of special expertise as a printing broker,
anyway, so there was no problem in leaving that to
him. Distribution is concerned with keeping the national distributor on his toes, checking his draw-and-
return figures to see that copies of the publication are
going more or less where they might be bought instead
of to six all-night delicatessens in LaPorte, Indiana.
Bob was less good at that, but even so, better than I
was.

Dealing with distributors is not the most fun there
is. The standards of the trade are higher now than
they used to be, but there was a time when your

average local wholesaler had got most of his training in the newspaper circulation business, in the days when the standard ploy for bettering your sales was to tip over the other fellow's delivery trucks. One national distributor of a few years ago was run by a troika. Two of them had served time in prison, and the other had got his start peddling pirated song sheets. I took a couple of local wholesalers to a science-fiction convention once and showed them the costume ball. One femme fan had a lovely butterfly costume, weeks of painful sewing and a lot of creative thought; the two wholesalers showed their first signs of interest when she came by. One said, "Hey, I like that," and the other said, "Me, too. Will she fuck?"

Bob was not too rarefied a soul to be exposed to such crudities, but even he came back from some excursions into distribution with horror on his face. There was a large newsstand near his summer home; it sold six or eight hundred copies of *The New York Times* every Sunday . . . and two copies of *Galaxy* every month. Bob suggested to the dealer that he ask for more. The dealer said he had, dozens of times. The two copies he did get he kept under the counter for regular customers, and he was sure he could sell plenty more. But the distributors would not be bothered. So Bob took fifty copies out of the warehouse and put them in the back of the car, and the dealer put them on his shelves. And forty-six of them sold. And so Bob went triumphantly to the wholesaler and said, "See? Why don't you ship them fifty copies every issue now?" And the distributor said (paraphrasing out some of the more colorful parts), "Why, no, Mr. Guinn, I wouldn't care to do that, and because of that dealer's presumption we won't ship him any copies of *Galaxy* at all any more."

Well. That was a while ago, and the elder statesmen of the distribution business have now largely retired to their villas outside Palermo. The new generation is a lot easier to get along with. But still it is no job for an amateur.

So when Bob proposed to employ a professional publisher, I was all for it. In due course into the office came Sol Cohen, former VP at Avon Books, recently retired with enough capital-gains on his stock participation to be in little need of employment, but not ready to quit working entirely.

I spent a lot of time with Sol over the next couple of years. He has strengths and weaknesses. In the right place he would be a valuable natural resource for a publishing company. I don't think Galaxy was the right place. The size of the numbers involved was an order of magnitude smaller than he was used to. His experience was with paperback books, rather than with magazines. And he had much too much interest in the editorial aspects of the business to suit me. We had that out early. After a few tentative engagements he never interfered with my editorial decisions on the magazines but took out his ambitions on side ventures: a series of anthologies for a small paperback house; a book-magazine hybrid of our own called "Magabook," which struggled through a couple of issues but never really got off the ground. What he did do was spend a lot of time with the distributor, which I welcomed a lot. What I welcomed less was that on any major changes of policy I now had two people to convince instead of one.

My big remaining ambition was to make both *Galaxy* and *If* monthly. I had totally failed to persuade one person. Confronting two was disheartening. But I wanted it too much to accept defeat. While both magazines were in the red I could see that it wasn't a good idea to lose twice as much by bringing one of them out twice as often. But then, when *If* struggled its way into the black, I announced that it was now time to switch it over to a monthly schedule. "Oh, really?" said Bob, and "That's a big step, Fred," said Sol; and the two of them went off and conferred. They came back with the decision that it wasn't a good idea to mess with a profitable proposition by making a change in frequency, either. Oh, shit, I said, look! If you don't want to go monthly when it's losing *because* it's losing, and don't want to go monthly when it's making *because* it's making, then when, pray, is the time when one *does* go monthly? They admitted that was a good question. They talked it over for another eternity or two and then, reluctantly, agreed to roll the dice for an experimental period. We'll make *If* monthly for six months, they said. No promises beyond that! If it's doing all right at the end of the six months, we'll keep it up. If not, back to bimonthly and no more arguments. Fine, said I, my heart singing.

That meeting took place in the afternoon of the last Thursday in August of 1962. I know the date well, because the next day I was to leave for the World Science Fiction Convention in Chicago. In fact, that was why I had pressed the issue at that time. What I was trying to do was to generate and maintain momentum. I had bumped the rates, improved relations with a lot of writers, got some talk going, acquired some significant stories. The next thing I wanted was to be able to tell that convention that *If* was going to be monthly again. Happy as I knew how to be, I went home and packed, collected Carol, caught a plane, and arrived in Chicago to find a telegram waiting at the hotel:

ON NO ACCOUNT MENTION POSSIBLE
MONTHLY SCHEDULE FOR IF PENDING
FINAL DECISION.
                             SOL

"Possible" monthly publication? I got on the phone. But by then, of course, it was Labor Day weekend. I couldn't reach either Sol or Bob to ask them what the hell they thought they were playing at. When the convention was over and I was back in New York, I found out: they had got to thinking after I left. And they had chickened out.

I've said that Bob and I got along well most of the time, barring occasional yelling. That was one of the times for yelling.

Although I had been talking about it for months, I think they had never really perceived how important it was to me. They thought it over for a while and then decided to placate me. Look, said Bob (or Sol), we're just scared to make a move with either *If* or *Galaxy*. We're sorry we are, but we are. But if you're all that ape-shit for a monthly magazine, we'll tell you what we'll do. We'll start a third magazine for you. We'll make that one monthly.

That took me aback. The last thing I wanted right then was another magazine. It seems to me that a magazine, any magazine, is or at least ought to be a living creature. It should have a personality and an identity of its own. Not part of a litter; an individual. I was a long way from attaining that with either of the two magazines I already had.

On the other hand, my bluff was called. It was an offer I could not turn down. I figured, fuzzily enough, that maybe I could start the new one and make it work as a monthly, then merge it with, say, *If*. I would insist on maintaining the monthly schedule with the new composite, I dreamed; and then, when that had been shown to work, it would be easy enough to get *Galaxy* back up there, too. . . .

So I accepted the deal and got to work. We picked out a title: *Worlds of Tomorrow*. We designed a logo.

I bought the stories. We signed a distribution contract. We sent the first issue off to the printer. . . .

By then I was beginning to see flaws in my rosy reasoning. Suppose it *did* work as a monthly. I had had no luck at all in getting Bob and Sol to change the frequency of *If* or *Galaxy*. Just what would be my chances of getting them to *kill* a moneymaker in order to merge it with another book?

But in the long run it didn't matter. The problem never came up. By the time *Worlds of Tomorrow* came out, Bob and Sol had had another failure of nerve. The test project designed to establish the potential of monthly publication, too, was a bimonthly.*

Worlds of Tomorrow lasted several years, and even published some pretty good stories that I might not have been able to get into either *If* or *Galaxy*. In order to distinguish it from the rest of the herd, I had decided to feature long, complete-in-one-issue seminovels, and there were some fine ones by Gordon R. Dickson, Philip K. Dick, and others. But I had also decided to try to include some material on extrapolative science— not exactly fact, but not exactly science fiction, either. They were, I thought, among the best things in the magazine. We had a series on future weaponry written by someone who knew the subject so well that he could not use his own name. And we had freezing.

Shortly after the magazine was born, I found in the slush pile something that was not exactly a manuscript. It was a privately printed, spiral-bound book called *The Prospect of Immortality*, by someone called Robert C. W. Ettinger.

One of the interesting fringe benefits of a career in

---

* I did, finally, get both magazines on a monthly schedule, but not for a few more years. It made little difference one way or another to the sales.

science fiction is that one gets to hear from a lot of geniuses, and from a lot of nuts. It is not always easy to tell at first encounter which is which. I looked at the book without much enthusiasm. Then, as I began to read it, Ettinger began to come through as a person who had had a wild idea that might—that just possibly *might*—really work.

The argument of the book was easy enough to follow:

If you wanted to live forever, there was at least a reasonable hope that the technology to make that possible was already at hand. By following certain simple directions, you might never die—or, more accurately, if you did die now and then, it needn't be fatal.

How was this to be achieved?

By means of the deepfreeze, said Ettinger. Go ahead and live your life. Die when you have to. Then, at the moment of death, have your body popped into a freezer. A *cold* freezer, around the temperature of liquid nitrogen, maybe even liquid helium. You could keep an organic substance—including your very dear own personal body—at liquid-gas temperatures without essential change for a long time. No physical change. No chemical change. No chemical processes taking place at all, except for a little free-radical activity, glacially slow and not to be worried about. There might be a touch of radiation damage from prolonged exposure to cosmic rays—but not quickly. Not for days, weeks, months, or centuries. Perhaps not even for millions of years.

And this, said Ettinger, was not theory, it was scientific fact.

That was one of the two bases his plan rested on. The other was not exactly a fact, but it certainly seemed at least a good gambling bet. That was that medical science would continue to learn. Sooner or later, Ettinger said, doctors would know how to do three things at present difficult or impossible: (1) how to cure or repair whatever damage had killed you in the first place; (2) how to repair whatever additional damage had been done to your body by the freezing process itself—mostly cellular damage from the phase-change of water to ice; (3) how to start you up again (as we now are able to start up again people who through drowning or electroshock or heart arrest would once have been buried instead). All this might take some time, he conceded. But dreaming away in the deepfreeze, time was what you had plenty of.

Was this science fiction or a real hope? Did it mean that some real person now in the agony of terminal cancer could really have some expectation, however slim, of living once more in health and comfort?

I was no authority on any of these subjects. I am no real authority on most subjects, for that matter; but the nature of an editorial job is that ignorance is no excuse. Whether you know enough to make a decision or not, you still have to make the decision. And I was impressed by the amount of homework Ettinger had done. He had calculated the replenishment rate for liquid nitrogen as it bubbled off the cooling jacket around the corpsicles and had looked up the market price for LN2. The idea was science fiction. In fact, I had read it in a story by Neil R. Jones back in the early 1930s.* But Ettinger had put numbers into it. He had gone beyond that. He had considered the religious, moral, political, and ecological consequences of what he proposed, and found the arguments for all of them. His own credentials were satisfying. He was on the physics faculty of a respectable university; and in every case where I knew enough to decide whether a statement of his was true or false, it was true.

* "The Jameson Satellite." It turned out little Bobby Ettinger had read the same story at around the same time.

None of that proved that freezing would work. But it was not to be dismissed as a crackpot pipe dream. So I made arrangements to publish an extract from his book, and it appeared in *Worlds of Tomorrow*.

When I finally had the printed issue in my hand, I perceived, a little belatedly, that here at last was a chance to do what I had always wanted to do: to use the electronic media to publicize science fiction.

By then I had become fairly accustomed to microphones and cameras. In particular, I had become a regular on the all-night radio talkathons run by Long John Nebel in New York City.

Long John was (and is) the king of nighttime radio. He is a legend in his own right, professional photographer and roadside auctioneer turned radio personality, with a slavishly devoted audience of all-night short-order cooks, nurses, night watchmen, students, and insomniacs. First to last, I've done the Long John show maybe four hundred times. And maybe four hundred times I've asked myself what I was doing there.

One reason, I guess I have to admit, is that I seem to have a fondness for the sound of my own voice. Another reason is Long John himself, marvelous quirky man that he is. Most of all, it is because I have met a great many interesting people in Long John's studios: scientists, writers, politicians, flying-saucer nuts (and also, I add at once, UFO experts who are not at all nutty); that human killing-machine, Roy Cohn; the late H. L. Hunt, roly-poly right-wing Santa Claus who called himself "the richest Gentile in the world"; * Gene Leonard, the cybernetics-systems genius who single-handedly caused New York City's worst news-

---

* I thought his political notions were pathetic when they weren't despicable, but I must say that I thought H. L. Hunt himself was rather sweet. We had coffee together. Guess who picked up the check. I'll give you a hint: it wasn't the richest Gentile in the world.

paper strike by automating the composing room of
The New York Times; Mel Torme, the great old
"Velvet Fog" himself; admired comedians like Phil
Foster and Victor Borge—well, for four hundred shows
I imagine I could think of four hundred names. Some
have become good friends, and one or two I will consider myself very fortunate if I never see again. Collectively it was like an immense, never-ending cocktail party. I've appeared on several hundred radio and
TV shows in perhaps twenty countries, but the one I
keep coming back to is Long John. If I'm not on it
for more than a month or so, I get withdrawal symp-
toms.*

What I did *not* do all those Long Johns for was to
sell my books.

I may have had some such notion in the beginning,
but I learned better. I'm not sure that it's possible at
all to promote science fiction by radio or TV exposure.
The electronic audience is too broad-based and, forgive
me, too ignorant. Ignorant of what science fiction is all
about. I don't mean to put the mundanes down, but
science fiction is a special taste. Most people who don't
read it anyway are not going to be moved to do so by
hearing me chatter between midnight and six A.M.

But freezing—ah, that was something else! That was
the *exact* kind of thing that one could promote on
radio and TV, and Long John had exactly the right
program to do it on.

I was in a peak period with Long John at the time,
doing the show at least once a week and sometimes
three or four times. When I mentioned Ettinger's idea
to John, he jumped at it. We scheduled a show right
away, and the response was immense. The phones at
the Galaxy Publishing Corporation office began ringing as soon as the doors were open, listeners who

* As this book was in proof Long John died of cancer. For
millions of listeners, the night air will be bleaker.

wanted to know where they could buy the article we had been talking about. We did a repeat show, and then another, and then got Ettinger himself on the air for one of them. By phone. John had no budget for flying guests in from Michigan, and neither did I. I took the show on the road, to other radio and TV shows in New York. A year or so later I wrote a lead *Playboy* article about life prolongation in general, and *Playboy*'s fantastically competent public-relations person of the time, Tania Grossinger, booked me onto every radio and TV show I had ever heard of, and some I hadn't, from Johnny Carson on down. And on all of them I talked about Ettinger's freezing program. After I had done this maybe fifty times, it began to enter my slow, tiny mind that maybe Bob Ettinger would feel a little resentment at somebody else's taking his very own idea and running around the country with it. He came to New York around then and we had dinner.* I waited for a suitable moment and then asked him if he, well, minded my talking so much about his brainchild. Bob smiled his slow, gentle smile and said, "Not a bit. You see, I'm very selfish. I want to be an immortal superman. In order to make that possible, it has to be possible for everybody else to be one, too, and any way that happens is all right with me." So the Chautauqua went on. It didn't do an awful lot for *Worlds of Tomorrow*. That one first issue had a hell of a sale, but little of it carried over to any other issue. It did, I think, do something for the freezing program.

Because of all this, a lot of people I meet seem to think that I am one of the elect. I'm not. It isn't that I don't believe it might work. I thought the chances

* His uncle joined us for dinner. This is not the sort of thing that I usually think worth mentioning, but Bob Ettinger's uncle is Peewee Russell, who just happens to be maybe the greatest jazz clarinetist who ever lived.

reasonably good when the whole notion was only a gleam in Bob Ettinger's eye. Now there is a lot more substance for the opinion. There are freezing organizations in half a dozen countries. They publish journals. They conduct research. They've even frozen eighteen or twenty real people who are now lying in their big thermos bottles with the liquid N2 percolating around them,* waiting for that great thawing-out day. There are thousands of card-carrying immortals in the United States alone. The cards are real. They look like Medic-Alert IDs, and they say:

NOTICE!
If you find me dead, *immediately* pack me in dry ice and call the number below. On no account autopsy, embalm, fold, spindle, or mutilate me.

Or words to that effect. To be sure, nobody has yet been defrosted. And yet I still think it's a good enough gambling bet, viewed as a sort of Pascal's Wager. As Ettinger says, the worst that can happen is that it won't work, in which case you are no deader than you would have been anyway.

The reasons I have for not signing up to be an immortal superman are philosophical and economic. Philosophical: what makes my life desirable to me is the network of relationships and the endless iterative series of projects that I am always involved in. Stop them and restart them at some future time, and they are no longer the same. Economic: freezing *costs*. I estimated when I first heard of it that it would take easily fifty thousand dollars cold cash to make and protect a corpsicle. Now I would put it a lot higher. So buying the chance of a future postfreeze life costs

---

* If you are astute enough to have noticed that I said "helium" earlier, you can also probably figure out that the reason for the change to nitrogen was financial.

some sacrifice in this one; and it seems to me that I'm more interested in the quality of my life than in the quantity of it.

As I indicated a while back, Bob Ettinger was not the only person to turn up in my life with something to say that he wanted the whole world to hear. They come in all shapes and sizes. Some are obvious crackpots. With some it's hard to tell. You never know. Maybe this year's Newton or Faraday is sitting in your waiting room, dabbing Clearacil on his chin. I have had at least five visitors and correspondents who had worked out the long-sought replacement for Einstein's Unified Field Theory, a dozen who have solved all the secrets of the mind, twenty with new religious revelations, and God's own horde of flying-saucer people. Some I can dismiss pretty easily. If they speak in koans and giggle at the doorknob, I just don't listen, especially if they tell me they know someone who can read minds, or bend keys, or foretell the future. It isn't that I am certain none of this is possible. Au contraire. I hope; and I wish with all my heart that it were real. But all the evidence for ESP, any kind of ESP, is terrible. It isn't just that it is bad, it is evidence of that special kind, like the evidence for Laetrile or for the existence of God, which is utterly conclusive to people who are already convinced, and not worth examining to people who aren't. As far as I know (which is far), there has never been a test of ESP ability conducted under conditions of enough rigor to eliminate the chance of cheating. Most of the great psychics have been caught faking. Most of the serious researchers, however bright and honorable, have shown themselves pitifully gullible. I'd *love* to believe in ESP, but the frauds and the dupes won't let me.

In this arrogant, hard-nosed skepticism, which has won me many enemies, I am aided and abetted by my friend and neighbor, The Amazing Randi, who is even more hostile to the whole paranormal performance than I am. Randi has a standing offer to me to duplicate any "psychic" feat I can describe, under the same conditions as it was done by the alleged psychic. He has made good on it so many times, that I no longer bother to test him out. He has even taught me how to do some of the simpler routines, including the Uri Geller metal-bending event (with which I dazzled Arthur Clarke first time out), the Moscow-Leningrad Ladies' Paranormal Tube-Spinning Feat (that takes a little more skill, but sometimes I can make it work), and the jazziest demonstration of infallible mind reading I have ever seen, so good that I hate even to talk about it. If I ever find myself weakening and beginning to believe in ESP, all I have to do is call Randi up, and at any hour of the day or night he will come over and talk to me until I am through the crisis. And yet—

And yet, well, look, folks. There is still that little part of the inside of my mind that *wants* to believe in ESP. And it is not entirely unsupported by my observation of the world. I have as many anecdotal experiences of ESP as anyone else. I can clearly remember a number of occasions when I *knew* what the next card in a deck was going to be. (But there were also a lot of occasions when I knew it just as well, but was wrong.) I have called friends to have them say they had just been thinking of me; burst into song at exactly the same moment as a companion burst into the same song; had a flash of inspiration that told me where to find a lost object. A few years ago, in Barletta, Italy, my wife and I were walking aimlessly about, and I mentioned to her that when I had been there last, twenty-odd years before, I had had a friend who lived in an interesting apartment on a courtyard. What kind of a courtyard? she asked. Well, I said, a lot like *that*

one. And it turned out to be the very house. I can
multiply anecdotes as long and as tediously as you
can, whoever you are. But anecdotal evidence isn't any
kind of proof. As the French say, even a broken clock
is right twice a day.

But then there's the case of the ESP teaching machine.

In 1972 I was invited to a National Aeronautics and
Space Administration Seminar on Speculative Technology. It was a great weekend, one of the most exciting I've ever spent. A physicist from Stanford Research
Institute named Russell Targ turned up with what he
called an ESP teaching machine.

That was not the only attraction of the weekend;
in fact, it was only a little extra helping of dessert to a
marvelously stimulating meal. But I was taken with
the machine. It was about the size of a bedside clock
radio. The front of it displayed four colored slides,
with lights behind them. Under each slide was a button. Inside the machine was a random-number genera-
tor, on the basis of which the machine would decide in
advance which slide it was going to light up.

What one did with the machine was to try to guess
which slide that was going to be. Having made your
guess, you pushed the button for the slide you expected. Then the machine lit up the slide it had decided on. Sometimes it would be yours, of course. More
probably it would not. You only had one chance in
four of guessing correctly.

At the top of the machine a counter registered how
many times you had guessed, and how many of those
times you had been right. It was set to record a run of
twenty-four trials—in which, of course, chance expec-
tancy was that you would get six right. If you did get
six, or five, or seven, that was all that happened. If you
got substantially more (or less) than chance, the ma-

chine would light up a panel saying "significant to one standard deviation," "to two standard deviations," etc.*

It was a fun machine.

I played with it a lot—when I could get it away from the fifty other invited attendees at the seminar, Arthur Clarke and Marvin Minsky, Wernher von Braun and Krafft Ehricke, Bob Forward and Ed Mitchell. The first run I tried was significant to two standard deviations! Wow! My second run was a little on the low side. My third was lower still. I didn't really keep a careful count, but actually after about ten runs the pluses and minuses pretty much evened out, so that there was no significant indication of anything happening one way or another.

All that is true, but in the interest of accurate reporting I must record one additional datum.

I am not *sure* nothing significant happened, because over the several hundred trials there were a few cases, maybe fifteen or twenty in all, when what I did was a little different from all the other cases. In those cases I observed myself reaching out to press one button, drawing my finger back, and then pressing another. I don't mean that I just hesitated, or pushed a button I didn't intend. I mean my finger actually touched one, and then ultimately pressed another. And on those few trials, under those circumstances, I wasn't right just the chance twenty-five percent of the time, I was right more than half the time.

Does that prove anything?

No, not even to me. It is more anecdotage. I didn't keep a count, my impressions are subjective and, anyway, there simply were not enough trials to mean anything. But I sure would like to borrow that machine for a week or two and try it all over again, with an

---

* There is a more complete description of a slightly different form of the machine in Martin Gardner's column in *Scientific American*. Martin was not as impressed by it as I was.

objective observer to record what was going on and a
careful tally of results.

That sort of approach to ESP is fun. What is a lot
less fun is having someone tell me about the strange
experience his uncle had in Palo Alto, California (I
just won't listen), and what is hardly any fun at all is
having someone tell me about his own experience
when it is apparent that there is something going on
beyond the objective interest in ESP. A majority of
ESP proponents make me feel acutely uncomfortable.
Some are plainly and offensively out to hoodwink me
and the world. Some have hoodwinked themselves. A
lot are just pathetic. One of the unhappiest hours I
ever spent was with one of the pathetic ones, a nice-
looking, middle-aged lady who came to the *Galaxy*
offices one day with a tale of woe.

It seemed she was being victimized by a ring of
telepaths in Short Hills, New Jersey. The telepaths
were all young and male. Some of them were black.
They were listening in on all of her most secret
thoughts, especially sexual ones. They were spying on
her every hour of the day and night, and she could
feel them ridiculing her and treating her with contempt. It was hard for her to discuss the worst parts
of it with me, a strange male, because she was too well
brought up to say the specific things easily. But obviously she was in serious torment of the soul.

I really did not know what to do with her. I tried
to suggest that she might be imagining the whole
thing. Oh, no! She was certain it was all real. I hinted
that she might find it useful to talk to a doctor. The
doctors hadn't been able to do a thing for her. She
was at her wit's end. After an hour or so of her gentle
weeping, I found a solution—not to her problem, just
to mine.

I said, yes, thinking it over, she had actually made
a wise decision in coming to the editor of a science-

fiction magazine to tell her problem to. The only mistake she had made was in choosing the wrong editor. And I sent her up to John Campbell's office.

Having alienated maybe a third of potential friends by saying that I don't think the evidence for ESP is any good, I think it is now my obligation to alienate another third by saying that I think the evidence for flying saucers is even worse.

I have to admit that my early exposure to flying-saucer people was not, on the whole, the kind that conduces to reasoned investigation. Most of them I met on the Long John show. John made his reputation with them in the early days, people who claimed the saucer folk had flown them from the White Sands Proving Ground to lower Yonkers and back, people who had been given the ultimate secrets of the universe to pass on to the rest of us. ("Love thy neighbor and eat lots of yogurt.") I hate myself when I attach pejorative labels to any group of human beings. So it is hard for me to say that all those early saucerers were either nuts or con men. But that was the way to bet it.

And one time on Long John's show, just before we went off the air, I said so.

Before I was out of the studio the phone was ringing. It was from a man named George Earley, Connecticut State Chairman for the National Investigating Committee on Aerial Phenomena. "See here," said George, "NICAP has in its files thousands of reported UFO sightings. Have you investigated them all? Come to that, have you investigated any of them? Or are you just taking the word of such notorious saucer skeptics as Willy Ley and Lester del Rey?"

Well, he had me fair and square. I had to admit it. I had never for one minute believed that any of the flying-saucer reports were really related to visitors from another planet, and I had not bothered to check any

of them out, or even, really, to think about them much.
It is an interesting fact that almost all science-fiction
writers are UFO skeptics. They always have been.
Even John Campbell, who was perfectly capable of
swallowing astrology, dianetics, and the Dean Drive,
gagged on the saucer people. I think I know why. You
cannot spend a large fraction of your life reading and
writing about life on other planets without absorbing
the notion that (as Einstein put it *) "the universe is
not only stranger than we know, it is stranger than we
can know." Stories like Kenneth Arnold's "disks that
moved with a saucerlike motion," the contactees' pale,
somber humanoids in Grecian togas, machines that
stop car motors—they aren't too fantastic for science-
fiction people to believe in; they aren't fantastic
enough. A diet of ionized intelligences from the electri-
fied planets of Betelgeuse immunizes you against little
green men with red eyes.

The other thing that has turned so many of us
against the UFO reports is that so many of them are
pathetic and palpable frauds. But that's not important,
George Earley responded to that. There can be a million frauds. But if there is one true, indisputable account of a visitation from another planet, that is the
most significant event in human history, and it out-
weighs all the frauds a millionfold. And that is true
enough; and before I got off the phone, I promised
George that I would either look into the matter seriously or keep my mouth shut.

So for two or three years, as time permitted, I looked
into the flying-saucer world. I read all the recommended
books. I went to UFOlogists' meetings. I interviewed
celebrated contactees. I even visited the scenes of
some of the most famous sightings to glean what
wisdom I could from the physical surroundings.

---

* Ben Bova says it was J. B. S. Haldane.

Since I put in so much time on it, I would like to salvage something from the effort and tell you at some length about the flakes and frauds I met along the way. But I don't think it would interest you. It doesn't even interest me. There were a lot who were just not able to distinguish between fact and fantasy, and another lot whose dull lives had suddenly been brightened by the attention they got from claiming to have met aliens. There were also a few who were making a solid buck by preaching to the gullible, and I liked them least of all.

And then there were the ones who were simply uncritical, and maybe a little ill-informed: a lady at a cocktail party who said, gosh, she'd seen plenty of UFOs in her time; there were quite a lot of them, flashing red and green lights, almost every night, over near where the helicopters landed. ("You mean you saw flashing red and green lights over near where the helicopters land and you call them *Unidentified* Flying Objects?") And there was the New Mexico state cop in Socorro, showing Jack Williamson and me around the site where his colleague, Lonnie Zamorra, had had a famous sighting just a short time before. He also had seen UFOs, he said proudly, pointing off past the drive-in theater in the general direction of White Sands Proving Ground. He had seen one just the night before. It started out as a fairly bright yellowish light, zigzagged around the sky, growing dimmer and oranger, and finally disappeared. Jack and I looked at each other. As former Air Force weathermen, we had launched enough pilot balloons to recognize the description at once.

I must not give the impression that every UFO person I met was wicked or dumb, or even careless. George Earley is not at all like that. Neither was the aforementioned Lonnie Zamorra. I didn't ever meet him face to face, but I spoke to him by phone, talked to his colleagues on the police force and people in the town, and I have to say he has the best testimonials to his honesty of anyone I can think of. ("Lonnie could be wrong, but he'd *never* make anything up.")

Barney and Betty Hill, the famous "interrupted journey" couple from New England, were not only decent and respectable people but, in the short time I spent with them, made me think of them as friends.

I believe that Lonnie Zamorra saw something; I just don't think it was an alien spacecraft. The late Dr. Donald Menzel thought it might have been a dust devil, which fits the facts at least as well as an alien spacecraft does. With the Hills, the story is a little more complicated. As it is reported, they were taken from their car one night, hypnotized, introduced to aliens in a spaceship, commanded to forget the whole experience, and returned to their car. Obediently, they had no conscious recollection of any of this. Then, much later, Barney had occasion to visit a shrink, who put him under hypnosis for other reasons, and the whole story came out. (And was confirmed by Betty, also under hypnosis.) What Barney said to me was that he was sure *something* had happened that night, but he was not entirely sure whether it happened in objective reality or only in their minds. And if he wasn't sure, how can any of the rest of us be?

The Hills offered me a chance to listen to their tapes next time I was in Boston, for what help it might give me. We actually made a date to do it. But my plans changed, I didn't go to Boston when I thought I would, I put off making a special trip; and then I learned that Barney had died. I wish now I had gone a little farther out of my way, not only to hear the tapes but because I *liked* Barney and Betty Hill.

UFOlogists complain that there is damn-all thorough and objective independent investigation of the saucer

situation. They're absolutely right. The only people
who are motivated to put a lot of time into it are
those who are already believers. Skeptics and the uncommitted may poke around in the field for a while,
as I did, but then they get bored—as I did. J. Allen
Hynek is one skeptic who became a believer. He is a
smart, sane, and well-informed person, and he has a
project which I would like to see tried. The FBI, says
Hynek, graduates a new class of agents every few
months. For a graduation exercise they assign them an
event—maybe a real crime, maybe a made-up incident
—and the whole class swarms out over the area, inter-
viewing everybody to put together a synoptic report
of the whole occurrence. Well, says Hynek, since
they're doing that anyway, why not one time turn all
that talent loose on a reported sighting? Talk to *everybody*. Balance the accounts against each other. Resolve
the contradictions. Sift out the facts. And, for once,
see for sure whether the thing happened or not.

This strikes me as an eminently workable idea;
I've already written my own congressman to tell him
I'd like to see it done, and maybe one day it will be.
I wish it had been done with the Hills, or Lonnie
Zamorra; and I'll admit that in my heart I kind of
wish that it had proved them right. I wish, in fact,
that I could believe *any* of the stories about sightings
of alien spacecraft, because it would give me pleasure
to have some proof that we are not alone in the universe.

But I don't.

The statistics are against it. Even without a full-
dress FBI investigation, confirming witnesses should
have turned up to Zamorra or the Hills. None ever
did. And with all those thousands of sightings, there
should have been *one* that simply could not be dismissed. But there isn't.

Logic is against it, too. Put it this way: if there really

is an intelligent alien race capable of building ships
of any of the sorts described, they would have to be
pretty smart, right? At least as smart as, say, you and
me? Well, then why don't they act that way? I promise
you that if I were an alien intelligence interested in
finding out about the Earth, I would find a hell of a
lot better way to do it than those dummies have.

So, after a couple of years of this, I wrote George
Earley a letter:

Dear George:
    I kept my promise. I looked into the evidence.
And I still don't believe.

You can't stay in the same house for more than a
quarter of a century without putting out some sort
of roots into the community, and by the early 1960s
I had acquired a couple. We had a bad fire around
then: a defective electric-blanket switch started a bed
smoldering when no one was looking, and by the time
anyone perceived something was wrong, the master
bedroom was in flames. Luck was with us. We had
elected to have our fire on a Thursday evening at
eight o'clock, which was when the local volunteer fire
company held its monthly meeting, so they were all
right on the scene. As soon as the alarm went in they
were on their way, only a block away. They saved the
house. In the process several thousand sheets of paper
in my office just above the burning room were seriously
scorched or trodden by firemen's boots, and the whole
house was well soaked; it took us a year to rebuild,
and a lot longer to deal with the consequences. (Some
manuscripts were destroyed forever; and for years after,
on wet nights, you could smell the char.)

But they had done a fantastic job, and I owed them
something. Money? Well, sure, I made a contribution.
But what they needed more than money was man-

power. So I joined up. For the next few years I woke
with the sirens and got myself thoroughly smudged,
scraped, frozen, and exhausted in several score fires,
great and small. It was interesting. It was socially very
useful; but I sure don't want to do it any more.

Being a volunteer fireman did have some fringe
benefits. At the beer busts after the monthly meetings,
from time to time someone would bring along a reel
of Tijuana's best imported porn, the first I'd seen
since Army days on Mount Vesuvius. And my local
volunteer company, like nearly every other volunteer
fire company anywhere in suburbia, had been just
about one hundred percent registered Republican. As
a known Democrat, I broke the line.

This meant something to me, because I was gung-ho
for the Democratic Party. I can't say I always thought
the Democratic candidates for office were really very
good. I only thought what I have always thought about
party politics in America; bad as the Democrats often
were, point for point and office for office the Republi-
cans were usually just that tiny bit worse. On those
grounds I had been a Democratic County Committee-
man for several years—the absolute lowest elected
office in America.* I worked hard, took no bribes, got
the vote out; and after some years of this was rewarded
with a political patronage plum. It was the best job
I ever had in my life. I held it for only two weeks,
and had to quit because of pressure from my family;
but if I had my druthers I'd probably have it still. Our
local leader was a street-smart old Irishman from
Jersey City, with the brain of a Mayor Daley in the
body of a retired jockey. He called me up and said,
"Fred, you been doing a great job and I wanna show
the Party's appreciation. You show up at Freehold

---

* All that anyone would possibly want to know about this is
in my book *Practical Politics*. If you can find a copy. Which I
doubt.

Raceway Monday morning and they'll put you to work. Say I sent you."

"But I already have a job editing a magazine, Artie."

"You call that a job? I'm talking twenty bucks for fifteen minutes!"

"What kind of job is that, Artie?"

"It's better if we don't go into that part right now," he explained. "Just show up."

So I showed up. The job turned out to be collecting urine samples from the trotting horses.

Look, I have as many middle-class hang-ups as the next man, and I had never considered a career in horse piss. Apart from anything else, it was easy to imagine the comments, the jokes, and oh! the belly laughs from all my friends. But the money was good. I liked being around tracks. It piqued my curiosity. And, considered objectively, what was so bad? After changing diapers for ten years, a little horse urine didn't seem too frightening. Besides, there was not much chance I would get any on me. The specimen goes into a sort of aluminum soup can on a five-foot pole. All you really have to do is hold the can in the stream long enough to collect an ounce or two. . . . Well, no. There's more to it than that.

What you have to do is know when the flow is going to commence, and how to coax the horse into making nice for daddy when he doesn't particularly want to. In case the problem ever comes up for you, I will pass along my hard-won knowledge. Female horses sort of squat down on their hind legs before they do it; watch for the squat, stick in the pot, and you're home free. With male horses you can tell at once when something is about to happen, as that majestic equipment starts to engorge; the horse is going either to urinate or to make love. At that point you want to be fast on your feet whichever way it goes.

Usually a horse who has just trotted six furlongs is

about ready to relieve himself. Unless he has done it
on the way back to the barn—bad luck!—you can count
on something happening in the first five or ten minutes.
If not, you have to use psychology.

I became quite good at chirping, whispering, and
shuffling the straw in the stall with my feet. I don't
know why that worked, but it usually did. I never had
a failure, never had a real bad time; but then I never
happened to get an Ohio horse. Ohio horses had a
very bad reputation in Freehold. In Ohio there was
a compulsory urine test for every horse. In order to
make sure they got samples, Ohio urologists equipped
themselves with electric cattle prods. Zap the horse
where it counts, and urine flows. The other thing
that happens is that for the rest of that horse's life,
if he sees you coming toward him with a specimen
can, he will try to kill you.

Easy work, warm summer afternoons in the open,
all the tips I could use on the races—that was one
fine job. But Camelot ended. I had expected to have
one day a week off, which I could use to go in to New
York and edit *Galaxy*, but it turned out that wasn't
possible. And the public pressure from my family in
particular got hard to bear, especially when the kids
started answering the phone with, "This is the residence
of the peepee collector."

So I gave it all up to concentrate on editing *Galaxy*,
and often I've wondered if I made the right decision.

Thinking about the stables leads me for some reason to the Milford Science Fiction Writers' Conferences.

That's a cheap shot, isn't it? And irreverent, too.
Milford is supposed to be the great sacerdotal shrine
of science-fiction writers. After you attend it you are
allowed to wear a green turban and call yourself *hajj*,
and for the rest of your life you are just that little

bit likelier to appear in *Orbit*, and to have an edge in
the voting for Nebula awards. There are writers who
swear that they owe Milford all they own of the power
to express themselves. And there are writers who come
away from it gaunt and stary, and don't write at all
for weeks or months afterward. One or two have
hardly written at all after an exposure to Milford,
and they of the best and most prolific. Even in the
case of Damon Knight, Mr. Milford himself, you can
divide his writing life into two periods: the copious
and good, and then, later, the sparse and maybe less
good; and the dividing line is pretty close to the time
when he began running Milfords.

Now, most Milfordites would deny that any of this
is true, or anyway, that it is relevant. A characteristic
of in-groups is that their members do not ordinarily
think of themselves as in-groups. There was never any
organized conspiracy at Milford to vote themselves
awards. (One writer did, in fact, telephone a lot of
Milford associates to ask them to vote for him, and
he did by a narrow margin win a Nebula that year;
but that's just one individual.) But the objective facts
speak for themselves. Milfordites were activists, and
voted heavily in the Nebula balloting. Milfordites won
a large proportion of the awards. When I first observed this and pointed it out, I got an immense
amount of flak from Milfordites, including Jim Blish.
Happened I saw Jim in Washington shortly thereafter,
at a time when that year's balloting had been completed but the results had not yet been made public.
I asked him to tell me who had won, and, quite properly, he refused. I then asked him to tell me at least
how many of the awards had gone to Milfordites. He
hesitated, and then grinned and shrugged. "Well, all
of them," he said.

The Milford Workshop came about when Jim, Judy
Merril, and Damon Knight found themselves all resi-

dent at once in the tiny town of Milford, Pike County,
Pennsylvania. All of them knew something about
writers' workshops. Either they had personal experience, or they had heard the accounts of friends who
had been deeply involved—Fletcher Pratt, for instance,
was a mainstay of perhaps the best of the lot, Bread
Loaf. They felt there was money to be made from a
summer workshop. Milford was resort country, which
was ideal for the purpose. They were none of them
more affluent than they wanted to be; and so they
issued a call to all sf writers who were interested to
sign up for a week or so in the beautiful Delaware
Valley.

In the event, the triumvirate did not survive as a
team very long, nor was there all that much money
to be made. But Damon continued it as a labor of
love. When he moved away from Milford, the Milford
Conference followed him—in Florida, in Michigan, in
Oregon; they all continued to be called Milford Conferences, long after the geography ceased to be real.
Even England developed its own "Milford," seeded
from a spore Jim Blish brought over when he ex-
patriated.

Milford is partly like a course in creative writing,
partly like an encounter group. The workshop procedure is highly refined and works well—to the extent,
that is, that any form of teaching writing ever works
well, which can be argued. (I use the same procedure
myself when I teach college classes in writing.) Every
registrant has to submit a work in manuscript. Every
registrant is asked to read every submitted work, and
usually most of them do.

Then all the workshoppers gather in a circle. The
conversation goes around the ring, one by one. Each
workshopper says what he thought about the story,
where it succeeded for him, where it failed. The author

is the last to speak—he is forbidden to speak at all until everyone else has had his say.

Passions can run pretty high. It is a shattering thing to see your infant's limbs gnawed away by a circle of ghouls. Writing is a private act; parts of it are painful to expose in public, and the workshopped have been known to weep or storm away. The full treatment runs a week, and for all those days the Milfordites live in each other's pockets: eat together, drink together, play together. The invasion of the ego goes far beyond literary matters. Some persons find it almost a mystical experience, others think it purely hateful.

I said Milford was partly like an encounter group, and this was not meant as a metaphor. I think it is true. Several years ago, when I was going through a more than usually troubled time, I signed up for an encounter weekend. I drove to a big old house on the Jersey Shore where ten or twelve other dissatisfied souls were looking for some sort of easing. We did mock wrestling and bioenergetic exercises. We closed our eyes and communicated by nonverbal gropes. We were encouraged to say whatever we felt, however odious or sad, to vent whatever pain we could squeeze past the guards of the subconscious. Unclothed, we gathered in a blood-temperature swimming pool and passed each other tenderly down a long line of supporting hands. Some of the people there were old pros who had been through a hundred such weekends. Some, like me, had never experienced it before. One or two were there for professional reasons: the dean of the Psych Department at a little Midwestern university, proper-straight fundamentalist methodically broadening his experience to help him communicate with the unruly kids; a grad student from a nearby school researching her doctoral dissertation. Some opened facilely to every new experience. Others stayed closed up for all the seventy-two hours, as armored in nakedness as any knight in mail. A couple were primal-scream junkies, bitterly jealous of their minutes on the mat. We ate the same food, slept on touching mattresses in the same great commons room. Sometimes there was hysteria, and a fair amount of gentle tears.

What did it accomplish? I don't know. I know that for me it was a special experience which I will never forget, like the time I had my tonsils out at the age of six. But I've never had the impulse to repeat it. I've never had the desire to have my tonsils out again, either.

Milford is a lot like that, except that I have never personally observed nude bathing in a warm pool. (A little skinny-dipping in the Delaware River, maybe.) The invasion of the personality is almost as complete —less so on the psychosexual level, but more so in those creative centers of the heart and mind which, to a writer, are perhaps comparably vulnerable and complex. Even the house is much the same, or was when Milford was in Damon's immense old place. The critics' circle was in his two-story living room, limited to participating writers only. Wives and other civilians were banished to the kitchen. (That wasn't exactly sexist. Nonwriting husbands, on the rare occasions when any showed up, were also kicked out. But, like most things that aren't exactly sexist, it worked out that way.)

And in both cases, over and above the presumptive therapeutic sessions, there was a hell of a lot of fun and games.

What happens in an encounter-group setting is the powerful emergence of a collective identity. We individuals suddenly and deeply become *us*. Relationships that begin in this setting carry over. The encounter sessions reliably produce a fair number of broken marriages and new pairings. Milford does not

do that exact thing as frequently (I wouldn't say
never), because of its literary orientation, but in the
area of writing it breaks and makes relationships in
plenty. Any writer who feels he is not moving ahead
rapidly enough might be well advised to spend a week
at Milford, because of the relationships formed. I'm
not talking about any impropriety, only about the self-
evident fact that an unsolicited manuscript from somebody you were drinking with till three A.M. gets read
in a different way from one that just comes over
the transom.*

Not content with creating Milford, Damon r'ared
back and passed another miracle: the Science Fiction
Writers of America. In the early stages it was hard
to distinguish between them. SFWA grew out of
Milford, and Milford was the closest thing to a meeting
place SFWA had.

This was by no means according to Damon's design,
and in fact he labored hard to expand SFWA beyond
the limits of Pike County, Pennsylvania. At the time,
I was publishing a new writer in every issue of *If*,
and every month, as soon as the new issue came out,
I would get a letter from Damon, addressed to the
novice in care of me, inviting him to join SFWA.
He proselytized every writer he could reach, and by and
by enough of them signed up to make SFWA reasonably broad-based—as much so as any organization of

---

* I'll give you an unassailable example. By the time you read
this, Bantam will have published a remarkably impressive first
novel called *The Short-Timers*, by Gustav Hasford. The chain
of causality is complicated, but it comes down to this: Bantam
would not have published that book if Hasford had not met the
editor at Milford; and I know this is so because the editor is
me. (The reason in this case is not that I would not have read
it sympathetically if it had been from someone I never heard
of—the novel made its own appeal—but that the author would
not have considered submitting it to me if we hadn't met. It
isn't science fiction, or anything like it.)

such thorny individuals as sf writers can ever hope to be, anyway. Damon was not alone in his efforts. His principal associate, working as hard and as effectively in his own sphere, was Lloyd Biggle, who lived in faraway Michigan. Even so, the focus and nerve center of SFWA remained in Milford.

From the beginning I had ambiguous feelings about SFWA. Partly it was because of my own dichotomous nature: half of me was blood-brother writer, the other half class-enemy editor. Partly it was because I felt (and still feel) that when writers join together for any purpose, they are subject to strange follies. As time went on, some of the activities of SFWA seemed to me to be of dubious value. I began to question some of them, which led to a long correspondence with Damon and other officers, past and present, which led to acrimony, which led to a catfight. So in disgust I quit the organization.

This is not an unprecedented act. A fair share of SFWA's best and most committed members have resigned from time to time. It is a normal activity, both an accepted form of political statement, like trashing the dean's office, and a sort of maturation rite, like a bar mitzvah.

Then time passed, and a new president, Jim Gunn, gentlest and most politic of men, invited me back. It was lonely out there, and I accepted. I was prepared to forgive and forget. I expected as much from the other side, but I was wrong. They bided their time. Then, a year or two later, they got back at me in a typically subtle and agonizing way: they elected me president.

The early 1960s was a period I enjoyed a lot, but there was a shadow. Around that time our youngest daughter, Kathy, began to fall down a lot.

She was only about three. All three-year-olds bash

themselves from time to time. Kathy's falls seemed excessive; in fact, scary.

Since I worked at home, I was a pretty fatherly father, on hand for most of the major events of the children's lives; kept odd hours, and so was a logical candidate for the two A.M. feedings and to soothe the middle-of-the-night frights. I saw a lot of all of them when they were small, including Kathy. But I didn't see that about her. Carol had to point it out to me, and at first I didn't believe it. Kathy was too pretty, healthy, loving a baby to have anything *wrong*.

But she did keep on falling down. Trot a few steps across a room and drop; pick herself up after a second, looking a little dazed, and then trot on. We told our family doctor about it. He looked grave and recommended a specialist.

Over the next year and more we took Kathy to a dozen doctors, hospitals, laboratories. At every step of the way we built up doubt of medical infallibility and loathing for medical brutality. If they had been kind to Kathy, perhaps we could have forgiven them for their lack of answers. But some of them were the opposite of kind. She had to have a skull X-ray. Well and good; but she did not have to be held down, screaming, by three orderlies. She had to have an electroencephalogram. But she did not have to be shouted at by a nurse who appeared to have completed her training in Belsen, because the sedatives the nurse had given her were having the wrong effect. (As I would have been able to tell the nurse, if she had told me what she was doing.)

Or, if they had been able to help Kathy, perhaps we could have put up with the meat-grinder callousness of their behavior toward her. But they couldn't. What we got were suggestions for further tests, and mumbles about "God's will." When medicines were prescribed, they worked in reverse. Sedatives revved her motors up and intensified the seizures. For a time we had to put Kathy back in a playpen, padding the sides so that when she fell down, which she did every few minutes, at least she would not split her head open on the furniture. Change the medicine, and the seizures begin to happen every few seconds. For a week or more the only place it was safe for Kathy to be was in her own bed or on someone's lap.

Meanwhile, Kathy was being so terrorized that when any woman wearing a white dress came into our house, she would run and hide. I didn't know the right thing to do for her. But I was sure that terrifying her had to be wrong. So for some months I simply refused to do anything, called off all further tests, stopped the medication, and just let her relax as well as she could.

I cannot tell you how much anger and resentment I felt toward the entire medical profession at that time. The individual doctor, whether in his professional capacity or otherwise, is usually a decent person, and sometimes a lot better than that. Collectively, in the concentration-camp milieu of a hospital or clinic, they are nearly to be despised. I am sure that not all the doctors, ward boys, technicians and nurses are evil people, and I even think that some of them are close to saints. But what I am also sure of is that the good ones tolerate and even protect the bad.*

At the end of nearly two years of trotting Kathy from place to place, at great cost to her and to all of us in every way, what we had to show for it was a name. They said she suffered from "petit mal."

Petit mal is not related to grand mal. Grand mal is

---

* There are two reasons for the explosive growth of malpractice suits in America, and only one of them is the cupidity of the lawyers involved. The other is the existence of a lot of malpractice, by medical personnel who are either incompetent or uncaring, and who are rarely restrained by their colleagues.

epilepsy. It had been established that Kathy was not epileptic. But, like an epileptic, she had seizures. They were relatively mild and brief, but they were seizures all the same. She would black out. In that moment she had no control over her limbs; they would collapse under her, and she would fall. When the seizure was over a moment later, she would pick herself up, perhaps not knowing what had happened, and try to remember what she had been about to do. It is not called "petit mal" because the term describes the etiology or helps to determine therapy, but only because it happens and therefore needs a name.

At the point of despair, we were at last referred to the New Jersey Neuropsychological Institute. For the first time we found a team who not only knew what they were doing, but knew enough to consider Kathy a person rather than a lump of meat. They gave her the same battery of tests—humanely administered, and with the cooperation Kathy had always been willing to give if allowed half a chance. Then they called us all together for a conference, Kathy and Carol and I and six or eight specialists, and told us what had gone wrong in her nervous system.

"Neurological impairment" does not really mean much more than "petit mal." But they were able to pinpoint the specific area in the brain where it had occurred. How had it occurred? It was far too late to tell that. Probably there had never been a time when anyone could say for sure. Kathy's had been a difficult birth, and that was a likely candidate, but it could have been some prenatal chemical antagonism, a genetic miscoding, a fall, a fever—it could have been anything. But at least there was that much understanding, and there was something more. The seizures, they said, would probably stop of themselves when she reached her teens. That was still years off. But meanwhile, they prescribed a different drug. We took the prescription and had it filled, and when Kathy popped the first pill in her mouth the seizures stopped. She has never had another.

Kathy has still not achieved her full potential. The strangeness of brain injury is that in some areas the brain simply does not work, and so some kinds of functions do not occur. Over years the brain is sometimes able to reroute its information-handling into other areas. Some of that has occurred with Kathy. She walks, she talks, she learns, she enjoys life. She is able to travel thousands of miles, from one country to another, by herself. She is a healthy, tall, good-looking young lady with a keen sense of humor and a disconcerting ability to understand nuances of behavior. Much is difficult for her, but we have not yet found anything that is impossible. And what is left of her problems is no longer as much due to brain injury as to the fact that so much of her early life was spent coddled and protected, so that she was not able to experiment on her own.

Because of Kathy, Carol and I have found ourselves involved in programs to help handicapped children. Because of that, we have discovered how many of them there are. There isn't a block in America that doesn't hide some children who are spastic, or emotionally disturbed, or perceptually impaired, or somehow, somewhere, cheated of what most of us take for granted. Ten percent of all children are significantly handicapped.

It is important to know that *all of them can be helped*. For a few, tragically, not much more can be done than to relieve a little of the pain and despair. For some, they can be brought to complete and normal lives.

But there is always something.

It isn't always easy to find. I was going to say something about that, and then I remembered it had been said already:

> Another blind alley, he had thought in despair. Another, after a hundred too many already. First, "Wait for him to outgrow it." He doesn't. Then, "We must reconcile ourselves to God's will." But you don't want to. Then give him the prescription three times a day for three months. And it doesn't work. Then chase around for six months with the Child Guidance Clinic to find out it's only letterheads and one circuit-riding doctor who doesn't have time for anything. Then, after four dreary, weepy weeks of soul-searching, the State Training School, and find out it has an eight-year waiting list. Then the private custodial school, and find they're fifty-five hundred dollars a year—without medical treatment!—and where do you get fifty-five hundred dollars a year? And all the time everybody warns you, as if you didn't know it: "Hurry! Do something! Catch it early! This is the critical stage! Delay is fatal!" *

That's from "The Meeting," one of the posthumous collaborations between Cyril Kornbluth and myself. When Cyril died, he left a good deal of incomplete work, some almost-done stories, some just fragments. One was actually a completed manuscript (or would have been, except that somehow a page or two had been irrevocably lost) about a meeting of a parents' association of a school for handicapped children. It wasn't quite a story. It was a scene, but a powerful and beautifully written one, and it had come out of Cyril's own experience of just such a school. Over the years I tinkered most of Cyril's fragments into

* From "The Meeting," by Frederik Pohl and C. M. Kornbluth, Copyright © 1972 by Mercury Press, Inc.

stories and had them published. "The Meeting" I
left alone. At first it was too foreign to my experience
for me to know how to handle it. Then it was too
close. Of course, "The Meeting" is fiction. The child in
it, and the school, are fictitious; but all the schools
share the same hope and pain. And, a decade and a
half after Cyril died, I perceived how I could make the
scene into a story, and did, and Ed Ferman published
it in *The Magazine of Fantasy and Science Fiction*
in 1972.

Sometimes, when one reads a story, there is a sense
of identification and revelation: what is happening in
the story is what has happened to oneself, and some
painful lump in the subconscious shifts to a more
easeful position. Catharsis? Therapy? It is the same
for the writer as for the reader. Cyril and I had dealt
with frustrations in fiction before—our not-very-suc-
cessful hurricane novel, *A Town Is Drowning*, was an
act of revenge on a storm that had ripped off my
roof and flooded his home a year earlier. "The Meeting" was harder to deal with, but I am sure that it
too was a kind of therapy for both of us.

The year after it was published I went to the World
Science Fiction Convention in Toronto with some
hopes of coming back with more than I had had
when I left. I had published a story called "The Gold
at the Starbow's End" the year before. In my vanity,
I really expected to win something for it. Nebula time
had come and gone, and somebody else had taken
away the prize, but it was up for a Hugo and I was
hopeful.

So were Ben Bova and Isaac Asimov, and the three
of us were sitting at the same table. Now, we are all
old pros, you understand. But as the long-winded
speakers wound down and handing-out time came
close, conversation flagged at our table. Even Ben ran
out of jokes. Isaac had to get up to go to the bathroom

six, count them, six times between the serving of the coffee and the presentation of the awards.

Then the awards began. Apart from the Hugos, there are a lot of them, and each speaker seemed impelled to carry on at insane length both in giving and in receiving them. But they came to Best Editor; and it was Ben, for *Analog,* and he got up to collect it and brought it back and plumped it down in the middle of our table.

Then they came to Best Novel. It was Isaac, for *The Gods Themselves.* And he too went up to pick up the trophy, and brought it back, and then there were two.

And then they came to Best Novella and it wasn't mine. It went to Ursula Le Guin's *The Word for the World Is Forest.*

I intensely admire Ursula Le Guin as a writer, and even like that story. But I could have wished very much at that moment that she had never decided to write it. Isaac and Ben were very nice about it, but I could see that I was bringing the class of the neighborhood down.

Then along came the award for Best Short Story. I had actually forgotten that "The Meeting" was even nominated.

But it had been, and it won in a tie with an R. A. Lafferty story, and honor was saved.

By the time I got back to the table with Cyril's Hugo and mine, my sunny nature had reasserted itself. I had had time to reflect that Cyril had had the bad luck to die before awards were common, and so this one was specially valued. I accepted the handshakes and kisses. But I was not prepared for the reactions of Ben and Isaac, who were both staring at the now four Hugos in the middle of the table. "Showy bastard," Ben hissed, and Isaac chimed in, "Yeah! We only got one Hugo. How come you get two?"

11

Have Mouth, Will Travel

In 1965 I encountered a new friend and a new way of
filling up my time. I had a phone call from T. George
Harris, then an editor for *Look* and later head honcho
for *Psychology Today*. George said that he had met a
fellow named John Diebold and thought the two of
us ought to know each other. So he had arranged a
luncheon.

George's instincts were exactly right, at least as far
as my own reactions were concerned. John Diebold
is a Renaissance man, a management Titan, a cosmopolitan gourmet; I had not met quite his like
before. His management-consultancy firm has offices
in nearly every city of the world worth living in.
Among other ventures, he conducts a Research Institute which tells management people the things they
will not learn from the B-School or the Kiplinger
Report. At the luncheon—it was at Lutece, of course—
Diebold asked if I had thought much about the future
of corporate management. I told him what had occurred to me. He invited me to repeat it at the next
Diebold Research Institute meeting, and I did, with
flourishes and variations. *Business Week* covered the

event, with a picture and a quote, and my phone began to ring.

So for the next five or six years I found myself talking to groups who didn't know anything about science fiction but were willing to listen to what I had to say, all over the map. Corporation presidents in Hawaii, architects in New Haven, Kiwanis in Alabama, international religious conferences in New York, life-insurance executives in Chicago, industrial chemists in Michigan, space scientists in Georgia, mathematicians in Washington, women's clubs, temples, rod-and-gun clubs, churches, interior decorators, soap and detergent manufacturers, science teachers, English teachers, for God's sake *kindergarten* teachers—it snowballs. The way it works, if you talk to a group of eighteen hundred management types, there are always ten or twenty among them who are themselves trying to book talent for the next meeting of their own group. So they are scouting for talent, and if when they catch your act you do not appear visibly drunk or demented, invitations follow.

Publicity helps a whole lot, and there I was very lucky. Sylvia Porter quoted me in her column, *The New York Times Sunday Magazine* ran a lengthy article, I was on a lot of radio and TV shows. It was all interesting. It got me to places I might not otherwise have seen (management people really do themselves well when they meet). But it was getting out of hand. I was occupying some very fancy hotel rooms, but the world outside the meeting places I was seeing only from the windows of a car going to and from an airport. On the day when I realized I had scheduled myself to speak at a luncheon meeting in Tuscaloosa at one and at a Columbia University gathering in New York City seven hours later, I decided I needed professional help.

The persons available for such help are called lecture

agents. There are scores of them. I didn't fool around.
I went right to the top. Armed with an introduction
from a writer who was both a good friend of mine
and a highly valued client of his, I spread my problems
on the agent's desk. He pondered for a while and
then allowed that he *could* help. But he wasn't sure he
wanted to, really. Did I have any publicity material?

With some effort I assembled a batch of clippings
and notices. (I don't like to keep those things—not
because I lack vanity, but because I feel I have too
much of it already; keeping a press book panders to
urges I had rather suppress.) He thumbed through
them, and we talked, rather inconclusively, over a
period of a month or two. Then he called me in to
say he had solved my problem. His son was just out
of Yale and coming into the family business. He had
decided to let me be his son's very first lecture client.
Gosh, I said, falling to my knees and kissing his ring,
when can we start? Right now, he said. And there was
a peal of trumpets and his son the Yale man came in
and whisked me away.

"Pohl," he said, "I've made a study of your case,
and I know what you want. You want to get into the
universities."

"Yes," I said, nodding feverishly. "I've always liked
talking to college audiences."

"Shut up," he said. "I'm talking here. You've got the
wrong act."

"But," I said, "I've never had—"

"Old stuff," he said; "you need to keep up with the
times. You don't know what's going on *now*. The
occult! That's what they want to hear about on the
campuses. I know this, because I've just graduated
from Yale. That's all they talk about there, Buckley
and the occult."

"I'll have to think about that," I said, and went
away.

I never went back. After a while I got a sort of reproachful note from the father, returning my publicity clips, and that was the end of that.

Since then I've tried a few other lecture agents, but they really are not any solution to any problem of mine, whatever they may do for Alvin Toffler and Arthur Clarke. I do a lot of talking, mostly to college groups (the Yale man was right about what I preferred), but seldom through an agent. I'll go on talking to colleges as long as they go on letting me, too, because, next to writing, it is my favorite vice. College students are about the best people in the world, and rapping with them from time to time is a bigger high than dope.

In the last few years I edited *Galaxy*, things were coming along. Both *Galaxy* and *If* were finally monthly. The paperback book sidelines, Galaxy Novels and MagaBooks, had faded away, but we began to add other magazines: first *Worlds of Tomorrow*, then a wild idea that I had dreamed up over a quitting-time drink with Bob Guinn, *International Science Fiction*. The idea was to publish science fiction from foreign authors, little of which had appeared in the United States at that time. It seemed to me that some of it was quite different from what we were reading from the Anglo-American school, and maybe worth showing to an American audience. Bob thought it was a dumb idea. Still, he mentioned it to our distributors next time he saw them, and they thought it exciting. So we brought it out, with stories by Soviet, Australian, French, German, Italian, and other writers, the first time most of them had been seen in the U.S.*

For most of this time the person who did all the manuscript reading, copy-editing, proofreading, blurb

* The sales were terrible. Bob had been right: it was a dumb idea.

writing, and general donkeywork was me, sometimes with a secretary, sometimes without. It now began to be more than I could handle, and I started looking for an assistant. The Hunter College placement office sent down a resume that looked interesting: Judy-Lynn Benjamin—a recent graduate, early twenties, specialist in James Joyce, some writing background; she sounded great. I arranged for an interview, and I hired her.

A little later we added another title, *Worlds of Fantasy*. I have written a little fantasy and read a lot of it; some of it I enjoy immensely, but it is not an area in which I feel very confident of my judgment once I get below the obvious masterpieces. So we took Lester del Rey aboard to edit that and for various kinds of expertise.

I thought they made a good team, Judy-Lynn and Lester, and congratulated myself on my wisdom in hiring them.

A dozen years later, I am not so sure. They thought they were a good team, too. Now married, they are collectively Del Rey books, an imprint of Ballantine Books. Lester is still handling the fantasy, and Judy-Lynn the science fiction. And they are the competitors I fear. In this week's *Times Book Review* the top best seller on the mass-market paperback list is Judy-Lynn's *Star Wars*, and still high up on the trade-paperback best-seller list is Lester's *The Sword of Shannara*. And one of these days I am going to have to explain to my employers at Bantam just how I happened to let these two books get away from me.

However antlike and industrious an editor is, the aphids that squeeze out the honey are the writers. Editing is such a big ego trip that it's hard to remember that. Sometimes I forgot. The telephone isn't congenial to me, and letters don't always say what needs to be said. I tried to spend as much time as I could with writers, one on one, face to face, and burned up a lot of jet fuel doing it.

One of the advantages to me of the lecture circuit was that it got me around the country a lot, and I used the opportunities to visit writers. Florida was Doc Smith territory; he and his wife, Jeannie, lived in a big, permanent house trailer in a park in Clearwater, and kept a smaller mobile one for dragging across the country when the wanderlust hit them. Every time I found myself nearby I stopped in to chat him up and enjoy his company and spur him on. The Bay Area was Poul Anderson and Jack Vance, and down the coast a way Bob Heinlein in his curious, new circular house with the pie-shaped rooms—a marvelous idiosyncratic home that I still envy a lot. Poul was one of the mainstays of my magazines, as he has been for everybody's for the past quarter of a century, always good, always meeting his deadlines; apart from which, he and Karen threw fine parties. Jack Vance and his wife lived just a mountain or two away, in the hilly parts north of the San Francisco Bay, in a house built on the side of a precipice. Jack wrote *The Dragon Masters* for me, a beautiful strange novella of odd creatures and their convoluted social lives, endless light-years and centuries from here and now. *The Dragon Masters* seemed to me the kind of story whose complexity and strangeness deter some readers. I didn't want my readers deterred if I could help it, especially since the story itself was a masterpiece of its kind. After some pondering, I persuaded Jack Gaughan to draw small figures of all the various kinds of creatures in the story and even to do a map to help follow the action on. When convention time came, *The Dragon Masters* won the first Hugo for any story I published, and Jack's illustrations were nominated for the art award, too—as far as I know, the only time ever that specific illustrations were nominated. In Washington I visited Paul Linebargar, better known as Cordwainer Smith, in his sunny home near Rock Creek Park, with the big gold-and-scarlet birth scroll from Sun Yat-sen in his living room.

Bob Heinlein and Poul Anderson, Jack Vance and the two Smiths, Doc and Cordwainer—all gave me first-rate work to publish. So did half a dozen others— so did a lot more than half a dozen others, one time or another but the mainstays were those five, plus Keith Laumer, Fred Saberhagen, Bob Silverberg, Mack Reynolds, Larry Niven, and Harlan Ellison. What Laumer and Saberhagen gave were series stories, really nice ones. They are the kind of thing that a lucky editor finds under his Christmas tree, almost as good as a serial at keeping the readers coming back, not as annoying to the readers who hate having their stories interrupted a month at a time. Of course, Santa Claus isn't real, so they don't actually turn up under a tree. You have to coax them along. When I saw Keith's first story about an interstellar diplomat named James Retief, I bought it at once and wanted more, and consequently devoted a lot of thought to persuading Keith to make it a series. I couldn't do it in person; he was in the Air Force, in some strange overseas place like England, and none of my lecture dates seemed to be taking me in that direction. What I didn't know was that Keith perceived those potentials just as clearly as I did, and in fact the one I bought was actually the second of the series. He cooperated cheerfully, and for several years Retief was a big part of the glue that kept the *If* readership sticking with us.

Fred Saberhagen turned up as a brand-new writer with a short chess puzzle story. I wasn't too crazy about the chess, but as a little fillip to the background he had thrown in a maniacally murderous, preprogrammed automatic space battleship which he called

a "berserker." The chess game was only limited fun.
The Berserkers were a great deal of fun; and when
I suggested to him what he could make of them he
saw the point at once, and we published a great deal
about them, to the delight of both readers and me.

Toward the end of my tenure with *Galaxy*, after
Lester del Rey had come aboard, he and I decided to
run our own "best of the year" award. The Nebulas
and the Hugos already existed, but the Nebulas were
being given on the basis of tiny votes—as few as half
a dozen appear to have won at least one of the early
Nebulas. The Hugos were perhaps more representative,
but the difficulty with the Hugos is the difficulty with
the World Science Fiction Convention committees
that give them. Each is a brand-new group every year.
There are continuing rules to govern the handling of
the awards, but each committee has its own personal
style, and some are a lot more diligent than others.
We decided to conduct a mail survey of subscribers,
and give away a few thousand dollars in prizes to the
writers the readers said they liked best.

Most of the stars did well, as we had expected them
to do. But the writer who did most surprisingly well,
with every story rated high by the readers—and we
had published a lot of his stories that year—was Mack
Reynolds. I think Mack may be the most underrated
writer in science fiction today. As far as I know, he
has never received any of the ongoing awards, perhaps
has never been as much as nominated for one. What
was he doing beating out so many of the Big Names?

And then it penetrated my tiny, torpid brain that
Mack had in fact contributed quite a lot to science
fiction. I remembered telling Robert Theobald about
some of the interesting political-economic ideas in
science fiction, and realizing that they had all come
from Mack: the credit-card economy, the Minimum

Basic income, "Common Europe," some fancy variations on today's political systems—all Mack's. I was at first surprised that he had done so well, and then surprised at myself for being surprised.

Mack is a heavyset, hard-drinking, no-frills guy, and he writes the kind of prose you would expect. No one would call him a stylist. The "New Wave" hypertrophy of literary values left Mack untouched. But if you consider language as a tool for the communication of concepts, then Mack uses it better than most of us.

The writer who came in almost as well as Mack overall (and carried off one of the prizes, too) was his exact opposite, Robert Silverberg.

Soon after I became editor of *Galaxy* and *If*, Bob made me a proposition. He had been out of science fiction for a number of years, concentrating on writing the shelves of quickie books that made him rich before he was thirty. He wanted back in. But, for personal reasons, he wanted a deal. He wanted to know that I would buy every story he sent in. If I really hated one, I could call off the deal at any time; but I still had to buy that one. It is not the kind of arrangement I would make with every writer, but, thinking it over, it seemed safe enough with AgBob. He was a hard-nosed professional. If he had a professional's weakness (at that time, for example, a mournable tendency to milk wordage, so that a lot of his stories turned out fifty percent over their best fighting weight), he also had a professional's virtues. It was exceedingly unlikely that he would turn in a manuscript that would disgrace him or us. And he was capable, I knew he was capable, of really great work when he chose to do it.

So I agreed, and for most of the decade of the 60s *Galaxy* and *If* had a lock on every word of science fiction Bob wrote. We published it all, and I never regretted the deal. There is no question that Bob is one of the larger talents ever to hit science fiction.

I don't think he has always realized that talent. His early work is padded, and most of his major writing of the 70s is so searingly, soul-depressingly *down* that I find it hard to read; Tolstoy and Céline are Mary Poppins compared with Bob Silverberg when he gets a good grump on. But when he is at the top of his elegant, world-weary form—"Nightwings," say, or parts of "Shadrach in the Furnace"—he is hard to beat.

For a while it seemed that the Silverbergs' lives and ours were inextricably meshed. Carol and I had a death in the family, then a fire that seriously damaged our house and almost leveled it entirely; shortly thereafter, so did they. He wrote me a letter to complain, with that special kind of irony that contains serious pain, that he didn't like being condemned to recapitulate all the tragedies of my life, and would I please tell him what I was contemplating next so he would know what to expect?

Larry Niven did well in the voting, too—and has gone on to do even better in the decade and more since then. I have always had a special attachment to Larry's work. He was one of the first of the "*If* Firsts," the stories by previously unpublished authors I had running in every issue of *If* for years on end. Larry had an advantage denied to most would-be writers. He had chosen for one of his grandfathers one of the oil kings of southern California, the very Doheny whom Doheny Drive is named after, and he could be philosophical about the relatively low cash rewards of his apprenticeship. It didn't keep him from working. He was one of the most prolific of our writers. Because I had published his first story (as well as his second, third, fourth, and *n*th), he gave us first look at everything.

Larry is the best of the recent hard-sf writers, and I felt a little guilty about keeping him from being published, at least once in a while, in that quintessential hard-sf periodical, *Analog*. It wasn't just conscience. It seemed to me that Larry could reach a somewhat different audience now and then, with happy results for himself and, indirectly, for us, too. So I encouraged him to offer one or two stories to John. Queerly, John would have none of them, though at least one of them, "Slowboat Cargo," was one of Larry's best, and placed high in the readers' voting.

To everyone's astonishment, most of all his own, Harlan Ellison did not do particularly well in that year's voting. It wasn't entirely fair. The period of the voting happened to be one in which Harlan had published only one or two stories, and those not of his best.

I must confess, as evidence of the existence of grievous character flaws, that I was not as unhappy as I should have been to see Harlan taken down a peg. It isn't that I don't like him. Harlan is an exciting, talented, fun person to be around, a brilliant writer and capable of great exertions as a friend. He is also one of the twentieth century's greatest sources of *tsoris*. For most of that decade I published nearly all the sf Harlan wrote, and I would estimate that, taking everything together, Harlan was as much pain and trouble as all the next ten troublesome writers combined. If I tried to change a title, the calls started: "What do you mean, just 'Repent, Harlequin'? Has to be 'Said the Ticktock Man,' too, otherwise you wreck the whole rhythm of it." When he judged I was editing an issue's copy, he'd be on the phone: "Just wondering, Fred; any, uh, changes you were thinking of making? What? Fred, I don't understand you; *why* can't I have one character call another one a douche bag?" Usually he won those arguments, and maybe he should have; the case *for* is that an author should have control over what he is represented as saying, the case *against* is that a magazine should have some sort of consistent personality of its own, and any time you want to debate, I'll take either side. But he was not always reasonable. Somehow he got his hands on a copy of *Scientific American* containing some pretty, spectrum-like bands of color. He wanted to use them for decorations in one of his stories. I had to say no. For one thing, we didn't own them. For another, it wasn't physically possible. Neither argument satisfied Harlan: "*Why* can't you use the lines?" "I keep telling you, Harlan, we don't have four-color printing inside the book." "Right, you haven't had *so far*, but what I'm suggesting is—"

Harlan offended is not a temperate person. Neither is Lester del Rey, and one of the ghastlier memories of my life is a dinner in a restaurant at the Statler-Hilton in New York. It was worldcon time, and everyone knows that all hotel restaurants grow faint and collapse when a science-fiction convention is near. But I must say the Statler-Hilton set new records for awfulness. It was the night of the costume ball, and we all wanted to be there for it, so we allowed three hours to eat. Not enough. You would not believe me if I told you all that happened; the core of it is that everything was unbelievably late, and when it arrived part of it was the wrong thing and the rest was pretty awful. (Carol had ordered escargots, but they had been allowed to sit for most of an hour before the waiter could bring himself to deliver them. Have you ever eaten room-temperature snails?) Harlan had ordered popovers, and didn't like them; Lester had gone to some length to describe the chef's salad he wanted, and got instead some wilted lettuce and a pale tomato. It was so bad that I, even I, was moved to complain, and so I rose to explain to the maitre d' that not only was his staff hopeless but he himself should return to the tire-refinishing industry he had obviously just left. But he wasn't listening to me. With an expression of horror on his face he was staring past my shoulder, and I turned to see Lester skating the plate of salad across the floor while Harlan, on the other side of the room, was bouncing his popover against the wall to prove his point about its texture.

It does not pay to fool with Harlan, and although I found our little editor/writer encounters stimulating, I began to wonder how long I could stand the loss of blood. What I didn't know was that Harlan was planning a role reversal. I began to hear about an anthology he was planning to edit, something called *Dangerous Visions*. The publisher involved said that, as near as he could figure out, what it mostly was, was stories that had been rejected by everybody in the business. Told that that didn't seem like the best idea anybody had ever had, he added, "Well, according to Harlan, it's because they're so *good* and so *different* that everyone is afraid to print them. Except me," he added, turning pale.

It is an article of faith with some writers that such stories exist, kept from an eager audience by the poltroon editors. It is an article of faith with *me* that this is hogwash. Some editors do hesitate to publish off-track stories, but if the story is any good, some other editor, sooner or later, will snap it up. Then Harlan called me up:

"Fred, I want a story from you for *Dangerous Visions*, the kind of story that no editor dares to print."

"Harlan, I don't know what kind of story that is."

"Shit, man! Of course you do. Like you've been printing all along in *Galaxy*!"

Actually, I think *Dangerous Visions* was a pretty good collection, and I'm pleased to be in it. My story is called "The Day the Martians Came." Or should be. What it says in the book is "The Day After the Day the Martians Came," because when Harlan realized what opportunity lay before him, he couldn't help himself; he changed the title.

The 1961 World Convention was held on the West Coast. For Carol and me, it was our first real look at the area. We loved it, especially San Francisco and Washington State, and whenever the chances came from then on, we commuted back and forth. In 1965 the convention was in London. Not counting World War II for me, it was our first look at Europe, and we loved that, too. As one who firmly believes that all our energy reserves are being bled white and disaster is only a few years away, it sometimes troubles my conscience that I have become such a jet-fuel addict, but I do love traveling.

One of the great good things about my world is that a lot of traveling goes with the job. There are lectures to give and conferences to attend and meetings to be met. It isn't all joyriding. A lot of hours of work go into, for instance, the sort of tour I have done once or twice for the State Department, culturally exchanging views on science fiction from Skopje to Leningrad. Three weeks into the last one, I counted up and realized I had totaled less than seventy hours of sleep in the preceding twenty-one days.

But usually it's a little more relaxed, and in and among the talks to Bulgarian professors of English and the panels on the New Wave in Chester and Toronto I get a chance to see things I would not otherwise have seen, and meet people I could not otherwise have known. The circumstances are not always ideal. I have observed that my wanderings follow the seasons, but the wrong way around for my maximum pleasure: it is customary for me to need to go to Minnesota in January, and Miami Beach on Labor Day. No matter. The company is usually good. We've seen Stonehenge with Jack and Blanche Williamson, and spent a weekend

on a Japanese lake with Brian Aldiss and Arthur Clarke
and Judy Merril, not to mention some truly wonderful
Japanese hosts and Russian co-guests. I don't ask for
better companions.

Well. No one wants to see anyone else's travel slides,
and I don't suppose you would sit still for very much
reminiscing about Caribbean cruises with Carl Sagan
and Isaac Asimov and the Heinleins, or about the
quaint old man who was curator of a rose garden outside Tbilisi, in Soviet Georgia. I don't blame you. I
wouldn't want to hear it, either. But the point is that
toward the end of the 1960s I was beginning to get
bored with my job. Traveling made it bearable. But
most of the traveling was only indirectly connected
with editing *Galaxy* and *If*. I would lose little if I left,
I pondered. So why was I staying on?

I do like being an editor. But I also like ripe avo-
cados and chocolate malted milks; but when I have
had enough of either, I have had enough. I was beginning to have had enough of the joys of editing *Galaxy*.
Besides, it was beginning to interfere with my writing.

There is an obvious conflict between editing and
writing. What I am not sure I understand is why sometimes the conflicts do not seem important and at other
times they are almost insuperable. For the first five
years as editor of *Galaxy* and *If*, the disease was in re-
mission and I managed to do both with no particular
strain. Bob Guinn had asked me not to write for the
competition. Except for one or two stories in *Analog*
and *F&SF* over that decade, I was willing to oblige
him. If there was a story I felt like writing for its own
sake, I wrote it. If there seemed to be an ingredient
missing in the mix I was getting from other authors, I
wrote something to fill the gap: I liked to see more
"nonfact" articles than we had, so I wrote "The
Martian Star-Gazers" and "Earth 18," wished for
science-based comedy-adventure and wrote "Under Two

Moons." Now and then I would do one for *Playboy*
or some other noncompeting periodical, and altogether
I managed to keep comfortable about writing while
meeting the magazine deadlines. But then that began
to be hard. I began to miss the dialectics of the author-
editor confrontation, often an annoyance but always a
spur. (The disadvantage of being your own editor is
that you have no editor.) And there began to be simple pressure from time. Even with Judy-Lynn and
Lester, nine deadlines a month were a lot. Galaxy was
taking more than half my working time, some months
nearly all of it. It wasn't paying proportionately, either;
there was never a time when my writing income did
not exceed the salary Bob Guinn paid me. I began to
mutter in my beer about quitting this lousy racket
and going off to write *really*.

Early in 1969 I got an invitation to attend a World
Science Fiction Symposium in Rio de Janeiro. Every-
body was going to be there, Poul Anderson and Forry
Ackerman, A. E. van Vogt and Bob Bloch, Brian
Aldiss and Alfie Bester, Jim Ballard and Arthur Clarke.
It sounded like fun, and it was.

Because I had an unbreakable speaking date in Key
Biscayne, we had to come a day or two late, but Rio
was an enchantment. The SF Symposium was only an
added afterthought to a major world film festival, and
the city was full of superstars and starlets. Fritz Lang
was staying at our hotel, nearly blind, living legend who
had actually made those films I had seen only as resur-
rected antiquarian art. Carol and I went to a party at
an embassy, and sitting next to us was, for God's sake,
Nijinsky's nephew, while just across the table was a
slim young man in a peekaboo black shirt named
Roman Polanski. (I had never heard of him; a month
or two later all the world heard of him when his wife,
Sharon Tate, was murdered by the Mansons.) The
Ouro Verde restaurant fed us the best meals I have

ever had anywhere in the world, with a view of the
Copacabana Beach and, once, one of the most impressively beautiful thunderstorms I have ever seen out
over the bay. I stole time from the symposium to fly
up to Brasilia, strange futuristic city on the *planalto*.
It is the only place I have ever been where the guides
point to an intersection and tell you, not what happened there in 1066, but what is *going* to happen next
year. (It has an impressively cantilevered building called
The Museum of the History of Brasilia. It was empty.)
Rio was exactly what a tropical vacation should be,
swimming on the famous beach, wandering among
the tourist traps, dancing in the nightclubs, and, of
course, participating in that permanent floating encounter group of the science-fiction community on the
move.

And when it was over I came back to the *Galaxy*
office and got some surprising news from Bob Guinn.
He had sold the magazines to another publisher while
I was away, he said. And what, exactly, were my own
future plans?

12

How I Re-upped with the World

If I were ever going to make the break, there would hardly be a better time. My bluff was called.

But my pride was also involved. For several days I waited, irritable and anxious, for the phone to ring, to see if I was going to be invited to go with the magazines. When it turned out I was, it also turned out that the new publisher, Arnie Abramson, had the quaint idea that his editor should be in the office from nine to five. That settled it. I agreed to stay on as "editor emeritus," a title without duties, devised primarily to keep me from signing up with a competing magazine, and within a few weeks the editorship had passed to Ejler Jakobssen.*

I wasn't particularly hurting for money, so I gave myself a month or two off, deferring the day when I would have to face my typewriter in earnest. Before the time was up, Ballantine began a reissue program which brought eighteen of my earlier books back into print in two or three large clumps. That produced an instant year's income, or a little more than I earned

* Who, as it happens, had also followed me as editor of *Super Science Stories* twenty-five years earlier.

in an average year, and so there was no particular incentive to start writing then. So I gave myself a little more time off. We took the family to London and Paris that summer, closed the house and spent the Christmas vacation in Bermuda. Back to Europe in the spring. To the Orient the following summer. Now and then, between trips, I would sit at my typewriter and play with some words, but nothing much came out; I know I finished two or three short stories (but they weren't any good, and I have never even shown them to an editor). I started thinking about several novels. But whatever I put on paper seemed to twist itself in directions I didn't like. I gave a few lectures; wrote some articles now and then when someone called up to ask for a piece and the price seemed right. But what I mostly did, as far as I can now tell, was wait for the world to clarify itself, and that it refused to do.

Personal troubles began to crop up, some big, some small. My dear friend Evelyn del Rey was killed in a car accident; her husband, Lester, stayed in the house down the road for a time, but before long he moved into New York and I lost his companionship, too. My children were suffering various sorts of growing pains; they dealt with them as wisely and well as any other young people growing into a complicated world, and maybe somewhat better than most, but there were strains. My own general dissatisfaction did not help matters. Carol and I began having marital difficulties; there were all these clouds, none of them bigger than a man's hand, but among them they shut out a lot of the sun.

Part of the trouble, I am sure, is that I was turning fifty, and not liking it a bit. I had somehow got it firmly in my head that I would never live to half a century. As it got closer it seemed less and less desirable. *Everything* seemed less desirable.

I don't mean that my days were all misery. There were good times, but they never lasted very long. There weren't really any very bad times, just gray, dull, stagnating times. About the only thing I could count on for a lift was travel. When Carol and I went to Japan in the summer of 1970, it was a ball. I've seldom enjoyed myself more. We grooved on Japan. We were delighted with all our hosts, Tetsu Yano and Hiro Hayakawa and Aritsune Toyota and, perhaps most of all, Hiroya Endo. It was an international conference, and there were some old friends to share Japan with us: Brian Aldiss, representing England; Judith Merril, Canada (having given up her birthright U.S. citizenship to become a Canadian landed immigrant); Arthur Clarke, representing more or less everywhere, but domiciling himself in Sri Lanka, née Ceylon. (They were having some sort of halfhearted revolution in Ceylon at the time, and Arthur spent a lot of his time trying to get news of how close the fighting was to his scuba-diving school.) The Japanese had invited the Soviets to send some writers, and they sent a delegation: Yuli Kagarlitski, most amiable and best informed of East-bloc sf literary critics; Vassili Zakharchenko, tall, imposing writer-editor, with the courtliest of manners and the most commanding expertise on a hundred different subjects; Yeremy Parnov, the one member of the team whose writing I knew at all first-hand (I had published one of his stories in translation in *International Science Fiction* a couple of years before); a Ukrainian sf writer; a girl translator. Carol and I had met Kagarlitski a few years earlier in London, when he was there for the H. G. Wells Centennial (one of his books was a Marxist criticism of Wells) and we were on some sort of junket. The others were all new to us and, at first, rather remote.

We had all traveled a minimum of five thousand miles to get there and were accordingly fatigued. Before we had a chance to rest up and get comfortable with each other, the symposium started. For a while it looked like heavy going. The Japanese chairman gave a welcoming speech—in Japanese; then followed by consecutive translations into English and Russian. Arthur gave a rather formal talk on science fiction and the space program (followed by translations into Russian and Japanese). Vassili Zakharchenko gave an even more formal address on the necessity for international cooperation and the special qualities Soviet science fiction could add to world literature—in Russian; then into Japanese and English. All this took forever, or somewhat longer than that. We had signed up for two weeks of this! Carol and Brian and I looked at each other with dread. There had always been the chance that it would be a crashing bore, of course. It was the first time in history that the Soviets and the West had participated in a formal sf conference. Detente was still a couple of years away; international relations were touchy. We could not blame the Japanese for keeping it formal. It is hard enough to put on any kind of science-fiction conference. They not only had the problem of arranging logistics and providing a program, they ran the risk of starting World War III.

But they were more perceptive and more daring than we knew. As soon as the formalities were over Tetsu Yano took the stage. We Japanese, he told us (in English), have a tradition. You may think it silly or childish, but we would be grateful if you would humor our customs. We want each one of you to come up one at a time, and we will ask you to do something. And they had each of us, one by one, do a sort of vaudeville turn. Kagarlitski sang a little song. Judy was asked to give a two-minute speech on how it felt to be a grandmother. Arthur gave his version of a South Sea Islands hula. We all did something, all pretty silly; then we played a sort of group game (each of us required to say all the Japanese words we knew, as quickly as we could think of them); and then it was no longer possible for us to be stiff and formal with each other. For three weeks we lived in each other's pockets, and loved it, and each other.

We left Japan in a golden glow, on a JAL 747 to Hawaii. (It is an interesting experience to come into Honolulu on a Japanese plane, low over Battleship Row in Pearl Harbor.) Hawaii is perhaps the most beautiful place I've ever seen. We stayed at one of the tourist traps on Waikiki the first night, a typical hard-sell Hilton where you have to pass a dozen boutiques to get to the registration desk and where every petal in the lei has a price tag. We were both tired, and resentful of the Miami Beach tinsel, so the next day we flew to the big island and stayed at what I have always thought the most beautiful hotel in the world, the Mauna Kea Beach Hotel. I had been there before, lecturing for the American Management Association, and for four or five years had been looking for a chance to stay there again. Palms grow through the open central courts. Every night two or three mantas fly through the underwater lights at the end of its dock. If you rent a car and drive along the roads, you pass unexpected valleys and waterfalls. Its beach is unfailingly sunny, and the water always gentle. But even Mauna Kea was a letdown after Japan, and we cut our visit short for home.

I had business to transact in Los Angeles, so Carol went on ahead and I checked in at the Century Plaza. Unfortunately, the people I most needed to see were out of town, and Los Angeles itself was in an early fall heat-and-smog cycle. They laid on a small earthquake for me, which was interesting enough because it was the only one I have ever experienced (not counting the odd volcanic shudder on Mount Vesu-

vius), but the visit was a washout and I caught a red-
eye flight home, feeling tired, gritty, and depressed.

Hawaii was a letdown from Japan, California from
Hawaii, New Jersey from California; things slid down-
hill, all together, like a glacier creeping down a moun-
tainside. Every day seemed a little grayer and grimier
than the day before. A few weeks after I got home I
was invited to take part in a New York Academy of
Sciences planetology meeting at the Waldorf-Astoria.
Even that went badly. October, November, December
. . . do you know, I cannot think of anything good that
happened anywhere at all in those last few months of
1970. Wherever I looked, things were grimier and more
unrewarding than I could remember. I picked up a
cold somewhere or other, and it turned into a persistent, hacking cought. I began to put on weight. Not just
a little plumpness; I was fat, nearly forty pounds more
than the 175 I had weighed all my adult life. Carol and
I were growing more remote every day. I fiddled with a
little writing, but it was hard and scant and slow, and
none of it came out to suit me. I began to have money
troubles. I could hardly believe that the money was
running out; but some money that was due was slow
coming in, some that I had expected turned out not
to be going to happen, work that I had contracted to
do wasn't getting done, and so I wasn't taking in very
much. I let my bank balance get low. I sold the little
stock I owned—I know full well that I am too ignorant
of the market to invest sensibly in securities, so I don't
invest at all; but I had accumulated a little as payment
for services rendered. And Christmas came along, and
there were four kids expecting goodies; and there was
a point right then at Christmas when I was so broke I
was going around the house emptying the jars and
drawers of pennies tossed in them, to roll and take to
the bank and convert to bills. The last week or two of
1970 and the first of 1971 were about the lowest point

in my life. Nothing went well. Everything went badly. I felt exhausted most of the time, and the cough became a griping hack, and I began to think that there was a good chance that all the half million or more cigarettes I have smoked in my life were finally performing as advertised and I might very well be not far from dying. The worst part was that I didn't really mind. I found so few satisfactions in my life just then that departing from it was no sweat. I knew, in the forebrain part of my mind, that life might seem worth living again: that there might very well be fun to be had, relationships to explore, stories to write in which I might even feel pride, rewards to be obtained. But it seemed to me that it was highly unlikely that any of it would be *new*. I had tasted all those things already, and even though I recognized that I might enjoy tasting them again, it seemed little more than a summer rerun of a life I had already lived and didn't especially want to repeat.

Perhaps it is what is called the "male menopause." I don't know. I was fifty-one, which is the right time for it, I suppose.

Then a fellow knocked on my door and wanted to sell me life insurance.

I thought it was pretty funny. I really didn't think I was a good prospect; was a little sorry for him for wasting his time. But he was as persistent as an insurance salesman is supposed to be, and more or less as a joke I agreed to take the physical. I passed. I was astonished: no lung cancer, no emphysema, no hypertension, no nothing? I was, to be sure, a little overweight, the doctor said, and recommended I lose some.

So I went home, and paid my premium, and poured myself a cup of coffee and thought things over. It occurred to me that I might go to my own doctor and see what he had to say. I was pretty sure I knew what he was going to tell me. Assuming he didn't find something terminal, he would say I should lose weight, get more exercise, drink less coffee, smoke fewer cigarettes, and sleep more regularly. All right, I thought, let's try a little of that. So I did. And after a little while I began to feel somewhat more alive. I sat down at the typewriter and tried stringing some words together: they strung pretty well, I thought.* I took the family to the Soviet Union, partly on business, partly because I'd promised my son I'd take him to any country of which he learned to speak the language (expecting French or Spanish; but he picked Russian), and that was almost as high a spot as Japan.

And after a while it came to me that I had reenlisted for another hitch with life.

Reality is a terrible annoyance to a novelist. It does not come in tidy packages. What I want to do is to shape the events of my life to fit a dramatic pattern. They won't shape. Pieces don't fit in, others protrude and spoil the symmetry. I don't even know how to end this story. The time to stop, says Mark Twain, is with a wedding or a funeral. I am not presently in the market for either, but I think it's time to stop.

By now it is clear to the slowest observer, even to me, that I have committed my life to science fiction. It is fair to ask why. I mean, I'm smart enough. I could have had several quite different careers, and some of them, at least at the time, looked a lot more attractive in terms of dollars and pride. When you come right down to it, is making up lies about things that have never happened really a respectable way for a grown man to spend his days?

I have been asked that question. And yes, dear

---

* That year I wrote "The Gold at the Starbow's End," "Shaffery Among the Immortals," a large part of *Man Plus*, and about a dozen smaller pieces . . . very close to the best year's production I had ever had in my life.

friends, there have been times—a whole lot of times, though not so many of them recently—when I have asked it of myself. The question is rational enough, but it has only a nonrational answer: love. I do it because I'm in love. A long time ago, maybe when I was twelve, maybe even younger, I fell in love with writing science fiction. Through many turpitudes and dalliances, I have stayed in love ever since.

Let me tell you how falling in love happens, because of all the points of decision human beings ordinarily encounter, the act of falling in love is the least rational and the least understood. It goes like this:

John and Joan meet—it doesn't much matter where, or how. They notice each other. What John notices about Joan is that she smells good, has an inviting figure, laughs nicely when he wants her to laugh, and looks upon him with a rewarding show of interest. What Joan notices about John is much the same. On these flimsy data they each construct a private image of the other. They make each other up! What they know is very little. They fill in the rest of the picture by inventing qualities to match some private daydream. John has always wanted a girl to listen to violin concerti with him, who liked to make love in the morning, willing to walk five miles at a clip just to see what a stroller might see. He doesn't know these things are true of Joan. But he doesn't know that they aren't, either, and maybe? who knows? So he lays on her the traits he would like to find; going to bed with her will be like so, lounging on a beach will be thus; and the rest of the date, maybe the rest of the year or the rest of the life, is spent mapping reality against the hypothesis. The fit is never perfect. But as long as it is not too discordantly wrong, the love lasts.

And that is how it was with me and science fiction. When I first fell in love, I did not know that the creature sweated and snored. I just loved, and dreamed.

It is now clear that that first infatuated fantasy was very wrong in detail. I had the magnolious notion that there was some secret skill to writing science fiction. All sf writers had learned it, I supposed. Once I had acquired it, it would always be there, like riding a bicycle, so that writing the second story would be easier than the first, and the third easier than the second. . . . It isn't that way at all. Barring a few monkey tricks, some of which I learned with great effort and then had to unteach myself with even more, it is as hard for me to write today as it was when I was twelve. I would like to think that the end product is by some standard better, but the act of producing it has not become effortless with time. There is more drudgery than I had expected. There is a hell of a lot more frustrating boredom. But there is something else that I had not anticipated, and that is that I need it. This drudgery, this frustration, this tedium of staring at a typewriter and wishing I knew which key to hit next—this miraculous, liberating sensation of lightness and joy, when, once in a great while, it comes out almost as it should —I need it to live on.

Is spending one's life writing science fiction rewarding?

Why, sure. In all the ways I have said and many more. But that doesn't have much to do with it. You don't love a person just because she rewards you. The person is rewarding because you love her. So it is with me and science fiction. For the gifts she has given me I am truly grateful. But I loved her on sight, giftless, and it looks as if I'll go on doing it as long as I live.

Red Bank, New Jersey
1977